Peter

C000177510

TWO WORLDS

The Story of an Edinburgh Doctor

Peter Hoffmann was educated at Hunters Tryst School Oxgangs Edinburgh and Boroughmuir Senior Secondary School. After graduate and post-graduate studies in Edinburgh he worked for SCVS; the Scottish Episcopal Church; the private sector and thereafter mainly in local government as a chief officer in education; culture and sport. He is the author of a number of books.

Cover Miss Freddie Royster and Arthur Philip Motley circa 1921 McAlester City Oklahoma U.S.A.

Dr Arthur Philip Motley 1976

Peter Hoffmann

TWO WORLDS

The Story of an Edinburgh Doctor

I would like to acknowledge the ongoing invaluable and generous help and assistance which I've received from Dr Motley's grandson Harold Motley as well as input from others including Ms Danielle Spittle; Mrs Betty Verrill; Ms Vicky Mount and my mother, Mrs Anne Duncan, who was a long-standing friend of Dr Motley.

This book is dedicated to the memory of Lewie Motley, the son of Miss Freddie Royster and the unacknowledged son of Arthur Philip Motley and also to the community of Oxgangs which exemplified Martin Luther King Jr's dream '...that my four little children will one day live in a nation where they will not be judged by the color of their skin but by the content of their character.'

Contents

Introduction

Listen with Mother

The Landscape the Farms and RLS

A Village Grows Up Overnight

I Have a Dream

The Hoffmanns

Transactions v Relationships

Ebony and Ivory

Prejudice and Discrimination

McAlester Cottage

The Finest of Medical Schools

1928 Yearbook

1907 Clarksville Red River County Texas

L'Ouverture High School McAlester City Oklahoma

Dr Willa Strong

1925 Wiley College Marshall Texas

Lincoln University Pennsylvania

1926

1928

Sherlock Holmes

Revelation

University of Edinburgh

Anchor Steamline Caledonia

It's Capital

An Edinburgh Autumn

The Big Freeze

Show Boat

Edinburgh Colour Bar

Edinburgh Tenement Life

Leith

Marchmont

Edinburgh Snobbery

Dr Jekyll and Mr Hyde

The Peripatetic Philosopher

The Doppelgänger

Homesick

Leerie the Lamplighter

Mince and Tatties

Into the Mist

Auld Reekie

A Spring in Arthur's Step

Medica Metrics

Facing the Music

Disapointment in Edinburgh and McAlester City

We Learn from Failure, Not from Success!

Annette – Sweet on You

Turn your Wounds into Wisdom – Oprah Winfrey

1929

Calvinist Edinburgh and Three Deuces

A Shotgun Wedding?

The Wedding

University of Edinburgh

Good Old (Young) Arthur!

Academia

The Great Crash of 1929

Annette Junior

Dr Robert Thin

The Juggler

My Boy

McAlester City

A Pyrrhic Victory

School Years

1929

No Appearance

The Gilt is off the Gingerbread

The Letters

Autumn 1930

To Study or to Work

An Edinburgh Boy

The End of a Dream

A Year of Crisis

A Change of Direction

Arthur - he is just like a Bird

Much left unsaid between the Leaves and the Lines

The Dark Ages

The Lost Decade

The Honorary Medical Officer

It's a Mystery

A Ripple in the Pond

The Heights by Great Men reached and Kept

At the Last Gasp

Royal Army Medical Corps

Harold Motley

A Dark Secret

Another Grandchild

Dr Motley – a Vignette by Artist Vicky Mount

Mrs Annette Motley

Late Summer 2020

The Year of the Plague

Yuletide 2020/21

Tulsa Race Massacre

Lynching of Laura and L.D. Nelson

Oklahoma Land Rush of 1839

Tulsa Race Riots

A Rolling Stone

Reverend Frank Motley

The Kings' Doctor

The Bluebell Girl

Tie a Yellow Ribbon round the Old Oak Tree

Thanksgiving Day

School Sweetheart

Miss Freddie Royster

Two Worlds

I Have a Dream – Nye Beavan

The War Years

The Land of the Pharoahs

A Baptism of Fire and Brimstone

Demob Happy

Open for Business

The Gate Keeper

The Apple of my Eye

21st February 2021

Betty Verrill and Rosa Parks

The Golden Years

The Oxgangs World of Dr Motley

Let it Be and the Elephant in the Room

Aye Working

A Fictional Hero Too

The 1970s

A Patient's Journal

The View from t'other Side of the Consulting Table

Out of Left Field

Two Roads

Introduction

The two major stories of 2020 were Covid-19 and the role of the medical fraternity and the Black Lives Matter movement.

These twin themes and at times inter-related stories made me think of a very remarkable Black man who moved to Scotia's capital seat in 1928 and over the following six decades made a significant contribution and impact upon a working class Edinburgh community.

January is often a good time to reflect on the year just past and the year ahead. And with the announcement of another Coronavirus lockdown and given it being the heart of midwinter when people may also have a little more time to read - and this is a long essay - nay a monograph - his story - history - as David Daiches used to pen - made me think that I must sit down and over the period of a few months record Arthur Philip Motley's story thinking it might help to pass an hour or two of a mid-winter's evening.

The monograph or chronicle is not just a brief sketch of a life well led but it's a story of hope and perseverance and resilience - a story about not giving up on your dreams but instead to see them through. As Harry Lauder used to *sing 'Keep right on till the end of the road.'*

It's the story of a journey - indeed two parallel journeys - in the main that of Arthur Philip Motley - an Okie - who grew up in McAlester City Oklahoma U.S.A. in the early decades of the 20th century and travelled halfway round the globe to change for the better the lives of thousands of Edinburghers - but also the journey of the author - an Edinburgher - following in Dr Motley's footsteps. And thus rather than his story being presented in a chronological fashion, instead it traces my somewhat scatter-gun approach in gathering information, so the tale is presented in the form of a Dali-like folded clock ebbing back and forward across over a century.

It's a story about social integration and about people from different backgrounds and hinterlands living harmoniously together side-by-side - respectfully and well-adjusted alongside one another where people recognise difference but in the key respect of difference as to how people treat one another in terms of their conduct and their personalities - how they behave with one another - what they bring to the table - how they conduct themselves - are they fun - is there a warmth and kindness to their personalities and in their actions – are they caring - and Dr Motley had all of these qualities and traits and in abundance.

Over the years his thousands of patients recognised these qualities as recorded in their favourable comments and memories of him: just to give a small flavour, here are but a few:

One anonymous man said *'Thanks for remembering Dr Motley. He did his best to help my mum. That trip to the cottage was a regular one with me in tow. We lived at 34 Oxgangs Avenue in the mid 70s/early 80s so far away now and a mostly unhappy time but it made me who I am.'*

Heather Macnaught *recalled 'I have fond memories of Dr Motley visiting my grandfather. It was because of Dr Motley that I decided at the age of six to go into nursing. I did my General at the Western General then moved to London where I worked at St Thomas's then I did my Children's at Westminster. I have since moved to the States and currently live in Colorado and Florida (depending on the weather).'*

Richard Cropper says *'I was brought into the world by this lovely man on 29/10/62 at 2B Oxgangs Green. My younger brother was also delivered by Dr Motley on 29/1/65. My late dad remembers rushing along Oxgangs Avenue when my arrival was imminent, knocking on the door of McAlester Cottage. Always unhurried, "Calm down Mr Cropper, I'll be there in a few minutes!" I continued as his patient up until about 1978 I seem to recall (we relocated to Murrayburn Park, Wester Hailes in July 1970 but still continued with AP as our Doctor). He was always referred to us boys as 'Professor' as perhaps to all young male children in his practice? I remember him fondly as the archetypal kindly family doctor "How are your parents? And your brothers and sister?" but I recall his diagnoses could be somewhat hit or miss.'*

These are but a tiny few of the hundreds of positive comments and memories about the good doctor that over the past few years have come through the ether about Dr Arthur Philip Motley.

And yet – and significantly - I don't recall a single one mentioning the fact that he was Black in what was and remains a 99% plus white community: and if we were to travel back in a time-machine to the

1940s through to the 1980s when he practised there, in that earlier period he may well have been the only Black man in the area.

When I first took up my pen to write about my memories of Dr Motley and of how I held him in such very high esteem, as the years have passed I still feel exactly the same but as I discovered more about him on my journey I learnt that his story was much more nuanced than I could have imagined. I came to recognise that alongside all his wonderful qualities he had a more interesting hinterland than I could ever have dreamt and I guess like us all he had his flaws too.

But for me that made his life trajectory even more fascinating - being born at the turn of the 20th century in the American South to a family who originally would have been slaves and cotton pickers to living, working and building a new life for himself in Edinburgh, the capital of Scotland.

In his well mannered way his was a positive story of social integration – he was in his quiet way a pioneer breaking down barriers and his was a lesson too in how to conduct yourself with grace and with class.

But it's also a tale of a working class community responding like-wise, with a lot of class – something that others who might be quite judgemental about the area might have found quite unexpected when considering Oxgangs: I find myself feeling proud of the community in which I grew up.

Over the past decade I've written considerably about Oxgangs, one of Edinburgh Corporation's new housing schemes that were built in the decades after the Second World War on farmland on the southern boundaries of the capital set within the lea of the Pentland Hills.

And in writing about the area, of all the people who cropped up in the small vignettes that I wrote, the most remarkable story of all the individuals in the community was that of Dr Arthur Philip Motley – a young Black American student who in 1928 sailed across the Atlantic Ocean from New York to Glasgow and then took a steam train through to Edinburgh to fulfil his dream to study to become a doctor seeking his fortune in a new land over 4000 miles from his motherland and home, McAlester City Oklahoma in the United States of America.

Most of Dr Motley's patients wouldn't have given much thought or consideration to his route of travel assuming he had followed an effortless and traditional trajectory to become a local family doctor: but it was anything but and instead involved a tale of tenacious struggle against the odds, not qualifying until the very last gasp at the age of around 35 years in 1939 just before the start of the Second World War.

But in the four decades that followed (alongside the likes of the Reverend Jack Orr the excellent Church of Scotland minister) Dr Motley went on to become a legendary, popular and greatly loved local figure.

Those were the days when people from such professions as medicine, dentistry and teaching or some of the more charismatic local shop-keepers became some of the most recognisable and influential local leaders often making a powerful community contribution, impact and impression upon what was a new and very young community.

Listen with Mother

My mother knew Dr Motley perhaps better than most of his patients, especially as in later years after he retired in 1978 she became a friend rather than a patient.

By then he had moved house to pass out his remaining years half a mile uphill from his old surgery at McAlester Cottage to live in Caiystane.

Occasionally, if his name came up in any of our conversations she recalled various small stories about him.

For example she thought that during the Second World War he was a ship's doctor but we were unsure whether it was in the US Navy or the British Navy.

I assumed it would have been the American.

She also recalled that he told her that when on board a ship - was it during the war or on a cruise afterwards - was it in South Africa or was it another port? - but she said that when the crew - the sailors - encouraged him to go ashore and join them he replied 'No I'll have to remain on board'. When they asked him why, he replied that he was frightened he'd be lynched!

But if he had joined up to fight for America and the Allied Forces that begs the question why he came back to Edinburgh to set up in practice?

When we talked about this at the time we thought that perhaps by then he had met his wife Annette and rather than the couple choosing to live in America, the decision was strongly influenced by her wishing to remain in her homeland rather than them beginning a new life across the Atlantic Ocean in the Deep South of America and that it was primarily because of Annette that he chose to stay in Edinburgh, but Mother said to me that he loved Edinburgh too.

Despite the vagaries of the weather and the cold wind that often blows through the precipitous city where you can experience the four seasons in one day, the capital often has that pulling effect upon those who come to study in the city drawing them in then enticing them to remain and build a new life and career within her boundaries.

We spoke too of how when Dr Motley was first developing the practice in Oxgangs he could be seen out and about on his bicycle visiting patients. In the deep midwinter he must have cut a wonderful sight.

We assumed that he must have set up the practice after the end of the Second World War around the beginning of the NHS in 1947.

Up until then United Kingdom patients had to pay for treatment so people always thought twice about visiting the doctor or calling them out not to mention that such bills were often paid for in guineas rather than in pounds.

We discussed too how being married to a white woman must have made life challenging both socially and professionally for Dr Motley yet my mother says that she recalls back in the late 1950s and in to the 1960s how he regularly held large parties at his home and quite often a line of fancy cars could be seen parked outside McAlester Cottage.

Mother recalled too of how before moving to McAlester Cottage he lived in one of the Gumley houses at Colinton Mains across from what was known as The Store - the St Cuthbert's Co-operative Society supermarket.

In later years when Dr Shepherd joined the medical practice Mother said Dr Shepherd moved in there and Dr Motley thereafter moved home to both live and practice at McAlester Cottage before eventually buying the house at Caiystane.

The reason for buying another house was two-fold.

Firstly, as more and more doctors came to work at the practice and became partners more space needed to be found to accommodate them: also practice nurses came to be employed and based there too.

And second, as the decade of the 1960s moved into the 1970s he had to plan ahead for his retirement - and of course he and Annette would no longer be able to live at McAlester Cottage.

Living above the shop so to speak had its advantages and its disadvantages - to go to work in the morning he simply had to walk downstairs to the surgery, but of course it meant he was always on call with patients ringing the doorbell at all times of the day and the night.

His first main partner - certainly that I can recall - was Dr Shepherd who was an excellent doctor and superior in skill to Dr Motley. It was Dr Shepherd who delivered my sister Anne at our home (6/2 Oxgangs Avenue) on the 19th September 1961.

But in the decade or so prior to this it must have been very challenging for Dr Motley to learn all the skills required to become a good general practitioner.

There was no immediate access to IT and the Internet and being human he undoubtedly will have made mistakes.

Indeed on one occasion around 1965 when I was 9 years old I had a poisoned big toe. The poison left a yellow vertical line from my toe and had spread up a vein to my knee. I was delirious and there was a danger I could lose my leg. When Dr Shepherd visited on an emergency call out he immediately took control of the crisis and lanced it to release the poison.

But, over the years and the decades Dr Motley was very supportive of our family and as I discovered afterwards, similarly so to so many other patients too. Mother is glad that when she had to retire from the Civil Service on the grounds of ill-health he helped her to secure a small pension which she still enjoys to this day. When the authorities frowned upon this saying the government couldn't really afford it, he waved the letter in the air laughing with Mother saying 'Just imagine it Jo – the government can't afford it!'

He is also recalled by many patients seeking a sick line to be off work – he was perhaps too accommodating in this respect and I'm aware he had a certain poor reputation amongst the powers that be for distributing the government's largesse.

With an alcoholic father our family had more than its fair shares of ups and downs and Mother had various medical challenges over the years and he was always very supportive and kind toward her.

During the mid-1960s whilst coming home one summer afternoon from Hunters Primary School I had a badly gashed forehead – either from being hit by a stone or from banging my head off a gate whilst ducking from my classmate Alan Stewart throwing a stone at me – anyway it oozed blood and my mother took me the 100 yards to the surgery where Dr Motley put in a couple of stitches thereafter giving me a boiled sweet for being a brave boy.

In more recent years I became aware this was his common approach – did he buy the sweets in especially or were they one of the many items that came his way from the various medical representatives and salesmen who visited the practice.

Come the 1970s it was at his medical practice that I received a message on the 14th June 1976 that I'd been selected for the Great Britain Olympic Team in Montreal. Ironically I was there on the Monday morning after the previous weekend's Olympic Trials getting an injury treated. It may have been the receptionist Mrs Sibbald formerly one of our neighbours at 8/2 Oxgangs Avenue who passed the good news on to me after my grandmother had telephoned the surgery.

During this period Dr Motley regularly offered to get me a scholarship to Oklahoma University which I never really followed up. Two years later in 1978 when I moved up to 800 metres - the half mile - for a season I would have been ranked number one in the United States so undoubtedly a good scholarship would have been available, particularly so with his connections there.

As I was a relatively poor student, after being selected for Montreal he very kindly and thoughtfully arranged a collection for me to help support my athletics. Come the autumn I was about to set off to study at Loughborough University and before I left I received a sizeable cheque but we think it was perhaps Dr Motley who provided the bulk of the monies.

Mother doesn't recall ever seeing his daughter Annette Junior. I thought that I had, but my memory must be wrong. As we chatted I wondered if perhaps she had been sent away to boarding school and therefore wasn't in Oxgangs very much.

My mother thought she married someone from Scandinavia, possibly Sweden and settled abroad.

Mother said Annette Junior became estranged from her father and possibly became quite bitter toward him.

Towards the end of his life she wrote to him and made an attempt to get back in touch but Dr Motley said that although he intended to leave most everything to her he felt it was too late in the day and that there had been too much water under the bridge.

Mother remained good friends with him including walking his dog each Wednesday afternoon up to Swanston Village at the foot of the Pentland Hills. She thinks that back in the 1980s grandchildren came to visit him and that he took them for a bus ride - on a tour of Edinburgh on the top deck of the Number 32 bus which makes a wondrous circular route of the city taking several hours to complete – not only was it a practical route for many of the passengers, but it was in some respects fondly regarded as a 'tourist bus' too.

But whenever my mother and I think or spoke about Dr Motley it is with great fondness. The mere mention of his name brings a smile to our faces and a warmth to our hearts.

The Landscape the Farms and RLS

The flats at Oxgangs on the south side of Edinburgh were built on farm land, presumably on the former Oxgangs Farm in the lea of the Pentland Hills. Looking back, as there were no local industries, the air was fresh and clean and thus a healthy place to live and grow up compared to such town areas as Fountainbridge which were more industrialised. There were still some local working farms including Hunters Tryst Farm which was a dairy until it returned to being a restaurant in 1969. Back in the 1920s they delivered milk to as far afield as Morningside, Churchill and Marchmont. Further up towards the Pentland Hills was Swanston Farm which grew potatoes and turnips. It was also a pig farm and noticeably smelly.

Eighty years beforehand, Robert Louis Stevenson walked along Cockmalayne and on to the same dirt road going to and from Swanston Village where the family had a holiday house, Swanston Cottage. Perhaps it is a trick of memory but I remember seeing his initials carved on the door of the old Oxgangs Farm House, Oxgangs Road North. In later decades the farmhouse became the local police station. Comiston Farm also grew potatoes and turnips. A lovely stone built house was an integral part of this farm. At one time there were wild rumours circulating of a ghost haunting the farm. The ghost was known as The White Lady or The Grey Lady. This caused great consternation amongst the pupils at Hunters Tryst Primary School, which was adjacent to the farm.

A Village Grows Up Overnight

I grew up in 6 Oxgangs Avenue which still looks okay today even over 60 years after it was built a year or two after I was born in 1956. By then Dr Motley had been in practice for around a decade.

I don't know what the expected lifespan of these buildings was. They weren't built of the fine old sandstone of the Victorian or

Edwardian flats at Morningside, Bruntsfield and Marchmont.

The housing development was part of the legacy of the Labour Government which came into power after the Second World War and the implementation of Beveridge's proposals to end the general poverty that had impacted upon much of Britain.

6 Oxgangs Avenue is a block of eight flats. There are four identical such blocks located at the west end of Oxgangs Avenue where it formed a T junction with Oxgangs Road North. These are

numbers 2, 4, 6 and 8. A further five blocks of two were built behind stairs 8 and 6 accessed from Oxgangs Street. In each of the stairs five of the flats had two bedrooms whilst three had three bedrooms, with balconies. Unfortunately they are north facing: excuse the pun, but not very bright.

Of course there were far more people living in the area because these flats were surrounded by many other properties built in the early 1950s.

On the other side of Oxgangs Road North at Oxgangs Farm Drive were slightly older blocks of council flats containing six flats i.e. a ground floor with a first and a second floor whereas our flats had a third floor. Much nearer, off Oxgangs Street at Oxgangs Park, were a series of rows of blocks of flats identical to those at Oxgangs Farm Drive.

Across Oxgangs Avenue from The Stair were the prefabs - small cottages which had been thrown up after the War. As captured forever in Douglas Blades' photograph below these were quaint houses, but regarded as a temporary way of housing families. There were 229 of those prefabricated houses located in Oxgangs, sadly, now all gone. The ones at Oxgangs Avenue were all torn down in the 1960s and replaced by modern flats.

When the new flats were being built the building site was a great adventure playground; at one time we even had a front door key to one of the new flats!

Directly behind The Stair was a small enclosed rough field only used for bonfires. Behind this field lay an area of park land known as The Field, where we played hundreds if not thousands of games of football. Children can no longer play football there as the young trees which were planted in the 1970s have thrived and grown into a copse. I'm unsure how they ever survived local children's attentions. Today it looks pastoral and very pleasant, but at the time was an atypical example of a lack of communication with the residents i.e. removing a leisure asset and replacing it with something else - Big Brother knows best.

The Field and small copse forms a boundary between the road and the five rows of two blocks of identical flats on the other side which are approached from Oxgangs Street. Thus, there were 14 identical blocks of flats with 8 families in each making for a grand total of 112 families in this development, around 400 people - the size of a village, who all arrived around the same time, the mid to late 1950's, to begin a new chapter, forming new friendships, growing up, living together many of whom will have spent their whole life there and some who are still there today; others who died there and the many others who as they approached and reached adulthood left and moved away, to begin a new life for themselves - the never ending circle of life.

And these ever growing numbers were important because with the advent of the new National Health Service (NHS) general practitioners were paid on a capitation basis i.e. based on the number of patients registered at the practice.

In the decade after the Second World War the new Oxgangs and surrounding housing schemes were great places to live and to bring up young families - modern flats; indoor loos; open coal fires. Looking back we were also incredibly lucky to have both a new doctor's surgery and dentist's on our doorsteps; for our family at 6 Oxgangs Avenue it was less than a two minutes walk. When you're young you just suppose it was how it always was and should be, not appreciating our good fortune. Mr Russell was the local dentist for decades. His surgery was located next door to Dr Motley - happenstance or not, but a good arrangement.

I Have a Dream

In some respects this tale begins back in 2012 – nine years ago – when I first started a blog about the community of Oxgangs which the following year resulted in the book *The Stair – An Oxgangs Edinburgh Childhood.*

Dr Motley featured prominently and in the years since people have occasionally got in touch with me with their memories of him.

Distant Motley family members from throughout the world including the United States, who until I wrote about Dr Motley had tried in vain to discover information about their (long-lost) relative similarly contacted me as did a Norwegian lady with a family.

From time to time Dr Motley still 'puts in an appearance' on the Facebook Group - Oxgangs - A Pastime From Time Past.

Like a slow drip-feed further information has emerged even as recently as Christmas Eve 2020 from the University of Edinburgh.

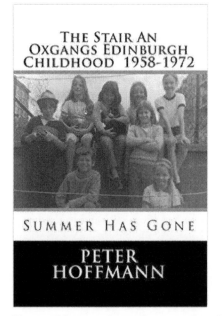

To me his story is much more than being a member of that wonderful fraternity and tradition – the family doctor – and instead his story is a larger one and something which is emblematic of something in life which is very positive – a good news story - one of an individual not being seen in terms of the colour of their skin but through the prism of their character – a real life example of Martin Luther King Jr's vision as articulated in his immortal speech of 1963 when he said '...I have a dream that my four little children will one day live in a nation where they will not be judged by the color of their skin but by the content of their character....'

Martin Luther King

I Have a Dream

Here in a small working class area of Scotland, King's dream was actively being lived out.

From the recorded comments of dozens and dozens of his patients' memories and eulogies this is what comes through time and time again - of what a greatly loved local character Dr Motley was in the community of Oxgangs, Colinton Mains and Firrhill. He is remembered for his kindness – his thoughtfulness – his gentleness – his pastoral care and compassion for all of his patients and local families.

This was very much an era when doctors, dentists, bankers and shop-keepers had a relationship with their customers rather than the more modern-day transactions. Relationships and transactions – a theme which I will revisit in this book.

From the age of 2 until I was 16 I lived and grew up in Oxgangs between the years 1958 and 1972 and despite moving in late 1972 the seven miles from the hills to the sea to Portobello Dr Motley remained as my GP until 1978.

And whilst I wouldn't have dwelt or spent much time reflecting on Dr Motley's route of travel, if I had, I would have assumed he was a bright individual who had become a general practitioner following a traditional route by passing his annual medical exams in the process of a relatively smooth journey to thereafter owning his own local practice in Oxgangs.

But instead, with the benefit of hindsight and the availability of further information and the time and opportunity to reflect, his route of travel was anything but smooth, indeed, at time it was quite rocky.

And here in 2021 I've now come to appreciate the remarkable journey of a young Black man in the late 1920s travelling across the globe to a predominantly white city to transform both his life and the lives of thousands of others for the better.

With the increasing awareness that his journey wasn't quite as straightforward as I'd first assumed it's this struggle which attracted me to write further about him.

His route of travel took a lot of determination and fortitude to fulfil both his dream – and the dream of his mother, Ethel Motley, back home in Oklahoma, for him 'to become a polished doctor'.

Like most mothers she did her very best to inspire and support the young Arthur to become part of that wonderful and most honourable of professions – a family doctor. And when he did pick up that wonderful sobriquet – Dr – after all the years of sacrifices, scraping and scrimping and worrying after him from so very far from home, in the days when communication was less than instant – oh how very proud she must have been of her beloved son when he became Dr Arthur Philip Motley.

The Hoffmanns

In late 1958 our family were the first occupants of 6/2 Oxgangs Avenue Edinburgh taking up residence in what was always referred to as *The Stair.*

I was but two years old. My brother Iain had just been born at the end of November 1958. Three years later my sister Anne would come along in September 1961 to complete our family.

My parents, Anne and Ken Hoffmann, had married in 1955 and after living at my maternal grandparents - Mother's parents - for a while before sharing a flat with Mum's cousin Margaret and Andy Ross at Duncan Street Edinburgh they picked up the keys to what was to become their first proper and indeed only family home together before they divorced 13 years later on my 15th birthday on the 1st July 1971.

I of course don't recall my first visit to see Dr Motley but for one reason or another I would have met him either as a patient or if I were accompanying someone else to the surgery. Those were also the days of home visits too. But for as long as I could remember he was an integral part of my young life all the way through until I reached the age of 22 when he retired in the late summer of 1978.

But even thereafter he would occasionally feature in my life. For example I still have a job reference which he did for me circa 1981. In the years after his wife Annette died my mother remained very friendly with him and each Wednesday afternoon she regularly walked his dog up to Swanston Village with its thatched houses nestling into the lower slopes of the Pentland Hills and from those visitations she might give me an occasional update on him and his retirement.

On other occasions he sometimes took her with him to the Edinburgh University former students' club for lunch.

In looking back to this period in the early 1980s I simply assumed he had of course graduated from the University of Edinburgh and he was enjoying return visitations to his alma mater, more of which anon.

This was still the era when knowledge came slowly – the Internet was still but the dream of a few star-gazers. Indeed it was only through the power of such a new research and communication tool that I was able to begin to slowly unravel and find out a little more about Dr Motley and piece together some of his story – something more than just my own personal experience or what had been passed down through family oral history and folklore.

And thus began the slow realisation of a far more interesting hinterland than I could ever have imagined.

Transactions v Relationships

I've long been interested in the concept and the difference between relationships and transactions and how this has evolved over the past half century.

Our family always had a relationship with Dr Motley: on any visitation he wasn't solely interested in you the patient, but it was also a useful opportunity for him to keep abreast of the lives of other members of the family too which might at some stage come in handy.

As former patient Richard Cropper recalled he never seemed in a hurry – even when a birth was imminent – 'Calm down Mr Cropper, I'll be there in a few minutes.'

Richard also remembers how on any visitation to the surgery he and his brothers always referred to Dr Motley as 'Professor' and how he was an archetypal family doctor always asking after his parents – his brothers - and his sister too.

Today, with all the pressures on the medical profession and the expansion of many surgeries into health centres with an expanded staff and often with general practitioners in double figures we no longer feel we have a relationship especially if we see a different doctor on each visitation.

That's no different from shopping – when we used to shop at the local grocer's who similarly interfaced with their customers rather than the anonymity of the supermarket checkout. And then we used to have our own local bank manager – today we bank online and through a call centre.

There are of course advantages and disadvantages to this, but being able to speed through a checkout in a supermarket, shop online or be able to bank from home gives us more time in our busy lives, but at the same time we lose something too – the confidence, the knowledge and the intimacy and the comfort that comes from having those who serve us in their capacity as a doctor, a bank manager or the grocer, who intimately know our needs and our overall family situation – there's more of a 360 degree perspective – one that's holistic - knowing the ins and the outs of our family lives helping enable them to provide a better more personal, empathetic and knowledgeable service without having to seek out basic information on each visitation or call.

Ebony and Ivory

As a wee boy Dr Motley was the first Black man I'd seen or met.

I couldn't take my eyes off this exotic man.

The fact that he was a different colour to me, Black to my white; then there were his hands - I noticed too the contrast of his palms which were of a much lighter tone. And of course there was his deep American voice – there was a lovely rich sound to it with its slow drawl, sweet cadence, musicality and mellifluousness.

I always found him to be a very gentle man - a gentleman - who was positive, empathetic and sympathetic to his patients. And despite the gravity of life and the gravity and ups and downs of his professional life experiences he struck me as being a very happy person - he laughed a lot. If only you could have bottled his cheerfulness and positivity and handed it out to his patients it would have been a cure all! But in a way of course he did because in some way – large or small – there was a positivity in visiting him for an appointment. You felt better for seeing him.

As I grew older I began to appreciate too just how immaculately groomed he was in appearance. In some respects he looked more like a specialist at the Edinburgh Royal Infirmary than a general practitioner in a local working class housing estate. He dressed in beautiful suits, shirts and ties and wore first class jewellery - a gold ring and a lovely watch and there was always a handkerchief in his top pocket.

He had a real sense of style and must have cut quite an exotic figure in early bleak grey 1950s Oxgangs. Although he wasn't tall, he was handsome with a gentle face and a gentle countenance.

Starting the Oxgangs practice from scratch around the late 1940s at the start of the NHS it's likely to have initially been a one man practice. This would have contributed toward me feeling that I always had a personal relationship with him. But as became apparent from the comments from hundreds of his other patients, they felt exactly the same way too.

But in reaching this juncture in his professional life and his developing practice, what a background story there was - what a tale - what a life trajectory - what a journey. Only, none of his patients really knew much about it and instead only some small select parts of his back-story.

Prejudice and Discrimination

But just for a small moment imagine how challenging it must have been for the young Arthur Philip Motley in the late 1920s to travel the thousands of miles from the American South to come to study here in Calvinist Edinburgh.

As a Black man in late 1920s Edinburgh he would have been in a small minority both at Edinburgh University and also within the city.

Over the years and across the decades he must have suffered prejudice and the vicissitudes of discrimination. Indeed, just this year, in January 2021 the Edinburgh World Heritage page gave many of the capital's citizens a bit of a jolt reminding and educating us of what Edinburgh was like at the time and in the years after his arrival and of how even a decade later- 'In August 1937, African American Bishop William Henry Heard travelled 3,000 miles from North America to Edinburgh with his niece to attend a conference. However, when they arrived at the North British Railway Station Hotel, both Heard and his niece were denied entry, due to the Edinburgh 'colour bar.'

The colour bar was a ban against minority ethnic people in Edinburgh's venues, cafes and dance halls. Managers at the time cited their reasoning as being to appease other - white patrons, who objected to sharing a space with people of other races.

Coming to the capital to train at the University of Edinburgh to become a doctor and also at the city's Royal Infirmary says a great deal about his character. But to thereafter go on to form, develop and build up your own successful practice at McAlester Cottage in the fledgling community of working class Oxgangs in the late 1940's and early 1950's must have been an even greater challenge and speaks volumes about Dr Motley and his character.

McAlester Cottage

My earliest memories of McAlester Cottage are of what a lovely house it was. When I was a boy it doubled up as both the practice and the family home, something which at the time I would have simply presumed had always been the case.

It was situated within an immediate local area of rapidly developing council flats at Oxgangs and Firrhill (but with private houses at Colinton Mains (usually blocks of four) and a few detached houses up the hill at Caiystane and Swanston, McAlester Cottage with its attractive white and red exterior was the finest house in the immediate area; in a small way it reminded me of the work of the famous English architect Sir Edwin Lutyens's, however it was designed by the architect A.A. Foot in 1927 for a J.C. Gibson Esq.

When combined with Dr Motley's immaculate appearance, really more akin to that of the image of a hospital surgeon – any visitation gave you a certain confidence – there was a subtle effect upon you when you visited the surgery.

You immediately felt that you were in safe hands.

For a short moment in time you had entered a remote, distant, safer land – an oasis of calm and civilised quiet conversation with other patients – whilst outside the front door was 'wild' Oxgangs.

As you climbed the two steps entering the waiting room between two white pillars into its open spaciousness and the perimeter of chairs there was an air of calm.

Alongside the pillars, two curling stones sat, one on either side of the entrance.

He must have employed very efficient and effective cleaners because the patients' waiting room was immaculate with its highly polished wooden floor, large mirror on one wall and seating – indeed, we kids could slide across the floor! And within the centre of the room were eight brightly coloured chairs for small children which were great fun to sit on beside a low table where we could draw or play games.

The Motley family lived at the practice although I don't recall ever seeing either his wife Annette nor his daughter (Annette Junior); they must have kept a fairly low profile.

When Dr Motley was building up the practice he was in his early to late 40s and he must have worked incredibly hard.

No doubt he would have been called out at all times of the day and the night. And initially operating as a one man practice with all the inherent stresses and strains must have been very challenging for him. And yet, whenever he saw you as a patient, he never exhibited any sign of this – indeed he seemed to have all the time in the world to inquire about your little world.

By the early 1960s he had appointed a partner: in later years this grew to having at least three GP's at the practice, extending still further into the 1970s with the introduction of new doctors including females such as Dr Sharon Gilmour.

Until writing this small monograph I had never thought about the name of his home and surgery practice - McAlester Cottage.

But if I had I wouldn't have thought anything of it - after all it's a good Scots name.

However, it's now occurred to me that the name was carefully and rather cleverly chosen – it was a reminder of his home back in America – McAlester City, Oklahoma. But to all intents and purposes it simply melded into the local landscape.

The Finest of Medical Schools

Back in 2012 when I decided to write about Dr Motley I tried to place myself in his shoes all those years ago – all the way back to the era of The Roaring Twenties - to try to re-imagine his thought process in deciding to apply to study in Edinburgh, a city 4351 miles away from his home town McAlester City, Oklahoma – and that as the crow flies.

Was it for entirely positive reasons?

Was it for negative reasons?

Or indeed was it a mixture of the two?

The New University Buildings and Medical School, Teviot Place, Edinburgh. Containing with its Laboratories, Class Rooms, and Surgical Halls of the Medical Faculty what is said to be one of the finest equipped Medical Schools in the world.

Did he decide beforehand that after his studies and qualifying as a doctor he would thereafter return home to the United States or was his intention to always remain here in Scotland?

I don't think we'll ever truly know the answer, but we can read between the lines and the route of his journey and surmise what his intentions might have been.

He perhaps chose to study in Edinburgh because it had long been regarded as being one of the leading medical schools in the world.

After all a medical degree from Edinburgh meant that in theory he could practise anywhere in the world although as a Black man this would undoubtedly have restricted many such opportunities.

However if many people had reservations about socialising with Black people then how might the same people feel about being treated by someone who wasn't the same colour - would they not have had even deeper reservations - nay horrors - about being treated by a Black man?

Choosing Edinburgh as a place to study also begs further questions as to why he wanted to travel so very far away from his home in Oklahoma or his alma mater, Lincoln University in Pennsylvania.

Why did he choose a city so far away and so very difficult and expensive to travel to?

Why did he wish to uproot from friends and family – we are aware he was clearly a popular outgoing young guy back at Lincoln.

It also begs key questions as to how did he ever manage to fund his studies thousands of miles away from home never mind coming up with the resources for the significant travel costs and then his accommodation and day to day living expenses, never mind the cost of academic fees.

In posing such questions I set forth to seek out some of the answers to these questions – a poor example of the BBC series *So Who Do You Think You Are* – but unlike the professionalism of The BEEB in following his trail I wasn't quite so well organised nor so well resourced or informed.

1928 Yearbook

I somehow stumbled across the 1928 Yearbook for Lincoln University, Pennsylvania, a leading Black university: it provided me with some very useful biographical information as did a United Kingdom Medical Directory; later on I came across a reference to Lincoln University Centennial Alumni Directory from the year 1954.

1907 Clarksville Red River County Texas

Arthur Philip Motley was born in Clarksville Texas on the 18th June 1904 and not 1907 as he maintained for the rest of his life. His mother was Ethel Motley. His father was a Frank Motley (as recorded in Arthur P. Motley's matriculation record at the University of Edinburgh). At the time I assumed Frank was his natural father, but more anon. At one time his father was a minister thus the Reverend Frank Motley.

Arthur's birthplace, Clarksville in Texas, is most famous for – at least to me as a former international athlete – as the birthplace of the legendary athlete and Black icon the great Tommy Smith whose gesture giving the Black Power salute on the dais at the 1968 Mexico Olympic Games 200 metres medal ceremony captured the imagination of the world - a moment in time and an image that will live forever.

When Arthur was born Clarksville's population was 2,000 with a mixed demographic of white and Black people: the 'city' had a relatively new limestone courthouse; five white and two Black churches; three schools; two banks; two flour mills, and a weekly newspaper, the Clarksville Times.

Tommy Smith 1968 Olympic Games

The town was established by a James Clark who moved to the area in 1833 and laid out a town site. When Red River County was organised in 1835 Clarksville was chosen as the county seat beating out the community of La Grange (later named Madras). The town was incorporated by an act of the Texas Congress in 1837 and within a few years it became an educational and agricultural centre.

Many of the town residents had fought in the Confederate Army during the American Civil War.

Economic recovery from the Civil War was stimulated when the Texas and Pacific Railway reached Clarksville in 1872 bringing new settlers and new businesses.

The 1870 census recorded a population of 613. By 1885, the population had grown to about 1,200. In 1914, the city now had 3,000 residents – a significant exponential growth - and had added a waterworks, two newspapers, an ice plant, and an electric power plant.

After that, outside events such as two World Wars, the Great Depression and increased competition from other cities (e.g., Dallas, Paris, Bonham, and Texarkana) began to slow Clarksville's growth. By the turn of the new century the population in 2000 had stabilised and was very near to that in 1920.

L'Ouverture High School McAlester City Oklahoma

L'Ouverture High School · 1908 · 1952

However Arthur didn't attend school in Clarksville but instead attended the preparatory L'Ouverture High School in McAlester City Oklahoma so at some point around 1908 the family must have moved from his birthplace in the state of Texas, 128 miles north to the state of Oklahoma to McAlester City.

We know that this must have been when he was no more than 3 years of age, but again, more of that later.

The 13th United States Census of 1910 records Arthur, his brother Harold, father Frank and his mother Ethel as now living at 118 Monroe Avenue, McAlester City, this but a short time after it received its statehood in 1907 through the Louisiana Purchase in

1803 that the United States had obtained what became the state of Oklahoma.

L'Ouverture High School opened in 1908.

It was an all Black school remaining so because of segregation until 1968 when it closed and a new integrated school opened in the city.

When Arthur attended the school there were four classrooms.

His grandson Harold Motley writes that the school was two-storied and included children from kindergarten through to senior grade classes within the one building and that the school's books, desks and equipment were hand-me-downs from local white schools.

The school was named after the great Haitian revolutionary, Toussaint Louverture.

Toussaint Louverture

The school came into being within a culture and tradition emanating from Haiti, maintained and carried through the Civil

War and into the twentieth century in response to racial discrimination.

Attending such a high school with its iconic name would have meant that Arthur would have had a deep knowledge of Black history and also United States, European and Native American history which were all part of the syllabus as was the Haitian Revolution. And thus despite the relative paucity of educational material it stressed the value and the importance of getting a goodeducation.

And yet when I recall any interaction between Dr Motley and myself I never got the impression that he was interested in this key social and cultural aspect – the struggle of Black people, never mind being any kind of an activist: instead it was the normal courteous interface between two individuals: and when it became a discussion on medical matters you were of course in the company of someone more knowledgeable than yourself – but around that there was usually a more light-hearted ambience and some banter.

Reflecting on this half a century on I wonder if that meant he was more comfortable in this specific environment which was very much a controlled one, but that perhaps he may have felt less comfortable outwith?

I don't know, but my gut feeling says yes, he was less comfortable in more open-ended situations and interfaces, but that said I have very little to go on. On one occasion we met up at the Pentland Community Centre and on a few other occasions I was very briefly in his sitting room at his home in Caiystane.

Shortly after Arthur left L'Ouverture High School a gymnasium cum auditorium was added to the building.

The design is of an Art Deco style. This was progressed during the Great Depression and through the Works Progress Administration it provided work for unskilled Blacks.

A Willa Strong was a member of Arthur's class in 1924 – remarkably she went on to become Dr Willa Strong and in later years went on to teach there before becoming the school's principal.

The school closed in 1968: in 2014 the building was purchased by two former class members to be preserved becoming a new community and cultural facility.

Dr Willa Strong

Dr Willa Strong was an inspiration to the Black students who attended L'Ouverture Elementary and High School in McAlester as well as being a Sunday School superintendent at the African Methodist Episcopal Church.

She was seen as being a very loving person - a caring but stern individual. Following in the school's tradition her raison d'etre was to help to ensure that her students aimed high and excelled through education to go on to lead a good life fulfilling their potential.

Dr Willa Strong - Arthur's classmate

She was born in what was then known as South McAlester on June 24, 1908, only a year after Oklahoma statehood.

Her parents were a William M. Strong and Wilma Johnson Strong, both from Texas so again there was another connection with Arthur Motley. Her father worked as a garage mechanic and her mother, Wilma, gave piano lessons and also taught music.

Strong went on to the University of Kansas in Lawrence earning a bachelor's degree returning thereafter to teach at L'Ouverture Elementary School in 1929 whilst doing graduate courses at the University of Chicago, earning a master's degree. A decade later in 1939 Strong was appointed principal at L'Ouverture High School and also the elementary school. Later on she was awarded a Ph.D. in education from the University of Oklahoma. She served as L'Ouverture's principal for 30 years – becoming one of the best well-known African American educators in the state of Oklahoma.

When inducted into the Oklahoma African American Educators Hall of Fame, it was mentioned how she developed a 'can do' sensibility and attitude amongst both students and staff at L'Ouverture.

When the schools integrated in 1968 Dr Strong served as vice principal at McAlester Junior High School before retiring a few years later at the end of June 1970. Sadly, she died but a year afterwards in 1971.

She was a strong advocate of Black, Oklahoman and American history once commenting 'Once you get it in your head, they can't take it away.'

She was posthumously inducted into the Oklahoma African American Educators Hall of Fame, is known far beyond McAlester.

Her record, like Dr Motley's, exemplifies the high standards and the cultural nature of the school, young as it was at the time.

Homelife

Compared to some of his school-mates Arthur and the Motley family were perhaps slightly better off than many other local Black families.

But that said, like all Black families it was within an environment of the Oklahoma Jim Crow code and culture which impacted upon every aspect of home-life and the interface between white and Black people in terms of access to work where the latter were discriminated against as well as in the quality of access to education, health, housing, recreation and other facets of life.

But that didn't mean that within the Black community there wasn't an active social and cultural life especially within the church environment – and for the Motleys - most probably the Baptist church – at the forefront of life offering a safe haven from the vicissitudes of segregation and discrimination.

Looking up Choctaw Ave. from Union Station, McAlester, Okla.

In the years between 1908 and 1925 when Arthur left for Wiley College Texas aged around 21 the family would have enjoyed some very happy times too.

They may have had access to and enjoyed a battery-powered radio and could listen to radio shows.

With his natural intelligence, inquisitiveness and interest in the world Arthur would have found this aspect of entertainment and education enjoyable.

And whilst come 1930 Ethel is recorded as being employed as a secretary, up until Arthur left home she and Frank assumed the traditional roles with Frank working long hours at the laundry whilst Ethel took on the primary caring role bringing up Arthur and his elder brother Harold alongside taking care of all the household tasks and chores such as sewing, cooking and canning.

And whilst there was a certain hierarchy at play – even the census denotes this with a Head of House category - family life was moving toward being more of an emotional approach with each member seeing one another as a friend too.

McAlester City Library

The advent of indoor lighting and indoor plumbing made life easier making it possible for people to stay up later into the evening in the winter months if you wished to read.

There was a small McAlester City library and at certain periods in the year Arthur may well have become a well-kent face looking in each week as he so wished to borrow books to stretch himself and satisfy a thirst for knowledge.

In 1920 a radical new magazine came out which was targeted at coloured children.

It was called *The Brownies' Magazine* and was aimed at Black and brown children as well as those who were yellow and all colours.

It was revolutionary and radical: part of the magazine's rationale was not only to entertain and to educate but to help children and young people to raise their horizons – to change their sensibilities to realise that it wasn't only the children of white people who could aspire to become architects, dentists and of course doctors too, so who knows, aged 16 this may well have been what lit the flame for young Arthur in his dream to one day qualify as a doctor.

The Brownies' only lasted for two years, but Arthur was at a key stage in his development, aged 16 to 18, so the magazine may well have shaped him considerably.

Prior to The Brownies' there had also been another magazine called *The Crisis.*

Within both magazines' pages there were features on art, sport, play, games, etc. But there were also occasional mentions to political life in America including references to the dreadful lynchings which were still unfortunately happening, all of which helped to shape and create that awareness and sensibility of life in America in Arthur's mind and as highlighted by his grandson Harold may have been one of the primary reasons that his grandfather moved abroad to another country to escape this stain on American life.

The editor of The Brownies' was a man called W.E.B. Du Bois and his vision was to help to instil some universal values within the readership including that being Black was nothing to be ashamed of and that instead that children and young people should grow up realising that they were beautiful.

He promoted a mode of behaviour and sensibility for young people to help them overcome the unfairness in life and ways to address the vicissitudes of what life might throw at them.

And certainly in looking back and recalling the way that Dr Motley behaved and inter-related with people he was a perfect living example of what The Brownies' mission was all about.

This may well have been an important part of the socialisation process in Arthur's young life.

Arthur's father was described as being white with Ethel, Harold and Arthur, Black - and not as mulatto as described in the earlier census of 1910 - but I think the boys' cultural identity and racial pride would have been important to them and to the family too.

Similar to thousands of other Black families who had moved north - the Motley's too had moved from living rurally - and were now technically more urban dwellers.

If they had continued to live down south Frank may have had to work on a farm, in the fields, repairing equipment or farm buildings.But given Dr Motley's sunny disposition, life in 1920s McAlester City wasn't all work and no play.

The family enjoyed school annual presentations where Arthur would have been a star and end of the year picnics where they could gather with their neighbours and friends.

Given Frank's strong interest in religion the church would have featured predominantly in the family's life what with gatherings, potluck dinners and ice cream socials as a way to bring people together in their leisure time.

And amongst it all he would be like others too - taking music lessons and maybe even attending camp. Dr Motley had a sweet tooth so no doubt enjoyed his candy and sucking on lollipops.

At some stage he would have been introduced to American Football as well as to baseball and basketball.

And at year end he would have posed for school pictures now sadly all gone including when he proudly graduated from High School.

1925 Wiley College Marshall Texas

Around the age of 21 Arthur left high school in Oklahoma returning to Texas but this time much further south to begin studying at the famous Black college, Wiley in Marshall Texas.

Wiley College is situated 109 miles from his birthplace in Clarksville and 211 miles distant from McAlester City.

In travelling there he joined the 'Wiley Express' a famous train that carried students back and forward.

I can only surmise as to why Arthur - or indeed his parents Ethel and Frank - chose Wiley College. Having reflected on this and exchanged views with Harold Motley the reason may well have been the revelation that after Arthur's school sweetheart became pregnant in 1924 his father the Reverend Motley took control of the situation and with the timing being right in terms of Arthur leaving school and going off to college he arranged to have him shipped out the 200 miles distant to pour cold water on the relationship and to help extinguish the passionate fire.

The college had an excellent sports programme including American Football so Arthur would have enjoyed this aspect helping him forget Freddie.

I recall on one occasion on a visit to the Oxgangs Surgery Dr Motley proudly showed me a trophy – a gold (American) football set on a plinth which he had been awarded: he said that he was a well regarded player and it delighted him that I too should so enjoy sport: for several years it provided a common link between the two of us.

After Arthur left the college, a few years later, during the early 1930s Wiley College became famous across America for the high quality of its debating team, indeed a film - The Great Debaters - starring Denzil Washington was made about the team's extraordinary record.

And in 1933 Wiley College was recognised by the Association of Colleges and Secondary Schools as an "A" class college of the southern states marking the first time any Black school had been rated by the same agency and standards as other universities.

Lincoln University Pennsylvania

1926

The following year, 1926, Arthur left Wiley College. I imagine he returned home for the summer before travelling east, the far distance to Chester County in the state of Pennsylvania to enrol at Lincoln University where he would remain for the next two years graduating with a Bachelor of Arts degree.

Two years later the Lincoln University 1928 yearbook records:

'Hoops' Motley, now living in McAlester Oklahoma also comes to us from Wiley College. He belongs to The Firm, to the Varsity L Club and to Alpha. Hoops has been among the honour group students since his matriculation. He is a profound philosopher of life and religion; a lover of women, Wiley, and Bull Sessions. A few years and Hoops will be an M.D. from Edinburgh, Scotland.'

After graduating from the university Arthur presumably returned home to McAlester City for the summer thereafter leaving home, probably for the very last time, to make his way across America by train before boarding a ship docked in New York to sail across the Atlantic Ocean to begin his studies in Edinburgh, Scotland.

In 1983, 55 years later and now retired, the 79 year-old Dr Arthur P. Motley would cross the Atlantic Ocean to return to his alma mater, Lincoln University for one last time to meet up with some of his former classmates from the year of 1928.

The LION newsletter of Summer 1983 records:

"DR.ARTHUR P. MOTLEY a medical practitioner travelled the long distance from Edinburgh, Scotland, to be present at Commencement and to celebrate his 55th reunion with his classmates. The Class of 1928 MOTLEY, Arthur Philip, physician; b Clarksville Tex June 18 1907; prep L'Overature HS McAlester Okla;'

So there we have it - the bare bones of Arthur Philip Motley's story – a life in a few pages – a swift journey through his early life trajectory.

I've no idea whether Dr Motley ever returned to America before that class reunion of 1983.

Did he ever pay a visit back home to McAlester City Oklahoma to visit his parents Ethel and Frank Motley?

Did he keep in touch with them by telephone or through correspondence?

Did he help to support them 'Magwitch style' (Dickens' *Great Expectations*) from a distance or was that vice-versa?

After graduating and qualifying as a doctor in Edinburgh was his initial plan to eventually return to the States to go back home - to work – to build a career – and to develop a family life in McAlester City. And if so, what diverted him from his planned route of travel?

We may never know the answers to some of these and other pertinent questions, but in the process I've managed to piece together some of his story.

And outwith that very late visitation to Lincoln University Pennsylvania in 1983 when he was aged at least 79 whilst we can surmise why he didn't return to America and why that should have been the case – why did he leave it so very late in the day to return to the land of his birth?

It seems strange because undoubtedly his mother in particular as well as his father must surely have been very supportive of him making great sacrifices along the way to help him on his journey through life trying to give him the kind of life which they had never enjoyed.

So, although the young 21 year old Arthur Philip Motley set out to study in Edinburgh, Scotland and no doubt will have had his dreams and plans, as one wag said 'God laughs at those who make plans' - or as the former British Prime Minister Harold Macmillan reputedly remarked to President Kennedy 'Events, dear boy, events.'

2018

In first sketching out a pen-portrait of Dr Motley in 2012 it was a

bit like throwing a pebble in to a pond, not knowing quite where the ripples might go.

Six years later, in 2018, I came across further information about him including a brief CV in the 1954 Lincoln Alumni Centennial Directory:

'MOTLEY, Arthur Philip, physician; b Clarksville Tex June 18 1907; prep L'Ouverture HS McAlester Okla; attended Royal College of Surgeons Edinburgh: LMSSA (London) 1939; m AnAve Corona LI NY 1/54) Annette T H Combe Oct 1929; chil-Annette. Gen prac of med. Mem Brit Med Assn; assoc mem Brit Assn for the Advance of Sci; mem Coun of Scottish Health and Soil SOC; foundation mem of the Coll of Gen Practitioners; mem Edinburgh Clinical Club, Edinburgh Internat Hous. Ch of Scotland. Capt Royal Army Med Corps 1940-46. Address: (res) McAlester Cottage Oxgangs Rd Edinburgh Scotland.'

This was very useful providing and re-confirming some earlier information, the detail of which I was already familiar with but it also added some new information propelling me forward to pursue one or two new avenues - new trails - allowing me to begin to both induct and deduct from these and other sources discovering some new and quite illuminating aspects of Arthur's life here in Scotland and in particular with regard to his wife Annette and their daughter, Annette Junior.

Sherlock Holmes

The new information which I did gradually elicit, given the era, was quite revelatory and astonishing.

However, whilst I'd donned my Sherlock Holmes deerstalker and felt quite pleased with myself, I hadn't been quite as incisive and sharp as I should have been.

The synopsis – of a life denoted in a brief CV – whilst it made me rethink some aspects of Arthur Motley's life trajectory, I didn't quite cotton on – I didn't twig - to a key part of his story.

And instead a further twist in the road awaited me a further two years later in the summer of 2020 when it occurred to me of something really quite significant – an incredibly important thread in the life of Arthur P. Motley and from the most important decade in his life, between the ages of 24 and 34 which would determine the course of the rest of his life was there all along – not hidden – but as far as I had been concerned, it was hidden to me, but instead it was in plain sight.

And further to that another revelation awaited me too but was hidden within the bowels of the Scotland's People website.

Revelation

Up until last year (2020) I had simply assumed that Arthur had graduated from the University of Edinburgh. And why shouldn't I have – after all, as a former student there, and as mentioned, in later years during the early 1980s he occasionally took my mother out for lunch to the Edinburgh University former students' club, then why should I have assumed anything else.

My natural assumption had been that because he had gone to the University of Edinburgh that he had naturally graduated from that august and esteemed old institution too – either M.B., Ch.B. or M.D.

He had studied at the University.

He had worked at the city's Royal Infirmary.

He became a doctor.

And after a while he set up his own practice in Oxgangs.

And that his route of travel had been smooth and seamless.

But no - instead, it had been anything but and his life could just as easily have taken a very different course altogether.

And as with us all the road taken was a mix of serendipity, ability, application and luck.

But eight years after first writing about him and appropriately given the year – I was now beginning to apply more of a 20-20 vision to his story.

And of how of a sudden a thought occurred to me - that perhaps Arthur Philip Motley hadn't graduated in 1932 from the University of Edinburgh after all and that he may instead have failed those notoriously ferocious, tough and much feared exams – he may even have had to give up the course entirely.

As you might imagine that thought and possible revelation hit me quite hard – I found it quite startling and if he had come a cropper then this would beg all sorts of new questions, once again leading to me to take down my metaphorical deerstalker hat from a hook in the hall setting me back off on the trail in search of Dr Motley's story.

And whilst I was aware that I might only manage to put a little more flesh on the bones I determined to do so, not with the smooth and efficient approach of the BBC's *So Who Do You Think You Are*, but one which was a little more scatter-gun in approach.

I was aware that where I'd gone awry was in not picking up – not cottoning on that the big clue had been staring me in the face all along – it was the gap – he had begun studying in Edinburgh in 1928 (straight into second year) and thus if things had progressed smoothly he should have graduated as a doctor in around 1932.

But instead, in the brief CV that I'd been aware of, there was no mention of him graduating in the early 1930s: and once I'd got my head around some of the acronyms denoting a doctor's qualification – at the time there were several - I was able to ascertain and become fairly sure that Arthur Philip Motley didn't graduate from the University of Edinburgh after all.

University of Edinburgh

But let's not get too ahead of ourselves and go back to 1928 and young Arthur Philip Motley's arrival in Scotland.

In that year he had successfully graduated from Lincoln University with a B.A. – a Bachelor of Arts degree from one of the foremost Black universities in the United States.

His parents must have been very proud of him: this was the completion of a big first step in their hopes for their son.

Interestingly, although he earned an arts degree, looking at the subjects which he studied (as listed in the University of Edinburgh Matriculation form) they are much more of a scientific bent rather than what we might have been expected from an Arts degree today - the qualification would surely have resulted instead in a B.Sc. - a science degree - and indeed in references within later U.K. Medical Directories it states that instead he has a B.Sc. - yet another Arthur Phillip Motley mystery.

But in those two years at Lincoln University between 1926 and 1928 he studied: Physics; Botany; Practical Botany; Chemistry; Practical Chemistry; Zoology; and Practical Zoology - so not much in the way of arts subjects there.

Thus by 1928 - most probably a goodly while before then - he had decided he wished to study medicine and at the University of Edinburgh.

As to how this came about we'll never know.

Did he discuss it with the academic staff at Lincoln University?

With Edinburgh being one of the most prestigious centres of learning and medicine in the world did this aspect enter into any such discussions?

Some form of extensive discussion surely took place between the 24 year old Arthur and his parents particularly as to how he - and no doubt they - because much of the financial burden would fall to Ethel and Frank were going to fund both the academic fees and his accommodation and living expenses in such a radical venture.

To enable Arthur to study at the University of Edinburgh he was required to sit a preliminary exam - the Scottish Universities Entrance Board in July 1928.

One would have hoped that Arthur was able to sit this examination in the United States rather than having to travel across the Atlantic Ocean to Scotland only to return back to America immediately thereafter.

It would also have been exceedingly expensive for such a short trip to have had to do so.

But the wonderful news for all concerned was that he successfully passed this exam which now qualified him to study at the university.

His final year at Lincoln University studying science subjects would have served him well for the University of Edinburgh examination: I wonder whether going into the 1927/28 academic year in Pennsylvania influenced his choice of final year subjects.

But he had cleared this next hurdle - the game was on!

Thus it was a very brave step by the 24 year old Arthur Philip Motley B.A. who now set out – possibly Magellan-like from New York to step onto Scotland's shores at Glasgow for presumably the first occasion on the 28th September 1928, well into a Scottish autumn.

Anchor Steamline Caledonia

S.S. Caledonia

What was that journey like for this young man as he boarded a ship for probably the first time?

No matter the size of a ship, crossing the Atlantic Ocean is quite a journey. Was the trip smooth or was it rough? Was he sea-sick as many people are? Did he socialise with others on board the ship?

What we do know is that he travelled as a student on the Anchor Steamline ship 'Caledonia' – rather appropriate as he sought out a new life here in Scotland.

On the ship's passenger list his occupation is recorded as being a student however his name is mis-spelt as 'Matley Arthur' rather than Motley Arthur.

Arthur may well have been the only Black man on board which may have led to some awkward interactions: some passengers may have been friendly with him whilst others may have chosen not to interact with him whatsoever and simply ignored him. And as to whether he joined fellow male passengers in the ship's smoking room who can say, but it's unlikely.

However as often happened on those journeys as the days on the Atlantic Ocean passed and the ship travelled further and further away from American shores people relaxed more and some of the prejudice and discrimination dissipated too and Arthur may well found himself enjoying some conversations with others who may well have been interested and fascinated by his back-story and his future ambitions.

The Smoking Room

Apart from it possibly being a rough passage on a choppy autumn sea it may well have been a rough emotional passage for him too.

Here he was setting out alone with no friends nor company. He was travelling to another country and to another continent.

Before he left home in McAlester City he would have been at the centre of attention – perhaps there was a leaving party for him where he was showered with good wishes and gifts too – did Ethel proffer a coat on him or was that something he would buy when he arrived in Edinburgh.

But as he looked out over the boat's rails he would have reflected on that last emotional and party family atmosphere and of just what he was leaving behind and all the while nervously worried and anticipated what lay ahead of him and how he might cope.

At that stage we have no idea whether his intention after qualifying was to create a new life for himself in the United Kingdom, perhaps with the idea of settling in Scotland or whether he instead thought he would simply return to America: my guess is it would have been the latter.

But Edinburgh has a habit of drawing her students into her bosom with the city gradually finding a deep part in former students' hearts. And Dr Motley would be no different in this respect, but his ultimate decision to do so would be a little more nuanced than simply a love for Scotland's capital.

After a week at sea when the boat entered port there would have been a great deal going on ashore.

He would have had to struggle through the crowds with his luggage.

In contrast to home he would have noticed that it was white people who were undertaking the more menial work in contrast to back home in distant America: there would have been many backs bowed as the porters struggled with the passengers' heavy trunks and luggage.

His first port of call would have been to the immigration office: thereafter having had his papers checked and requesting and receiving directions he headed off to the busy railway station.

On arrival at the grey station he would have been met by a similar cacophony of frenetic and vibrant activity with steam engines pulling in and out whilst close to the platforms the kiosks and trolley vendors were busy selling colourful newspapers, magazines, cigarettes, sweets and chocolates as well as flowers wrapped in cellophane.

He would have taken a carriage to travel the short 50 miles or so from west to east and quickly realised that there was no classification of Black and white on board – indeed the only classification was based on the size of your pocket and whether you had purchased a first, second or third class train ticket.

And when the steam engine pulled into the magnificent Edinburgh Waverley Station he couldn't but be impressed by it – indeed possibly slightly overwhelmed by the sheer volume and number of passengers and people milling around.

But one of the advantages for Arthur with all his luggage was that Ramsay Lodge was but a half mile away, albeit a stiff climb up toward the Castle Rock and the world of the visionary garden cities architect Patrick Geddes. And although being tight for money, in this first instance Arthur probably took a taxi.

After checking in he might have had the time to go for a short wander.

Behind him was the Old Town with the tenement 'skyscrapers' and little wynds off a busy Royal Mile whilst down below him was an even busier Princes Street and beyond the magnificent sun-lit Edinburgh New Town.

It's Capital

His address and therefore first abode in Scotland is listed as being Ramsay Lodge Edinburgh: what a wonderful introduction to the capital to be accommodated at the top of the famous Royal Mile with its astonishing views across the city, with the Firth of Forth in the background and the hills of Highland in the distant beyond.

Arthur wouldn't have been used to the closely aligned buildings but couldn't but help be impressed although many of them were a grey and black sooty colour caused by the city's industries and the smoke emanating from the hundreds of steam engines that came and went each day not to mention from the thousands of chimneys across Auld Reekie.

However when he first ventured down to the New Town what a contrast with the lighter sandstone buildings particularly when the rays of the sun bathed their surfaces - another aspect of the duality that is Edinburgh – the dark and the light.

Ramsay Lodge

Arthur's residence at Ramsay Lodge wouldn't have been for long.

And like thousands of other students he would have very quickly had to seek out more permanent accommodation.

Arthur would no doubt have joined many others obtaining such information from the College Board and also from the adverts in the daily Scotsman Newspaper columns.

It wouldn't have been quite so straightforward as for his white counterparts as not every landlord, landlady or family renting out a room would have been keen to take in a Black student.

However, once he did I'm sure they would have been quickly won over by his charm and that he was such an interesting individual who had come from the American South.

He was clearly successful as by the start of the new university term his matriculation record has him residing toward the top of bustling Leith Walk at 54 Brunswick Crescent presumably in a let out room c/o Foubister: so at an early stage he moved into new accommodation: but perhaps within a month or so after this he is then denoted by the university as residing at 25 Marchmont Road c/o McLeish.

Therefore within a matter of a few months it would appear that he has had three different abodes and addresses within the city and it's still only the autumn of 1928.

An Edinburgh Autumn

Starting at the University of Edinburgh in the early autumn of 1928 must have been an exciting time for Arthur and one of his first tasks after finding more permanent accommodation would have been to visit the medical section of the famous and well-established James Thin Bookseller to purchase his text books.

He would have enjoyed walking from Marchmont Road down toward The Meadows crossing under the whalebone arch following the path that dissects this oasis of greenery in the city toward university-land.

By this time in the seasonal year the temperatures would have begun to drop and then within a matter of weeks plummeted.

The leaves were beginning to change to a golden brown and then as the season moved into November a dirty brown: sometimes young Arthur would have walked through a swathe of such leaves.

Meadow Walk, Edinburgh

Like many others over the years and the decades, on such golden afternoons he would have thoroughly enjoyed those walks traversing back and forth, but on other days when the infamous Edinburgh squalls did their worst – when it was wet and windy – he would have had his head down as he battled against the city's elements – very different from Oklahoman autumn afternoons.

On those daily journeys back and forward his sojourns would have been taken amongst many other students: Marchmont has always been and remains to this very day a popular area to live in, particularly for those attending the University of Edinburgh as well as for trainee doctors and trainee nurses too.

It was a popular area for the aspiring middle-class's with men who worked in the city and were able to walk to their work and their offices within the city centre.

During the day it was often quite vibrant with either mums or nannies who would take their young children out to enjoy the green spaces on their doorstep or to the play-park areas with their swings, roundabouts and chutes.

The park was overseen by uniformed park-keepers with their black caps.

And when the weather was fine there were even local ice cream vendors out too.

There has always been a happy feel to The Meadows and I think Arthur would have enjoyed this lovely aspect of Edinburgh.

And whilst the city and its weather were very different from McAlester City or from Lincoln University Pennsylvania where he spent the previous two years, still, on fine days he would have enjoyed those walks as he began to become more and more familiar with the area and all the time enjoying the buzz – the thrill – of starting his journey to qualify as a doctor.

But Edinburgh's weather would have been hard for Arthur to endure compared to the humid sub-tropical climate of McAlester City, what with its milder winters, but Oxford Pennsylvania where Lincoln University is situated is more akin to Edinburgh so the previous two years between 1926 and 1928 would have helped to acclimatise Arthur; but Edinburgh is snell and known as the windy city and certainly there tends to be some form of a wind a-blowing each day and you could well imagine Arthur wearing gloves, a hat and a scarf huddled up to protect himself from the cold.

The Big Freeze

What he may not have anticipated was that that first winter for him in Scotland's capital city - the winter of 1928/1929 - was one of the severest in Britain during the whole of the 20th century matching the one of 1962 – The Big Freeze - when snow lay on the iron-hard ground from Boxing Day through to the spring – this was what lay ahead of him – what an introduction to the United Kingdom. And little did he know that his general practice would one day be out at Oxgangs in the lea of the snowy Pentland Hills.

January and February of 1929 were particularly cold months with sub zero temperatures which Arthur would have felt as he wynded his way going back and forward to university each week-day. And it wouldn't have been any balm to him that it was similarly bad back home in North America with Pennsylvania and the students at Lincoln University enduring similar such temperatures and also shivering with the extreme cold: meanwhile the rest of Europe was particularly badly hit too - welcome to another continent.

One of Arthur's first purchases was to buy a heavy overcoat from the likes of the Army & Navy store on busy Princes Street, the city's world famous and busy main shopping thoroughfare.

It's a thoroughfare that every visitor to the city experiences with its shops on one side of the street whilst on the other side Edinburgh Castle sits high above looking down upon the city and her citizens as they wander back and forth.

Not only would he have been keen to visit it, but at the far end of the street – toward what is known as the West End - was where the American Express building was located which played a small but important part in Arthur's life.

Show Boat

As a poor student it's unlikely that Arthur would have had much in the way of spare monies for entertainment but if he had, on the 1st October 1928 the newly re-furbished and re-named Empire Theatre on the South Bridge close-by to the University of Edinburgh had just re-opened after a lengthy re-fit and on its programme was a three week run of Show Boat which had come directly from Drury Lane, London's well-kent Theatre Royal.

As the novel on which the musical was based was only published two years before in 1926 with the musical thereafter opening to great success on Broadway the following year in 1927, the show had hit London and then Edinburgh with impressive rapidity.

In later years Dr Motley enjoyed attending the Kings Theatre Tollcross Edinburgh - more of which later - so it's a show that might well have appealed to him particularly with much of the content containing aspects of American life in the South that he could relate to.

The music was written by Jerome Kern and the lyrics by Oscar Hammerstein and P.G. Wodehouse: the musical followed the lives of the dock workers, the performers and the stage hands on the steamship The Cotton Blossom over a period of four decades to more or less the year of the show itself.

So, not only was it bang up to date but it also gave an interesting potted history into the lives of Black people that Arthur would have been very familiar with.

And thus whilst Arthur would have enjoyed the show and the music reminding him of home back in the United States - indeed he would have been able to relate to many of the characters and the stories including their love lives and the theme of racial prejudice – but at the same time it would have been a little unsettling for him too and a reminder of life back home in America.

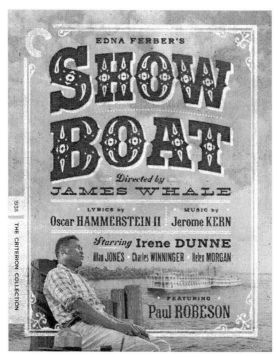

Edinburgh Colour Bar

And of course, it wasn't black and white so to speak, where his move from one distant shore to another would allow him to escape prejudice and its more active and ghastly form, discrimination, because like many other cities, Edinburgh too had its problems in terms of the prevailing social culture of the period.

When Arthur P. Motley arrived in Edinburgh in 1928 there was already a certain unfortunate culture within some parts of the city and from some of her citizens which had been growing since around 1920 as exemplified by the infamous Edinburgh colour bar – a badge of shame in the city's recent history especially in a city which was more widely and better known as the birth place and heart of the Age of Enlightenment – yet another example of the city of Jekyll and Hyde and the duality at her heart.

And whilst Arthur would have found himself in a distinct minority in a predominantly white local population, because of Edinburgh

Medical School's formidable world reputation it had been accommodating coloured students for at least 80 years.

In a great melee fellow young people had arrived in the city from not only the United States but India, Africa, Ceylon, Trinidad, Mauritius, Fiji, Egypt – there were Chinese, Japanese and Arabs. They were all colours – black, brown, yellow as well as white.

Such was Edinburgh's reputation that from the 1850s, Black students travelled from West Africa to train as doctors for the British Army's Medical Corps which of course Arthur would similarly join come the Second World War. Those earlier pioneers went on to work as medical officers in Sierra Leone, Ghana and Nigeria, but from 1902 a racist colour bar barred them from employment in the West African medical service.

But the Edinburgh colour bar was a stain – an unfortunate sensibility and mindset of various social and cultural institutions within the city as well as being a frame of mind of some individuals too.

This meant that in practical terms that when Arthur sought out accommodation in the early autumn of 1928 there would have been a distinct possibility of him being turned away. Don't forget that in Edinburgh's English counterpart – London – even into the 1960s lodging houses still displayed the infamous and egregious signage 'No Irish, no Blacks, no dogs'.

Some hotels and boarding houses had implemented a colour bar and this was also extended to places of entertainment including one of the city's largest and most popular places of entertainment, the Palais de Dance at Fountainbridge which could accommodate up to 900 young people.

It extended too, to some cafes and restaurants.

If queried as to the rationale for the rationale – appeasement (wasn't that concept ironic given a decade later Chamberlain's dealings with Hitler) – the managers and owners of such institutions responded that in turning coloured people away from the door was to keep their white patrons happy and to do otherwise would simply put them at the risk of going out of business.

Simply put, their predominant regular customers would not enjoy sharing such a space with coloured people – or at least they assumed so. And if they had to, they would instead take their business elsewhere.

It was rather ironic that Arthur Motley had left American shores where he had grown up and studied within a nation and a culture of deep and ingrained segregation only to arrive in the City of Enlightenment to unfortunately discover that he couldn't quite escape it and instead there were still vestiges of such a rotten culture prevailing within parts of Edinburgh.

Who knows therefore whether during those years Arthur went along to enjoy the musicals that were programmed at the Empire Theatre, but another irony is the name of the theatre too. An empire surely should surely reach out and be open to and welcome people from throughout the globe.

Such a prevailing culture is not just hearsay as on the 1st June 1927 just over a year before Arthur arrived in the city there was an astonishing letter published in the Manchester Guardian:

"I should like you to inform all members of the (Students') Union who use the above restaurant, on and after Saturday 23rd inst. admittance will be refused...I may add that this is not directed against the Indian community only, but includes all coloured patrons."

Jesu!

Thus Arthur would not just have felt vulnerable in moving so far from home, from continent to continent, but he was coming to a society where some individuals and some institutions not only displayed prejudice but acted upon it too by discriminating against people such as him and some of his peers.

And unlike other forms of this when directed against say Jewish people, Arthur could hardly go under the radar so to speak or disguise his background because being a Black man in a dominant white city he of course stood out.

In his day-to-day life it would have been difficult and challenging for him to ever escape from such an awareness and sensibility.

But Edinburgh wasn't all bad, indeed far from it and Arthur would have enjoyed the relative freedoms compared to some aspects of American life.

He was free to wander through the city's parks. There were no overt signs saying Whites Only.

There were other cafes, restaurants, dance halls, pictures and theatres that were open to him.

He may even have gone along at some stage to the Powderhall Stadium with some of his new friends and enjoyed a sixpenny bet on some of the greyhound dog racing.

And there were lots of university clubs and organisations several of which were based around those students who had travelled to Edinburgh from abroad.

And whilst within a generally more enlightened academic life and environment he would have been able to escape at least part of the time, especially because there would have been several others on the course who were non-white too, but as soon as he stepped out of the ivory towers of academia his ebony skin would have been only too apparent to others – indeed he would have been a novelty to many of those individuals with whom he came in to contact.

But more of Edinburgh's colour bar anon.

Edinburgh Tenement Life

Leith

With his initial brief residence perched up on the famous Edinburgh Castle Rock in his eyrie in Ramsay Place there was clearly no issue of discrimination or segregation from the university in providing accommodation.

Thereafter he stayed at Brunswick Street in Leith, but perhaps only for a month or so. I wonder why this might have been the case before he thereafter moved to the Marchmont area of the city.

With Leith having long been a port and a separate town from Edinburgh – indeed it was only eight years before in 1920 that it officially merged with Edinburgh - whilst being a predominantly working class area and because it was a sea-port it would have been much more tolerant and used to seeing such exotic individuals as Arthur what with the town and port trading with the rest of the world.

The town of Leith had a greater affinity with people from other lands who had immigrated there including some West Indian sailors who had settled in the area as well university student Indians who lived in the community.

Compared to Edinburgh it was slightly easier for Arthur to both secure accommodation and also to live there too.

But in the autumn of 1928 this was but for a brief period, although in later years the Motley family would return to live in Leith Walk for several years.

Marchmont

Marchmont Road with its Victorian and Edwardian tenements and wide cobbled streets and roads had been built for the growing middle classes and today a century later the flats are eagerly sought after commanding high prices.

They remain very popular with students too, although today it is more in terms of letting out a whole flat as opposed to when Arthur moved there to have a room let out to him but within a family household and home.

Renting out a room was a relatively easy and straightforward way for Edinburgh families to supplement their incomes allowing them to continue to live within a fine area of the town.

Marchmont Road, Edinburgh.

Most likely the flat at 25 Marchmont Road would have belonged to a reasonably well educated family – the McLeish's - who may have been more enlightened than others, but still they would have been ever mindful of what their neighbours may or may not have thought and said about renting out a room to a Black man: and no doubt when Arthur Motley first knocked upon their door seeking accomodation it would have made them pause to think.

Edinburgh Snobbery

It's impossible to really 'walk a mile in my shoes' if you generally haven't experienced prejudice and discrimination in your own life.

But in the City of Enlightenment this of course didn't and doesn't just relate to colour – living up to it being a a city of duality, it's a town where the old school tie still prevails.

Edinburghers on first meeting fellow Edinburghers for the first occasion, one of the first questions usually posed – overtly or subtly – is an inquiry as to what school you attended.

This allows some people to immediately pigeon-hole you – aah! he or she is or isn't one of us – we can feel safe – or better still, superior!

And if you attended one of the city's Merchant fee-paying schools such as Heriot's or George Watson's then you're fine – within Calvinist Edinburgh you're one of the chosen few.

'We' live in a different world to most other Edinburghers as exemplified by a certain class aloofness.

And when they engage with individuals from other city schools, whilst the likes of my former school, Boroughmuir - we pupils might just be generally acceptable – well, at least they – we - too play rugby to a good standard – but God help you if you attended somewhere such as Firrhill Secondary School, the secondary school in Dr Motley's future practice catchment area.

But ironically even in this world of the public school there is a ranking too – a social strata – an inverted snobbery - with those such as Fettes, where the former British Prime Minister Tony Blair had been educated – the Eton of the north – the school of James Bond – which alongside Loretto and perhaps Merchiston Castle see themselves as being a level up from the Merchant Company schools and therefore superior amongst superiors.

And whilst today things are miles better, unquestionably this still leads to some of the capital's sons and daughters being treated slightly differently from their peers within Edinburgh society influencing people's future life trajectories in terms of access to jobs and to careers.

There's still at play an aspect of who you know rather than who you are.

Dr Jekyll and Hyde

So, this was the city that Arthur came to study in – a city of contradictions and one which whilst vastly better and a great deal safer than the segregation that existed back home in America, yet within Edinburgh, prejudice and discrimination existed and occasionally raised its ugly head - it was just that most often it was something more subtle, but on other occasions could be quite overt and in your face.

In my remembrance of Dr Motley and those of many of his former patients the words used to describe him which crop up time and time again include how sensitive, gentle, caring and dignified he was as an individual.

As to how much that may be to do with nature rather than nurture is difficult to gauge.

Given he played American Football and was a young, virile, fit 24 year old man he would have had to contain some of the natural aggressiveness that comes with such territory, but certainly in the decades that I became more aware of him when he would have been in his late fifties there was no aspect of that whatsoever in his character.

Whilst growing up in Oklahoma the adoption of an at times subservient attitude and demeanour was probably the most rationale and pragmatic mode of behaviour to adopt within a highly predominant white culture - let's not upset the apple cart so to speak.

At times it must have felt like walking on egg-shells because even a decade later in 1937 there was an infamous incident that hit the news headlines throughout the world called Barring the Bishop.

Similar to Arthur P. Motley the African-American Bishop William Henry Heard had also travelled the 3,000 miles across the Atlantic Ocean from North America to Edinburgh to attend a Christian conference in Scotland's capital - how ironic - how Christian! He was accompanied by his niece. However, he ran into some unexpected problems.

On arrival at the city's top hotel, the North British Railway Station Hotel, both Heard and his niece were denied entry. They were turned away because of the afore-mentioned infamous Edinburgh colour bar.

The 87 year old bishop had perhaps hoped that he had left segregation, prejudice and discrimination far behind when he travelled to Bonnie Scotland which of course wasn't quite so bonnie after all.

He had ventured far across the sea to another continent only to discover that things weren't so very far different, leaving his niece to search out alternative accommodation in the city's West End finding a hotel there that would give them a room for the night. And still yet another irony given one of the key stories in the Bible - that of Mary and Joseph - seeking out a room at the inn only to be given a stable for the night.

Bishop Heard had arrived in Edinburgh to attend the World Council on Faith and Order Conference - not only had he travelled 3,000 miles, he had travelled a similarly long metaphorical journey as Arthur – indeed given his age an even longer and harder one as he had been a slave in the American South until the age of 15 and was one of the millions of slaves liberated during and after the American Civil War of 1859-1865.

However, unlike Arthur Motley – or perhaps they just had different approaches – Arthur's route of travel could have been argued to be more simple and straightforward – the African Methodist Episcopal Church Bishop was a loud and passionate advocate for civil rights so apart from the practical concerns of an old man securing a place to rest his head for the night it would also have incurred his ire and wrath stoking a natural sense of the great unfairness and injustice of life – and of how far he had travelled in life but of how much further he still had to travel because of the ongoing plight of Black and coloured people around the world – to become that society that didn't judge you on the colour of your skin but on the character of your behaviour.

Of course – and why not - it was also a useful opportunity to generate 'good' publicity for the great cause.

The Archbishop of York William Temple made an offer to Bishop Heard to come and join him to share his accommodation within the capital but Heard turned it down instead using the opportunity to make political capital in the capital.

On a more positive note, reflecting the duality at the heart of Edinburgh, in the days and the weeks thereafter the city revealed the better side of her nature and her split personality when Bishop Heard received supportive letters from the Scottish public giving him moral support and saying how ashamed they were of the hotel and of some of their fellow citizens and the way that both he and his niece had been treated.

As for Arthur we'll never know just how much prejudice and discrimination he suffered throughout his life but we can make an informed guess.

The Peripatetic Philosopher

Staying at Ramsay Place, Brunswick Street, Marchmont Road and then moving back to Leith Walk sometime in the early 1930s until circa 1936 when he and his wife Annette moved out to Colinton

Mains Road clearly shows Arthur had a roof over his head throughout the period, but as to whether he found such accommodation easy to come by, or only after walking the city streets seeking out flat after flat and being turned away because he was Black, only Arthur could ever have told us.

But when I recall his gentle countenance it made me think of the slings, the arrows and the brickbats he endured from people who were prejudiced and even worse, in the active sense of the word, through discrimination. But with his gentle manner and fine sensibility I suspect he often did what many smart people do in life - never reacting, never responding, simply just ignoring such things and instead getting on with the business of living and life. It's a philosophy I subscribe to but one which can be challenging to always live by - to live up to - and to adopt - and to implement. And yet I feel he was a master of such an intelligent and pragmatic approach which in a way was Gandhi-like.

But my mother made an astute point to me which in later years was echoed by Dr Motley's grandson, Harold Motley's view - when she said that 'Surely would it not have been a lot worse for him back in the States'.

Whilst I think the answer to that statement is most certainly yes, it was indeed much better than if he had lived an alternate life back in the United States - it wasn't a black and white issue - well it was - but the issues and the barriers that he would have had to address and meet and overcome in Edinburgh as he made his journey through life would not have been insubstantial.

The Doppelgänger

Young Arthur Motley aged 24 from McAlester City via Wiley College Texas via Lincoln University Pennsylvania arrived in 1928 into a so called City of Enlightenment, but one where prejudice and some active discrimination existed too - a city where some wags thought it clever to call Black people such names as Chalky White.

For those who are familiar with Edinburgh and know her intimately this might come as no surprise. Edinburgh has long been famous or infamous for its duality as expressed by writers such as Robert Louis Stevenson - Edinburgh and not London is of course where Dr Jekyll and Mr Hyde roam the streets of the Old and the New Town - yet another aspect of her duality - the city of Deacon

Brodie who was a town councilman by day and a thief by night –
and as written about by the great Karl Miller and others, the capital
remains the city of the doppelgänger.

Did Arthur find this contradiction – this strange dichotomy difficult
to cope with. And, how did he find his classmates and bedfellows
– were they similar or were they very different.

Homesick

Like any student, at times he would have been home-sick
exaggerated by the great gulf of the Atlantic Ocean separating him
from the land across the water especially when contrasted and
compared with most of his fellow students from the United
Kingdom who could at least aim to travel home at Christmas and
Easter.

But that wasn't an option for Arthur.

To an extent he was inured to this having been away from home
since 1925 when he first went to study at Wiley College in Texas
and then over the next two years in Pennsylvania, but still, at such
key occasions in the calendar year I would like to think that he was
welcomed into the bosom of the family lodgings at Christmas and
New Year or that he was able to enjoy key social occasions with the
new friends which he had made either at university or through the
local societies or organisations which he may have joined.

Over the course of the autumn of 1928 and then as it proceeded
into that severe freezing winter of late 1928 and into the first two
months of 1929 which echoed another crash, when not only was it
the temperatures that plummeted, but in the wider economic world
The Great Crash itself would impact upon the Motley family
similar to millions of other families across America.

Leerie the Lamplighter

During that first academic year in Edinburgh Arthur would have
soon got into a regular pattern of life.

Whilst living for the short time in Leith at 56 Brunswick Street, in
the early mornings he would have walked the two uphill miles to
the university.

Come the autumn the city's street lamps would be lit – and whilst
by 1928 the gas may no longer have been lit by Leerie the

Lamplighter made famous by Robert Louis Stevenson's poem - now replaced by a new automatic device, but still many aspects of pre First World War Edinburgh life in the form of its buildings and its streets remained much the same: indeed even today in 2021 Edinburgh is recognisable in a way than few other UK cities are.

My tea is nearly ready and the sun has left the sky;
It's time to take the window to see Leerie going by;
For every night at teatime and before you take your seat,
With lantern and with ladder he comes posting up the street.

Now Tom would be a driver and Maria go to sea,
And my papa's a banker and as rich as he can be;
But I, when I am stronger and can choose what I'm to do,
Oh Leerie, I'll go round at night and light the lamps with you!

For we are very lucky, with a lamp before the door,
And Leerie stops to light it as he lights so many more;
And O! before you hurry by with ladder and with light,
O Leerie, see a little child and nod to him tonight!

Robert Louis Stevenson

On some days, if Arthur felt lazy, tired or even flush he may have taken the rattling trams that operated between Leith and Edinburgh.

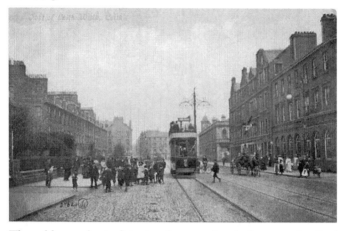

The cable cars he took to travel across the city began to be slowly replaced by electric trams which thereafter slowly gave way to buses when the last tram ran in the capital in the autumn of 1956 a few months after I was born.

And by the 1980s after he had retired it was rumoured that he enjoyed taking his visiting grandchildren on the famous number 32 bus which did a two hour circuit around Edinburgh's perimeter.

But back in the autumn of 1928 at the end of a day of attending lectures and studying he would have headed back to his lodgings wynding his way through Chamber Street or down The Royal Mile to the North Bridge before traversing Princes Street at its extreme east end walking down Leith Walk and back home to a room in the flat.

Mince and Tatties

Did his let room also include an evening meal courtesy of the Foubister family?

Perhaps.

And if it did, the fayre would have been very different from what Arthur was used to back home in America – there would have been porridge for breakfast and mince and tatties for dinner, or as it's termed in Scotland, your tea rather than your dinner.

Back home in Oklahoma he would have grown up enjoying Ethel's meals - dishes of rice and red beans, sweet potatoes, yams and sweet potato pie. Vegetables, pork and corn-breads and grits would have been an integral part of his diet too as would potato salads. Molasses would have been served in his iced tea and used as a sweetener in the cooking too.

But a dish common to both communities - America and Scotland - was that of macaroni and cheese, so if that were served up on a winter Scots evening after a day studying at university, it would have been a home from home treat for him.

Indeed macaroni was evidently a popular Christmas Day lunch in many of the Black States alongside other fayre: breakfast would have included eggs, bacon and sausages - something else he would have enjoyed in Edinburgh.

But if Arthur was able to partake of a family meal on Christmas Day in Edinburgh he would most likely have had roast turkey which is similar to the chicken he would have enjoyed back home in Oklahoma.

I certainly recall that despite having the most perfect set of teeth

even into old age, he did have a sweet tooth, no doubt from some of the afore-mentioned not to say the apple pies or brownies which Ethel would have served up back home.

Into the Mist

In that first year in Scotland's capital, no matter the time of the day or the evening the Edinburgh thoroughfares would have been busy with the sights and the sounds of the city.

On some days he may have swept round by his first lodging, that of Ramsay Place, with its panoramic views with Edinburgh Castle to the left, Princes Street down below in the valley with the Edinburgh New Town sweeping out behind and in the far distance the Forth and beyond that, on fair days, he could have glimpsed the hills of Highland in the far distance.

Taking in this panoramic view how Arthur's heart must have soared and lifted, at times gladdening his heart as he dreamt of a better future, and if not a golden one, then perhaps silver.

After he moved from Leith to Marchmont the journey was a different one from travelling up from working class Leith: now he was located in a more middle class area of the city and as he made his way each morning and evening, back and forward through the Meadows, this flatter route would have gladdened his heart too the way it's charmed so many of the university's alumni over the years, the decades and now the centuries.

Sometimes Arthur would have walked along and through the area's misty paths – those mysterious mists which descend upon the town which influenced an earlier more famous fellow Edinburgh doctor, the great novelist Arthur Conan Doyle.

Auld Reekie

Edinburgh wasn't just an autumn place associated with Keats's season of mists and mellow fruitfulness, but was for many decades known by the monicker 'Auld Reekie' because of the fogs that existed within the city emanating from the thousands of chimney pots – the smoke of the city from the fires in the hearth that kept her bairns and her citizens warm.

And whilst Edinburgh was nothing compared to London's pea-soupers – the city of the Empire that during the 1950s whose smog killed many of her citizens – but on late autumn and winter days the town was a place of mystery and shadowy figures which fired the imagination of Dr Arthur Conan Doyle when he came to write about the adventures of Sherlock Holmes and Dr Watson in foggy London town and given young Arthur something to think about, but on such grey afternoons Black and white simply dissipated.

So for Arthur, whilst his two winters at Lincoln University had inured him to a certain extent preparing him for the severity of the cold Edinburgh winters, the capital fogs would have been a revelation.

But what I do know from speaking to my mother is that Dr Motley had said to her how he loved the city and that love surely emanated from those early years on his youthful sojourns throughout the capital as he developed a greater knowledge and understanding of the city.

Because it was a practical and pragmatic choice in saving on the 'bawbees' - the monies for transport – this had the perk of him getting to know and become much more familiar with central Edinburgh than from sitting inside a tram looking out the window: when you walk you can lift your eyes to the heavens too and as you wynd your way in and out you come to know the city more intimately including her buildings, her parks and of course her infamous varying weather where you could experience four seasons in a single day and that in summer!

Whilst he may well have enjoyed living in Leith having to traverse the main thoroughfares of the city witnessing the vibrant street-life of the town, it may well have been when he moved to the leafier suburbs of Marchmont that truly cemented his great love for Edinburgh which grew and deepened with the decades.

He would have enjoyed these two distinct parts of the capital - Marchmont and the Meadows which acted as a green lung for the capital – and whilst not so colourful or vibrant as Leith - it has its own quieter and no less magical vibrancy too.

A Spring in Arthur's Step

As the long seemingly endless harsh winter of 1928/29 eventually turned to spring moving thereafter toward the summer of 1929 Arthur enjoyed taking in the local life in the Meadows which as the days lengthened grew exponentially busier.

Games of soccer and games of cricket would suddenly and spontaneously materialise consisting of local resident students as well as local young people, but alas for Arthur, there was no American Football, a great sporting love.

On bright sunny days students would sit out enjoying the better weather brought forth on the wings of early summer: the young men and women cemented and developed friendships some of which would last a lifetime. They would discuss university – their families back home – their hopes and their dreams for the future and perhaps if lucky, even fall in love too.

Floral Clock Willem van de Poll

And the Meadows were where the local children played as written about and so beautifully described and evoked by the writer and academic David Daiches in what remains the finest book written about the precipitous city – 'Two Worlds' – an apt title for any book about Dr Motley.

And Daiches writes too of the sound of bat on ball echoing across The Meadows' green pastures on late summer evenings.

And during that first spring Arthur couldn't but fail to love the displays of snowdrops, daffodils, tulips, hyacinths and crocuses.

And when he ventured along Princes Street he diverted into the gardens to see the floral clock and the music emanating from the Ross Bandstand.

And at least once he surely climbed up the wynding steps of the famous Scott Monument – a Gothic cathedral or 'rocket' to the sky –dedicated to Edinburgh's most famous son, the writer Sir Walter Scott from where he could have taken in the giddy surrounding views.

PRINCES STREET EDINBURGH

Medica Metrics

In his first year spent studying medicine or medica metrics he would have been expected to attend a significant number of courses and lectures putting in a considerable amount of hours.

And then at the end of that first year (Second Professional Examination) like every other medical student before and since, come the early summer, he was required to sit the dreaded examinations which were always on the near horizon and at the back of students' minds.

Unfortunately and worryingly for Arthur, at his first attempt he failed both the written and the oral paper in Physiology with marks of 45 and 31.

Within his University record in July 1929 appears the single word 'Resit'.

Not only had he failed, but he had failed badly.

Facing the Music

Resit - it's a dreaded word that thousands of students have seen and encountered over the years and the decades.

It's the stuff of nightmares that even after successfully passing exams many former students still awake during the night in a cold sweat seeing or hearing the word – RESIT!

It's a word that not only sends shivers down the spine but it spoils the eagerly anticipated summer holidays and the break from academia.

The Sword of Damocles is now hanging over you.

It was probably the first time that Arthur had ever failed an exam so that too would have taken getting used to – it was a blow to him but a blow to his self-confidence too.

Perhaps for the first time a doubt had now entered his mind – do I really have the ability to become a doctor.

Neither is it helped nor good for your confidence in that rather than receiving the news privately Arthur first received the news at the university at Teviot Place alongside and amongst his peers.

That's a hard thing to take.

And it's something which can strike at anyone's confidence.

And more than that it's a public humiliation.

But perhaps it's a subtle as well as a very crude university approach – it's a public lesson – it's a short sharp shock to the system – that if you hope to remain at the University of Edinburgh and hope to become a doctor – well, you'll need to pull your socks up if you truly wish to succeed.

And, there's nowhere to hide.

Amongst the 200 or so students Arthur of course wouldn't have been alone in failing his examinations, but looking at his marks, whilst he may have gone in on that early summer morning hoping against hope that he may have scraped a pass in the written paper, given he had got more than two-thirds of the oral examination wrong, if he had any self-awareness, he surely must have walked in from Marchmont through the greenery of The Meadows with the birds singing in the background on that long ago summer morning back in 1929 with a heavy heart, knowing that he was about to hear the worst and to receive the bad news. He had to face the music.

Disapointment in Edinburgh and McAlester City

Not only would Arthur have been disappointed, worried and felt bad about this, but being so very far from home may have been a bane, a blessing and a balm.

Many of us are naturally afraid to share bad news with our family and friends, particularly if we feel we may have let them down – we wish to protect them - so Arthur may have kept his results from Ethel and Frank back home in McAlester City.

We are unsure if this was the case, but in taking a resit he would have been required to pay to do this – an additional cost which he may or may not have been able to hide from his parents and their largesse.

But certainly, as will become apparent and like many students, in the immediate years following this Arthur would appear to have been poor in keeping Ethel and Frank up to speed with his life here in Edinburgh.

We Learn from Failure, Not from Success!

There may be a multitude of reasons for his failure and from this distant time – from the view in winter - moving toward a century later - we can only read between the lines in determining what happened to Arthur.

There are of course all the usual suspects.

When a student fails to pass their exams, given the premise that they've been competent enough to pass the Scottish Universities Entrance Board Exam – no easy requirement - and also given that Arthur already held a Bachelor of Arts Degree from Lincoln University with a science specialism, begs the question as to why he failed his exams and so spectacularly badly.

For many students it's because they get caught up in the distractions of student social life.

For others it's because they're too young.

For others still it's because it's their first time away from home and they're unhappy.

And for others it's because they lack the motivation to apply themselves.

Some students are found out – because of the nature and the demands of the course they're out of their depth intellectually.

For poorer students who also need to simultaneously work to support themselves economically whilst studying there's a fine balance to be struck not to be left feeling too tired and with not enough time or energy to study and apply themselves.

So, what was the reason for Arthur's failure?

What happened in Arthur Philip Motley's case that led to him to so spectacularly fail his first set of his exams in medicine, particularly in the oral examination?

Given the prevailing culture of Edinburgh it's unlikely that Arthur was tempted away and drawn into the distractions of late 1920s Edinburgh. But, it's entirely possible. After all Arthur's brief CV as recorded in the Lincoln University alumni of 1928 booklet says 'He (Arthur) belongs to The Firm, to the Varsity L Club and to Alpha. Hoops has been among the honour group students since his matriculation. He is a profound philosopher of life and religion; a lover of women, Wiley, and Bull Sessions.'

And of course Arthur loved sport too.

He was clearly an outgoing and sociable young man.

And this was still the age of The Twenties – the dying embers of the most distinctive decade of the twentieth century - the decade of exuberant release after the First World War - a decade when art, literature and particularly entertainment flourished and flowered.

And some social barriers were beginning to be brought down.

It was an era too when in this respect – in the field of entertainment - socially and culturally - Britain and America were drawn closer together and Arthur's arrival in Scotland coincided with this: we were coming to the end of the decade when many of those aspects were becoming embedded in society.

But change comes slowly.

This was also still the era of dour old Edinburgh – Calvinist Edinburgh – the city of the preacher John Knox, where a certain heavyweight culture percolated throughout Edimbra toon dampening down the city and her citizens under a sombre damp blanket and when allied to the weather were both metaphorical and literal.

Certainly on Sundays – the Sabbath Day - it was a city of The Gloom's when many people, soberly dressed, went about their business with a cloud above their heads.

It still remained such a place where on Sundays the church bells were the predominant sounds echoing across the city as it would continue to do so and remain for decades afterwards until toward the end of the 1960s – another period – another decade of great social and cultural change when social and cultural barriers and strictures began to be broken down and a colourful Glasnost broke out across the land.

But when Arthur arrived in the city, Sundays could be and often felt like very long days.

Thus for Arthur and for many others too once again the city revealed its duality – this was the city that Arthur had come to study in and to live within - a young man, full of life and charm, but a Black man within a predominantly white population set within the cultural changes of The Roaring Twenties, but in many ways it remained an island within a wider setting too.

In addressing his failure and what might have happened - whilst Arthur loved his sport, there was no American Football to be played here in Edinburgh, so sport was an unlikely distraction so he wasn't taking his 'eye off the ball' so to speak.

Was he therefore drawn into some of the university clubs and societies which took him away from his studies?

Whilst I don't know, still I would make an informed call, that no he wasn't. And that instead it was something other than this – something had made him take his eye off the ball – in fact in the common parlance of street-life Edinburgh and more crudely speaking it was another type of ball, but we'll come to that anon!

Were there any other reasons for his failure?

Was it being homesick?

I think not because he had spent the previous three student years away from home in McAlester City Oklahoma and become relatively independent.

And yes whilst things were different in 1929 compared to the three previous years when at the end of each of those academic years and terms he was able to return home for the summer, I really don't think that it was this that had thrown him off course.

If it had been a major reason for him failing – through being unhappy - I would have expected Arthur to have jumped on the first ship out and returned to America at the first opportunity and for good; and of course we know he didn't do this, instead remaining in Edinburgh for the rest of his life outwith several years abroad during World War 2.

Instead it would appear he only ever returned to American shores on that afore-mentioned single occasion – more than half a century later in 1983 for the 55th Reunion of his Lincoln University celebrations with his former classmates with no apparent sign of a visit to his home in McAlester City – but again, more of that anon.

I think this take on Arthur is backed up by the paucity of his writings home to his mother and his father during the subsequent years 1930 and 1931 when I discover his mother Ethel is desperately seeking out news and information on his progress at university in pursuance of a medical degree.

Did his failure therefore come down to competence or indeed incompetence – that he quite simply wasn't up to the task of passing those arduous medical examinations?

Based on my own and others' experience of Dr Motley and as viewed within the profession itself I would not describe him as being one of the better practitioners, indeed quite the opposite.

I don't think I'm being unfair here because as we've discovered he was unquestionably a gem of a bloke – an absolute diamond with many many wonderful personal qualities and traits which made him such a wonderful physician and family doctor, including his bedside manner and communication skills, but his clinical medical skills left something to be desired, even making allowance that within that earlier decade of the 1950s and 1960s when knowledge came slowly.

Whilst it may sound harsh he was perhaps of slightly less than average intellect compared to some of his fellow students, but nevertheless – a good Edinburgh and Muriel Spark word – the very fact that he had travelled so far to pursue a career in medicine – is suggestive that he was highly motivated and therefore with the right application could have successfully applied himself to the task in hand - to his studies and he really should have passed that first set of professional exams in 1929.

But instead, he failed.

It also brings into play his motivation and his choice of course too – was medicine his and his choice alone or as is often the way in life, university courses and careers are chosen and undertaken by many sons and many daughters purely to please their parents. Was this the case with Arthur?

It may have been so and in failing initially it may partly explain why he was such a poor correspondent with his parents.

Did he now regret going down this route of travel?

Did he regret his choice of course and hold it against them?

I don't think this was the case and that the motivation to become a doctor remained firmly ingrained within him, but it was certainly a wake-up call.

I think too that he felt ashamed at failing at the first real hurdle, for perhaps the first occasion in his academic life.

But still there remained a seed within him – a flame that flickered – a small dream that would one day lead to him eventually qualifying as a doctor.

My own take on Arthur falling at this first hurdle – failing both the written and oral paper in Physiology is because he didn't sufficiently or rigorously apply himself enough by keeping the main thing the main thing: and instead he was distracted by other interests and pleasures.

Put simply, Arthur had fallen in love – he had fallen under the spell of a 16 or 17 year old Edinburgh girl with whom he said to my mother over half a century later, reminded him of the film star, Betty Davis.

During Arthur's first year at university he had met a young lady – a local girl who was aged only around sixteen at the time. Her name was Annette Turnbul Combe and she would go on to to become a significant ongoing presence in his life.

As to when he first met her we don't exactly know, but given the nature of the relationship and what was to thereafter occur it would most likely have been at a relatively early stage in his first year at the University of Edinburgh, so perhaps during late autumn 1928.

By the start of his first academic year in October 1928 we're fairly certain that Arthur is now residing in lodgings at 25 Marchmont Road.

It's only an informed guess but it was perhaps whilst on his way to and from the university that he first met young Annette Combe within the general vicinity.

My mother seems to recall that her parents – or at least her mother - ran a sweet shop selling newspapers, cigarettes, confectionery, etc. Perhaps Annette worked part-time in the shop and it was here in the premises that their paths first crossed.

I suspect Arthur may have enjoyed both a smoke and a bar of chocolate.

When you visit a shop regularly it allows you to build up an easy rapport and quick relationship with the owners and the staff.

Each day you superficially pass the time of day - how you're getting on - and gradually as you get to know one another better you exchange what's going on in your day to day life too.

Here in Britain – and Edinburgh is no different to cities in England – such conversations famously begin with comments about the city's variable weather and before you know it you're discussing school, university, work and family background.

As a business one of the key tricks is to please your customer so that they come back time after time after time so that they become one of your regulars: it's not simply a transaction but instead you develop a relationship with your customers.

You want to be friendly but in doing so by trying to seek out the right balance – not being too nosey – too inquisitive, but being interested in your fellow traveller's life and when appropriate being supportive too.

If Annette worked in the shop she would have been pleasant to

Arthur. They were both young – Arthur was 24 and Annette aged around six or seven years younger. Indeed, she may still have been at school only helping out in the shop occasionally.

She would have found Arthur interesting, perhaps even an exotic creature – he was handsome – he was Black – he had an attractive personality and disposition – he was charming, fun, optimistic, with a ready smile and a hearty chuckle.

And he was different – very different to the other young Edinburgh men who frequented the shop and with whom she had come across, albeit, with students living within the Marchmont area and community, Arthur wouldn't have been the first coloured man that she had met. But nevertheless she was attracted to him and found him fascinating too.

But given the prevailing ambience and culture of Edinburgh, how on earth did their relationship develop beyond simply a short pleasant exchange, encounter and chat within the confines of a shop across the counter as Arthur passed his farthings, halfpennies, pennies, sixpences or shillings across to Annette in exchange for a bar of Cadbury's chocolate or a packet of Woodbine, Gold Flake or Players Navy Cut cigarettes?

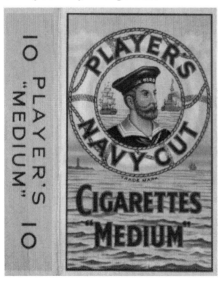

And in developing further the notion - the concept or theory of transactions versus relationships in the world of business and clients and customers - how on earth did they first move from it being a transaction to a relationship in its more fullish – or should that be foolish – sense?

At the time – late 1928 - the barriers would appear to have been insurmountable, but as the cliche goes, love will find a way.

Beyond the shop one other likely way whereby they may have met is if they had both attended the same local church.

I don't recall Dr Motley being of a religious persuasion but it does state in the Lincoln University CV that he was a philosopher of religion, so who knows.

With his father Frank going on to become a minister clearly his parents were religious. But outwith that unless there was perhaps a local party at around Christmas or New Year the only other possibility is that they may have passed each other in the local streets and got to know each other in brief little exchanges.

But beyond that, in Calvinist Edinburgh with its colour bars in some parts of the city, if they were to have been seen out and about as a couple together in each other's company, it would most certainly have turned heads.

They say Edinburgh is a village – that you're only one link away in the chain from knowing someone in common - and in a community such as Marchmont and given Annette's parents were shop-keepers, what with the regular flow of customers coming in and out of their shop each day, if the young couple had been seen out and about together, no doubt word would have spread very quickly and got back to them.

And whilst their colour difference at the time would have been a major barrier, this was further exaggerated by Annette being so young and still a local schoolgirl.

Annette may have attended the well regarded George Watson's Ladies College school better known as George Square named after its location in the city close-by the university: alternatively she may instead have been at the local school in Marchmont - James Gillespie School for Girls made famous by its most famous alumni

Dame Muriel Spark with the school becoming legendary as where 'Miss Jean Brodie' taught when she was in her prime.

Writing of this does of course raise the possibility that if Arthur and Annette had got to know each other through the shop, on occasion they may also have followed a very similar route home to Marchmont, she after school and he after being at university, giving them an opportunity to meet.

So perhaps on occasion they accidentally bumped into each other enjoying each other's company as they casually and easily chatted about their distinct and different young lives and backgrounds – she an Edinburgher and he an Okie.

And thereafter, as their relationship developed, rather than serendipity bringing them together, as the weeks and the months passed by, in the harmony of the Edinburgh seasons - autumn through the bitter winter of 1929 when Arthur kept warm in Annette's arms and sweet embraces and then into the darling buds of May and early summer, their love for each other grew and grew until their passion spilled over in that first week or so in May when they first consummated their relationship.

But certainly when Annette had started seeing Arthur it's something that wouldn't have gone un-noticed and it would surely have been spotted by one of the girls from Annette's school and no doubt word would have got out and quickly spread.

It would have been the stuff of gossip.

The Meadows on Sundays has always been a popular Edinburgh haunt for courting couples but it would have been well nigh on impossible for Annette and Arthur to have been like other lovers and instead they would have had to have conducted a more clandestine affair.

And yet, an affair there was – a love affair – so the young couple must somehow have managed to find a way because during the height of when Arthur should have been studying hard for his first set of medical examinations and sitting the written and oral papers he and Annette conceived a child.

Turn your Wounds into Wisdom – Oprah Winfrey

When I first became aware of this major event in Dr Motley's life, as you might imagine it came as quite a shock and I was a little taken aback.

Of a sudden I found myself seeing him in a different light. Not onethat diminished him in any way – after all, all his good qualities remained still intact – he was and would always be that wonderful gentle caring family doctor - that could never be taken away. But nevertheless – we're back to that tremendously useful Sparkian word – nevertheless – I did see him now in a different way and a different light. It made him seem more human.

That revelation emerging through the ether alongside Harold Motley's greater revelation that he was this unknown grandson I realised that like all his patients who came to visit him with their problems, their personal issues, their worries and the concerns in their lives, that he too was no different to the rest of us: indeed it may have helped expand that natural caring aptitude and empathy he had for his patients, some of whom in the decades ahead would no doubt have visited him with similar events occurring in their own lives – of falling pregnant outwith marriage - somehow he transformed such an event into a positive – it was very much a case of how can we make this thing good – how can we make things better?

And alongside that, it's only just occurred to me that another very strong and powerful aspect of his personality and approach and his strength as a doctor was that he was non-judgemental. He might have laughed or scorned at government bodies, but never you as an individual.

That's a very powerful thing.

So, when a distressed patient visited him he would have settled them, empathised with their plight and said, okay, how do we sort this – how do we resolve it – here are the options and how can I help you choose.

And when combined with his light touch and light manner and smile and optimism you left the surgery feeling better – that the world wasn't quite so bad a place as when you first went in to the surgery.

1929

So, back in the spring of 1929 when Arthur should have had his head in his books – and no doubt he would have for at least some of the time – his head and his mind were elsewhere too - he was in the midst of a passionate affair with a 16 or 17 year old white Edinburgh girl of school age.

When you are a student and in love it can often be a positive thing with one aspect helping the other leading to a lovely and happy balance in life – academia and love.

However, if it becomes unbalanced and this was at a relatively early stage in their romance, it can have the opposite affect – and it seriously impacted and contributed in some shape or form to Arthur failing his end of year examinations.

Calvinist Edinburgh and Three Deuces

Within a month or two of conception teenaged Annette would have begun to suspect and then realise that yes, she was perhaps pregnant.

But certainly after a summer of love, by the onset of autumn 1929, come September, when she was at least 16 weeks pregnant, she would have been fully aware of her condition and the situation that she and Arthur now found themselves in.

From the view in winter I can only imagine what went through the minds of those two young people – the conversations between them – and the further difficult conversation Annette would have had to have with her parents.

Tears would have been shed.

Not only had she fallen pregnant aged only seventeen, but she was unmarried too and what would have made that parental conversation even worse was that the baby had been conceived with a Black man.

In Edinburgh town it would have been very difficult to have come up with a worse permutation than that.

If she had been playing Three Card Brag she had just drawn three deuces.

A Shotgun Wedding?

Almost a century afterwards, from this great distance in time we can have no conception – forgive the pun - of how supportive Annette's parents were or were not. All that we do know is that come that September of 1929, but a year after young Arthur Philip Motley had first stepped onto Scottish shores he was about to be wed.

Crikey!

Did Mr and Mrs David Combe, Annette's parents, give their blessing to the marriage, hard as that may have been?

Or instead, was it a shotgun wedding?

Annette falling pregnant and marrying aged 18 were revelations two and three but revelation one was when Harold Motley had alerted me earlier to the astonishing fact that he was Arthur Motley's unacknowledged grandson back in America.

But here in 1929, unlike 1925 when Arthur was able to travel a few hundred miles south to Wiley College Marshal Texas to place a great distance between himself and his pregnant L'Ouverture High School classmate Freddie Royster, this time there was to be no escape, even if perhaps he wanted to do so.

Did Annette's parents attend the young couple's marriage?

In that era – in that Edinburgh year of 1929 – and at such short notice it's unlikely that it would have been anything but a very small affair.

And for many girls - not just those brought up in society at that time - but over the centuries before and in all the decades since, getting married is one of the most important and eagerly anticipated days of their lives not only for the brides but for the parents too - when the father symbolically gives away the bride - from his pastoral care to the loving and secure arms of her new life partner who will thereafter look after her.

Life was difficult for Annette and Arthur but it would have been similarly difficult for Annette's parents too.

Living in a small community in daily view of their neighbours it would undoubtedly have been the stuff of gossip with their peers, their neighbours and of course their customers.

If they were church-goers - and at that time most probably they would have been - it too would have been a major talking point amongst the congregation.

Have you heard the news! - a rushed wedding - and to a Black man too - and her so very young - and with him being Black.

Oh how some people must have had a field day.

And of course as September moved into November and beyond it would become increasingly apparent that Annette was indeed heavily pregnant - so the rumours were true! - the child had indeed been conceived out of wedlock.

Within most communities - and in Edinburgh society this would have been no different - their union would have been frowned upon.

And whilst Annette would have had some very mixed emotions at the time, it certainly altered her life trajectory.

Did she have other plans?

Was she keen to develop a career or to go on to university?

What were her dreams?

The Wedding

The couple married on the 8th October 1929 at 53 George IV Bridge. As the marriage was one described as 'Irregular' there is no Officiating Minister and it is simply stamped by the Sheriff-Substitute of the Lothians and Peebles office. The wedding was conducted by a J. Hetherington and signed as the Interim Registrar.

Arthur is described as being 22 years old although he was actually 25: his occupation is listed as being a medical student. Unusually, his address is denoted as being the University Union.

His father, Robert Frank Motley, is described as being a Real Estate Agent. A further interesting aspect is that his witness is a fellow medical student, an Ahmed Mahmoud Gohni who resides at 1 Argyle Park Terrace which may be the family home but more likely a student residence as it's part of the general Marchmont student land. Ahmed's father was a physician, but deceased. It's not unusual for fellow overseas students, particularly coloured ones to form a cluster and become friends and I would surmise this was the case between Ahmed and Arthur.

Meanwhile Annette Turnbull Henderson Combe is denoted as being 18 and her address is given as 16 Royal Crescent an affluential part of the city of Edinburgh and with its stone pillars and main door entrance a relatively smart address within the Edinburgh New Town with its Georgian architecture.

Similar to Arthur's part of the document it begs fascinating questions: Annette's father, David Combe, is described as being a retired architect. And yet there is no trace of him within the record of Scottish Architects and as he is only 44 at the time, it's a very early age to have retired. And even more strangely when he married back in 1906 his occupation is as a fireman at a steam laundry, so an odd career trajectory.

I can but assume the role of the fiction writer here.

Whilst on the surface it would seem odd that Mrs Catherine Combe, Annette's mother, would therefore be running a sweetshop if her husband is an architect but given his early retirement – perhaps because of ill-health – it may have been from necessity that she may indeed have done so, but perhaps not so far across the city as at Marchmont, but instead at neighbouring Stockbridge.

Annette's witness is an Edith Maud Crawford of 3 Marchhall Crescent and she works as a nurse whereas Annette is simply described as a spinster with no occupation. Is this perhaps how Arthur first met Annette, through a mutual aquaintance?

Based upon the Combe family's address rather than them living in the Marchmont area of the city they instead live on the fringes of Stockbridge. But what is interesting is that Royal Crescent dovetails into and becomes Fettes Row – more of which anon as this street surprisingly features again in Arthur Philip Motley's story.

University of Edinburgh

It's now mid-autumn 1929.

A full year had sinced passed since Arthur first enrolled at the University of Edinburgh and much water has flowed through the city's Water of Leith.

And what a year.

Come that second capital September he had barely survived a tumultuous year in the precipitous city spending an academic year studying medicine.

He had met a sixteen or seventeen year old schoolgirl.

They had embarked upon a a secretive relationship and passionate affair.

Annette had fallen pregnant.

He had failed his first set of examinations.

The couple had what might be described as a shotgun wedding.

And it would seem there was little contact between Arthur and his parents back home in Oklahoma.

And with his desire to recommence the third year of the course in October during this hectic period with so much going on in his life he also faced the burden and the worry of having to resit the Physiology examinations.

Good Old (Young) Arthur!

But buckle down he did and fair play to Arthur because he passed both the written paper and the oral examination with dramatically improved marks of 69% and 55%.

So, amongst everything that was going on at the time he had improved his marks and by a remarkable 24% in both sets of examinations.

Good old (young) Arthur!

At last some very good news for our young protagonist and the hero's journey, as his American peer, the mythologist Joseph Campbell might have penned at the time.

But in addition to having to now face the new academic year of 1929/30 studying the most demanding of all courses and degrees Arthur was now having to do so as no longer a single man who could be as selfish as he chose to be, including devoting as much of his time to studying as he so pleased, but now instead he was having to contemplate three lives – his own, his new wife, Annette and their baby due to be born early in the new year of 1930.

He was no longer single – life would now have to be considered and lived through the prism of being a family man.

In more normal circumstances in the young lives of new families, amongst all the joys, there are the challenges and worries and responsibilities too but for this family they were even more rigorous and challenging.

Academia

Annette was due to give birth in February 1930 at a time when Arthur should have been moving toward sitting the end of the academic year examinations in the spring.

It's moving toward the end of Arthur's second winter in Edinburgh.

His new small family are probably living snugly in a flat toward the top of Leith Walk, although perhaps not.

He's now mid-way through his second year, (but third year) of his medical studies at university.

And amongst all of the joys there are the responsibilities and the worries too.

Aged only 25 he's not only a student undertaking the most challenging and demanding of academic courses but he's now a father and he's over 4000 miles from home and the immediate support of his family on his doorstep.

He's now faced with an impossibly difficult and challenging task – balancing his studies with this new role as a father alongside the need to provide for his new family.

What a burden.

What a weight upon a young man's shoulders.

And on top of that the family will at times have to contend with being a mixed race family in an at times stern and judgemental Calvinist city where some people were prejudiced and discriminatory.

And, alongside all of this, Annette's own family is likely to be estranged from them too: and if they were so inclined disowning their daughter Annette and her new husband - given the era it's understandable if not forgivable.

Even a century later many parents would, whilst trying to be supportive had similarly concluded and worried themselves sick – is this really what I want for my young daughter – to fall pregnant aged 17, to be a mother at 18 and only recently married to an impoverished Black man from America.

Whatever the circumstances it's difficult to believe anything other than it dashed whatever dreams and hopes that they had for Annette and her future life in Edinburgh – they would have had great hopes for her future – and now their aspirations were dashed and life was taking a very different route from what they might have imagined and hoped for: over the coming days, weeks and years it would be a constant worry for Mr and Mrs Combe as to what lay ahead for their eighteen year old daughter and her young family.

Meanwhile back in the world of academia, for Arthur and his fellow students, the demands of medical students were as ever, fast approaching and very challenging.

He was expected to have undertaken 100 hours of Pathology and Bacteriology; 60 hours of Practical Pathology; 100 hours of Materia Medica; as well as 3 months of Clinical Therapeutics – a demanding schedule for a single care-free young man never mind a man with family responsibilities.

The Great Crash of 1929

Here they were – Mr and Mrs Arthur Motley - a mixed marriage couple living together in stuffy old Edinburgh.

Like every couple they would have had their financial concerns.

1929 was the year of The Great Crash which had greatly impacted upon and affected America with its reverberations continuing into the early part of the decade of the 1930s - would there be a similar knock-on effect that might also impact upon the lives of Arthur and Annette over 4000 miles away in Edinburgh, Scotland.

Even before their marriage Arthur struggled to support himself and pay his way through university.

Not only would this remain so, but he was now responsible for the lives of three people in this world instead of just one.

How would the family get by?

How could they survive?

Where would they live?

And whilst there's a reservation about pigeon-holing people and categorising them, given the particular nature of the situation one wonders just how supportive – or not - Annette's parents were?

They may of course have been wonderfully supportive either through providing a home within their own home or perhaps they helped them financially by helping them to secure a flat of their own.

Certainly that would have been the most pragmatic solution.

As shop-keepers and as a former architect they may have had a small amount of discretionary income and savings tucked away. And, such a course of action would remove Annette, Arthur and baby from the immediate and regular glare of their neighbours, their friends and their customers in Marchmont or more likely Stockbridge helping to take some of the sting out of the situation.

And it would have given the young couple and the new baby the chance to live on their own rather than within a strained household with three generations under a single roof.

Alternatively they may not have provided any support whatsoever and simply abandoned them.

We'll never know.

But what we do know is that by 1935 - six years later - the family were living in Leith, and for Arthur this time it was at Leith Walk rather than Brunswick Street.

Leith Walk is the main and noisy thoroughfare between the city of Edinburgh and the newly merged town and port of Leith. It was and remains a busy, vibrant and exciting place.

And somehow the Motley family would have had to find a way to fund this.

We don't know for how long they lived there - a year or six or somewhere in-between. I suspect it may have been closer to six, but who knows.

Annette Junior

It's likely the main burden of earning an income would have fallen upon Arthur's slim shoulders.

Whilst heavily pregnant and in the early months of the new year, 1930, Annette would have been too busy bringing up the baby and running their small household. It's therefore unlikely that she would have worked at this time. And whilst because of the nature of her parents' business they in theory could have been flexible in offering her some employment - a few hours of work - most likely they would have been glad that she was no longer living in Stockbridge.

And thus it was an intense period of mixed emotions for Arthur P. Motley. There was the excitement of becoming a father and living under the one roof with his new family.

He and Annette could be as passionate and loving as they so wished, but the intensive love life which they had enjoyed over the late spring and summer of the year before was now about to move toward a winter hibernation and intriguingly Annette Junior would be their only child together.

The baby was born toward the end of winter on the 5th February 1930. She too was called Annette - or within this tale and no doubt in day to day life, to be thereafter known as Annette Junior.

The thought just occurred to me, being and remaining the junior version of someone else - how does that impact upon you and affect you in life as the years and the decades go by - a smaller version of someone else - is it not something from which you might wish to escape or rebel from?

Annette Junior's birth was not straightforward and my mother said that Arthur had to call out a doctor from the Royal Infirmary.

During the birth poor Annette had a torrid time.

There was a danger that she might lose her life.

And it was for this reason that the couple decided not to have any further children for fear of an even worse repeat of the trauma that Annette and indeed Arthur went through - it was deemed to be too risky for her to ever contemplate having children in future.

It was only after this conversation that I became aware of Annette Junior's birth certificate and as ever in tracing Arthur Philip Motley's life it too came with surprises.

The document is a rather attractive one: it's an American Consular Services Report of Birth of Children Born to American Parents.

It records Annette's birth as the 5th February 1930 at the Simpson Memorial at Edinburgh Royal Infirmary.

Thus, Arthur didn't have to call a specialist out, but instead Annette Junior had been born in the hospital: given the difficulties in the birth this was clearly just as well placing Annette in the best place and safest hands to be cared for.

But as to whether they had been contemplating a home birth and she had had to be rushed to hospital, we don't know.

Within the document Arthur Motley is recorded as being a medical student at the time, but the biggest surprise of all is the family's address – 20 Fettes Row which is a relatively affluent address toward the boundary of Edinburgh's New Town.

But that said, they may just simply have rented rooms within a family's home or perhaps if they were lucky a small flat within the building itself, but nevertheless it did come as a surprise to me and yet another different address in the life of the peripatetic Arthur Motley.

It does also raise the question as to whether Annette's parents, Mr and Mrs David Combe had been supportive financially or whether Arthur Motley was somehow providing the monies himself. And it removed the notion and the assumption that they were living in Leith. So this was an interlude between Marchmont and thereafter returning to Leith Walk.

That Arthur's daughter has been registered as an American citizen begs questions as to whether during this period of turmoil in his life whether he now had some passing thoughts of returning to the United States and this would make his daughter's passage easier.

This is given further credence as at the same time there's another major revelation - it's recorded in Arthur's University of Edinburgh matriculation record for March 1930 that he hadn't sat his examinations.

Blimey!

Annette Junior's birth is registered at the Consulate on the 14th March 1930 at 9:30 a.m. more than five weeks after her birth.

Just before 5:00 p.m. she was allocated an American passport.

Dr Robert Thin

Dr Robert Thin

The Edinburgh physician whom Arthur had placed his faith in and the life of his wife Annette was a Dr Robert I. Thin M.B., Ch.B who is recorded as being the House Surgeon at the Infirmary.

He had qualified in Midwifery Practice from the Edinburgh Royal Maternity and Simpson Memorial Hospital but later on became a general practitioner and went on to become the first to be appointed President of the Edinburgh Royal College of Surgeons. So Annette was in good hands.

When Thin died, a 'Grateful Patient' wrote: *'In his visits, while he never gave the impression that he was hurried in his examination and advice, he never wasted his time.'*

That epitaph could sum up Dr Motley's approach too.

But in returning to my mother saying that Dr Motley had to call out a doctor I wonder if there remains a kernel of truth in this. After all Dr Thin worked from his home in 6 Albany Street which is but a ten minute walk or so from 20 Fettes Row, so perhaps he was also the Motley's local doctor.

The Juggler

Those first few years must have placed a tremendous strain upon the young couple, a strain which remained over the course of the decade of the 1930s.

And whilst in a household with a new baby there would have been much happiness it may have been tinged with the disappointment that there were to be no further children.

After all when their domestic circumstances changed and improved they may have been hopeful of having more children, perhaps a son too, but who knows. Certainly I think Arthur would have been a good father.

But given the period there would have been a general awareness that life would be challenging for any children of a mixed marriage as they tried to negotiate their routes through their young lives, so perhaps a small part of Arthur was pleased that a son would not have to encounter the same prejudice and discrimination that as a boy he had to face and to overcome.

But no doubt a multitude of thoughts and such reflections would have passed through his head.

Given the circumstances perhaps the last thing on Arthur's mind in early 1930 was therefore his studies.

After the birth of their baby in February, Annette had to be helped and nursed back to full health and strength in the coming months as spring moved toward Annette Junior's first Edinburgh summer.

And much of that burden would have fallen upon Arthur meaning that his studies took a back seat.

And whatever Annette's parents had thought of the wedding of their daughter it would have been as naught if they had lost her – if she had died whilst giving birth: and perhaps given what nearly happened it may have brought them closer to their daughter again, but at the same time it may have increased any antagonism and antipathy which they may most certainly would have felt toward Arthur.

And whilst they attached much of the blame to Annette for ending up in her situation, they would have pinned a greater blame at the feet of Arthur, who was at least six or seven years older.

My Boy

Arthur wasn't the most assiduous of correspondents with his parents back home in McAlester City. And of course those were the days when knowledge came slowly - it was easier to keep people at arms length and in the dark. Was there a certain estrangement between him and Ethel and Frank or was he quite simply poor at keeping in touch.

Ethel naturally and in the way of most mothers would have worried constantly about Arthur. Never a day would have passed without her thinking about him and his well-being and his welfare in far away Edinburgh town.

On the occasions when things were going well her heart would have sung – knowing that her boy, Arthur Philip, was thriving in far away Edinburgh at the finest medical school in the world would have brought a joy and a warmth to her heart improving her sense of well-being no end. But when things were going less swimmingly she would have worried herself to death.

When young Arthur was growing up in McAlester City and as one of her two darling boys he would have been her pride and joy.

Knowing him as I did in his later decades and based on his classmates' brief synopsis of his personality at Lincoln University I can but assume he was the same joyful, smiling, happy individual.

On top of that Ethel would have taken a particular pride that Arthur was a bright and intelligent young man.

And both she and Frank would be keen to steer him along the road to fulfil his great potential.

McAlester City

McAlester City grew considerably in the three decades after Arthur was born, from a small population of 646 to thereafter stabilise at between 10000 and 12000 people. It was therefore a small town – a town where many people knew one another.

The town had its history in the American Civil War and was named after a Captain J.J. McAlester who at the end of the war secured a job with a trading company – Reynolds and Hannaford - convincing the company to establish a store at Tupelo in the Choctaw Nation.

Whilst fighting in the war McAlester had become aware of coal deposits in the area and with the coming of the extension of the railroad (the Union Pacific) through the Indian Territory the local area had great potential for the location of a trading post and general store in 1869. The trading post was on the Texas Road – the very road that Ethel Motley would have taken with young Arthur when they re-located to McAlester City in around 1909.

Whilst on the theme of mixed marriage it's worth noting that J.J. McAlester married the 32 year old Rebecca Burney on the 22nd August 1872.

She was a member of the Choctaw Nation which made it possible for McAlester to gain both citizenship and to own property – including mineral rights to coal deposits, which begs the question as to how much their marriage was based on love, money and practicality – anyway, it suited them both and McAlester immediately afterwards purchased land close to the intersection of the north-south and east-west railroads where he opened a second store.

From there a small town began to gradually develop.

Miners arrived from Pennsylvania in 1874 to work and to the south the community of South McAlester developed at a greater pace than the North.

Alongside mining the fertile fields surrounding the town meant there was a considerable amount of farming and ranching too with cotton being the main cash crop. There were three cotton gins within the boundary of the town and a cotton press able to compress over a thousand bales of cotton a day.

In the year Arthur was born a few hundred miles south in Clarksville the two towns merged as one to become McAlester City.

This occurred on my birthday – the First of July. It happened just prior to Oklahoma becoming a statehood requiring the re-drawing of boundaries.

And by the time Arthur was 5 years old the town was well established with a population of around 13,000 with schools, a water system, factories and a grand hotel as well as a theatre and a trolley system linking the town with neighbouring towns.

A Pyrrhic Victory

As described after attending high school Arthur went on to study at Wiley College, Marshall, Texas.

At this time Wiley was a private Black college founded in 1873 by the United Methodist Church.

It was the first and oldest historically Black college west of the Mississippi River located in the town of Marshall Texas.

It was named after a white man, the Rev. Dr Isaac William Wiley who was a Bishop in the church.

Reflecting again as to why Arthur Motley, no doubt influenced by his parents, chose Wiley College in Texas so far from home when he could just as easily have chosen and attended other colleges much closer to home and within Oklahoma itself - it would have been financially better too, being less costly and onerous to fund takes us back to Arthur's sweetheart, Miss Freddie Royster and her pregnancy.

And there lies a tale and a number of mysteries.

He would still have been in L'Ouverture High School and in his final year.

Did Freddie, the mother of their baby let Arthur know of their situation?

Did young Arthur Motley know at the time or only after he had left for Texas?

Did his parents Ethel and Frank know?

What happened when Freddie became pregnant and what conversations took place or didn't?

And was it indeed through the strong influence of Ethel and Frank that Arthur was sent on his way to far distant Texas?

And was that choice to help to separate the couple - after all, if they were 200 miles apart they couldn't see each other.

This was of course long before the days of DNA testing: it was an age when such things could be (relatively) easily denied.

Did Arthur have a conversation with Freddie and refuse to take any responsibility for her falling pregnant?

Did Arthur's parents intervene taking a pragmatic approach that for Arthur to get married and become a father would stymie his career and life trajectory before it could ever get off the launch pad. And that given the circumstances they wished to send him as far away as practical down to the South to allow him to begin his college career?

As I've said we can only surmise about the agonies faced by each of the protagonists - Freddie, Arthur and their two immediate families.

On the surface and based on her own personal experience, Ethel Motley could both empathise with Freddie, but also given her love for her son, may have adopted a fairly harsh and selfish stance in being pragmatic, looking after Arthur's best interests.

But in doing so was it a Pyrrhic Victory in that the eventual outcome was that he never came back to her and that after 1928 Arthur Motley never saw his mother again - if so, as she lived for another forty years, for Ethel it would have been quite a penance.

And then what of Arthur's father who became the Rev. Frank Motley - what was the Christian thing to have done?

Having discussed and explored several of these questions with Harold Motley there can be little doubt that Arthur was aware of the situation and that he had fathered Freddie's son, Lewie Motley.

But that as hinted at earlier his father, Frank Motley, had taken control of the situation not only sending young Arthur 200 miles south to Wiley College but that come the following summer, rather than his son returning home, Arthur spent that vacation with relatives from the town of his birth in Clarksville, Texas thus keeping him apart from Freddie and helping to prevent any awkward inter-faces with the Royster family.

Given it was a small town and the boy, Lewie, had the Motley surname, there would be no escaping the situation other than by keeping your distance down in the state of Texas. In effect, Arthur had been run out of town, but by his father, neatly avoiding the possibility of a shotgun wedding.

But whilst Arthur was able to avoid the situation, poor Freddie lived it day by day and no doubt some people would have made her feel ashamed.

School Years

As mentioned earlier Arthur attended L'Ouverture High School in McAlester City.

With education being segregated (*Plessy v Ferguson 1896*) the school was for Black children only. That famous U.S. Suprene Court judgement case resulted in the separate but equal doctrine enshrining Jim Crow into law for half a century effectively leading to separate schooling for more than a half century.

In naming the school after the great revolutionary Toussaint Louverture there was a certain defiance in doing so and making that choice as with other similar institutions sending out a clear and loud message.

It's also likely that the school's curriculum would have addressed some of the inequalities that existed within American society educating the students to take a pride in Black culture and the philosophy that all men are created equal. Haiti of course was the first nation to abolish the crime that was slavery.

Four decades later with the advent of integration the school closed down in 1968 however over 40 years later it was purchased by two former school pupils and alumni and is now used by local people for community purposes.

But going back a century in time I have no doubt that Arthur would have thrived at school and this was echoed when his grandson Harold Motley said 'Some of the teachers I had at L'Overture taught Dr Motley too - they were always talking about how smart he was' as was Willa Strong.

His parents and particularly Ethel would have had great hopes for young Arthur's future and given the misfortune of him making a local girl pregnant this will have distressed them for a number of reasons.

But up until then I'm sure Arthur enjoyed his time at school, learning and devouring the curriculum - eating up knowledge – effortlessly passing his exams - the environment would have both engaged him turning him into an engaging young man and furthered his sensibility with distinct ambitions to challenge himself to try to build a good life for himself.

Harold is of course a direct link here where he recalls how this came about when he was 15. Up until then Harold had attended integrated schools in his home-town, Oakland, California; but after spending a summer vacation with relatives in McAlester City with his brother Marlon followed by a two month spell at L'Ouverture High School (the school term began two months earlier than back in Oakland) because he enjoyed the experience so much he himself wanted to stay on.

1929

Meanwhile back in Edinburgh town, outwith being occasionally sent monies to support him through university it would seem that Arthur had become somewhat estranged from Ethel and also his father Frank.

Why should this have been the case?

Did he want to leave his past behind?

Was he ashamed of his mother, Ethel?

For a man whom we always regarded as being a sensitive and caring individual that seems difficult to understand, but when you are young and less worldly-wise and empathetic to your parents and the love and concerns that they have for us, that can often be the case.

But the seed of this was first sown four years earlier back in 1925 when a girl had a child out of wedlock for whom he was the unacknowledged father: it was this that initiated the process of distance and estrangement.

Up until then Arthur was the apple of Ethel's eye.

He would have bathed in that glory and thrived on the positive attention.

And then, of a sudden, there came a jolt in the road – a jolt that had the power to send him off course foiling his parents' dreams for him and his future.

But of course, it didn't, but at what cost to Ethel, to his father Frank, to Freddie, to the child, Lewie Motley and also to himself?

Emile Zola highlighted in the novel *Therese Racquin* how we become different people when we go through extreme events and circumstances, so perhaps this was the first juncture in the road to a growing distance between Arthur and Ethel and Frank.

And thereafter with their son going away to study in Texas for a year followed by two years in Pennsylvania Arthur became independent rather than interdependent i.e. outwith the need for some monies to support him: and then when he left for distant Edinburgh Scotland, not only was he over 4000 miles away, but the distance reflected just how far apart they had grown.

No Appearance

In the month after Annette Junior was born in February 1930 and Arthur going along to the American Consulate to register his daughter's birth we come to another major crossroads in the life of Arthur P. Motley.

In March 1930 within his University of Edinburgh record are recorded two ominous words within the Second Professional Examination – the startling words are *'No app'* (No appearance) and alongside these two words under the Result column, there is but the wiggly stroke of the pen.

Arthur had been blown off course.

No appearance.

He didn't sit his examinations.

Indeed, did he ever start his third year academic studies back in October 1929?

Thus with everything that was going on in his life at the time - being newly married - with but a month or so old baby girl, Arthur had chosen not to sit the examinations.

What a worry.

What a disaster in his life and the lives of the immediate others who touched his – his wife Annette; his mother and his father; his parents in law; and for everyone else, family and friends, all those individuals with a keen interest in Arthur and his future welfare.

So, why didn't he sit either the paper or the oral exam?

Was it due to his new stressful family circumstances?

Or did he fear that he might fail?

Was it because he hadn't been in a proper mindset or didn't have the time to study?

Or was it because he didn't have the monies to pay to sit the examinations?

What this event confirms is that it is the first intimation that a gap – a separation - had materialised between Arthur and his parents: back in 1925 when he went off to Texas – and now here in Scotland five years later the distance has grown further. At this time his parents were unaware of what was going on in his life.

The Gilt is off the Gingerbread

The first written and confirmatory evidence of this comes in the form of a very poignant and heart-breaking letter dated the 18th

August 1930 from his worried mother, Ethel.

The early spring of 1930 had now become late summer in Edinburgh.

It's now five months since those fateful words 'No app' had been recorded.

Ethel is still living in McAlester City Oklahoma where she would remain for the rest of her life.

The Letters

Ethel picks up her pen and writes a letter addressed to a Professor Buckle, University Senior at the University of Edinburgh.

Ethel writes:

McAlester Okla

Aug 18th 1930

Dear Sir,

Just a word of information and it is this when do school opens. Also what will the bill be this year for my son. My money is limited this year haven't but a small summer. I believe my son will have to stop for a year or so. And try to help himself. I am almost broke so let me hear from you just saw your name .... and too would like to have Arthur's marks & how did he make out this last term. Thanking you for a reply please oblige

Ethel Motley

PS Arthur's mother

Reading this very beautiful, poignant and heartbreaking letter we can infer from it that she is now aware of Arthur's perilous situation and that he is in need of monies, but perhaps Ethel is not fully cognisant of the whole situation and story, thus her query about his academic progress. But more positively there has been some limited communication between her and her beloved son.

Arthur has apprised her of the situation that he may be about to take a year out of university to allow him to save some monies to allow him to return to university and be able to pay the academic fees.

But I think we may be able to take from the letter that he didn't inform her that this was partly caused by him failing to turn up and sit his examinations back in the spring: was this because of what was going on in his personal life or simply perhaps actually being unable to pay his examination fees back in March.

That does however need to be tempered in that her inquiry as to Arthur's marks was a more general query as to how his second (third year) year had gone. But I think it is indicative that Arthur had perhaps been somewhat economical with the truth perhaps keeping mum, so to speak.

I may be wrong on this, but I can't but wonder just how much information Arthur has conveyed to Ethel and Frank about his domestic situation - that he is not only now a married man – and to a white woman – but that he is the father of a six month old girl.

My own interpretation is that he hasn't informed them.

Those were the days when knowledge came slowly and it may well have been relatively easy to keep the dramatic change in his life quiet from his parents over 4000 miles away in the United States.

Arthur would of course have been influenced by what had happened five years earlier when he had fathered an illegitimate son back home in McAlester City and the upset and the worries and the massive fallout that that episode had caused. And now, here we are, five years later and not only is he in the same boat but in what might be described as an even worse situation – this time he was more in need of a lifeboat.

So the distance between Arthur and Ethel has grown larger.

And further, reading between the lines, Ethel and Frank Motley may have been hit hard by The Great Crash of the year before.

Harsh and cynical as it may sound, it would appear that from here on in, the only correspondence between the two of them may have been around the small amount of monies that Ethel wired - a few American dollars – around five dollars a week - sent to Arthur c/o American Express whose branch still remains to this day situated at the west end of Princes Street: with its handsome facade – a lovely building with its fine offices – for Arthur, what with its American staff outwith the American Consulate it was the nearest he would come to re-visiting the home soil of America.

Autumn 1930

The year 1930 was moving toward its end having been a very mixed year for Arthur.

Alongside the joys, the pleasures and the happiness he may have experienced as a husband and as a father it brought with it great worries too particularly financial and also that he had been blown off course in his ambition to qualify as a doctor.

And perhaps it was just as well that Arthur didn't know just how long that journey to become a doctor would take – almost another decade – ten years - and by a long, uncertain and circuitous route and journey.

I think that Arthur and Annette and their young baby girl may now be living in bustling Leith, but there remains uncertainty as to whether they're still at Fettes Row.

As to whether he continued to attend the remaining lectures and courses at the university at this moment in his story we can't say. Spring is now a distant memory and the summer has passed too – the traditional long vacation for students – Arthur would surely have desperately sought out work – no easy task in the Edinburgh of the period.

Ethel and Frank could only support him in a very minimal way which would have left only Annette to find some work and a source of income: and as to whether Annette's parents had become reconciled to their daughter's change of circumstance helping the young newly married couple out, we'll never know. But, in terms of a paper trail, we're fortunate to have some further information.

The following month, September 1930, almost a month after Ethel had written to Professor Buckle explaining their parlous situation and seeking out information on Arthur's academic progress and hinting that he may have to take some time out, she once again picks up her pen and now writes to a Mr J. Lenaim Smith at the University of Edinburgh.

Once again it's another letter that tugs at the heart-strings - a caring mother in limited circumstances trying to do the very best by her son – a story that echoes down the ages and through the years, the decades and the centuries. Your heart can't but help go out to Ethel.

McAlester Okla

Sept 27 - 1930

Mr J. Lanaim Smith

Dear Sir,

Your letter of a very recent date received glad to hear from you have been waiting for another letter fate against me in trying to finish my son, but will do the best that I can. I hope he passed as he will be admitted. I wanted to know so I could try and forward as much of his tuition as I possibly could. Many thanks to you for the info. which I received.

Yours truly

Ethel Motley

We don't have a copy of Mr J. Lanaim Smith's response to Ethel, but reading between the lines we can surmise that Arthur has been given the opportunity by the university to resit the Third Professional Examinations which he didn't appear for back in the spring.

Ethel has now been brought up to speed as to where her son stands on the academic front and is hoping against hope that he has both sat and passed the resit examinations, but it also indicates that Arthur himself hasn't been in touch with her during this worrying period.

It's something that every parent can relate to. Having a daughter or a son who has made fine progress only to face a crisis in their life trajectory – a major crossroads which can alter the course of the rest of their lives.

The third and final letter that we have from 1930 regarding Arthur's student life in the capital is dated a few weeks later, the 14th October. It's now well in to the autumn and the new university term has opened but unfortunately and rather sadly, not for Arthur as he hasn't sat the resit exams for the previous academic year.

The letter is addressed to Ethel and it's from the pen of the Dean of the University of Edinburgh. He writes:

Dear Madam,

I have your letter of 21st ult. (presumably September 1930)

Your son has not appeared for the Anatomy Examination. He has been interviewed in my office and states that he was due class fees to the University he was unable to take the Examination this year. He will therefore require to continue to study that subject during the winter and in addition he will be allowed to take the course in Meteris Medics.

The Matriculation and Class Fees payable for the Winter Session will amount to approximately £20.

Yours faithfully,

Dean.

For Ethel the Dean's letter will have brought mixed feelings especially with her living so very far away in McAlester City.

There would have been the great worry that her son had not sat the Anatomy Examination.

It would have worried Ethel further because she clearly had no overall idea of what was going on.

But it does indicate that there must have been some limited communication between herself and Arthur as she seems to have assumed he had said he would sit the Examination – and who knows, perhaps she had forwarded him some monies to allow him to do so.

Thus he didn't appear for the Third Year Examination for the academic year 1929/1930.

Despite Ethel's great disappointment she still held out a glimmer of hope as the university had agreed to allow Arthur to move into the fourth year of his studies albeit with the heavy burden of an already very onerous course that he would need to continue to study Anatomy – effectively doing two years in one all alongside being a husband and a father.

It was a fearsome propect and an impossible task that in all likelihood would have overwhelmed him, particularly in the context of his family's financial worries too.

I can imagine and sympathise with the nature of the Edinburgh Motley family's up and down life.

Arthur and Annette were on a high octane journey. What a roller-coaster ride.

There was the excitement of their early relationship which had turned into a passionate affair.

Annette had fallen pregnant.

She had married at eighteen years of age.

And now here she was having to quickly move from being a carefree girl to take on all the responsibilities of being a married woman – a completely new and very different mode of life.

There must have been tension within the household fuelled by their worries and their concerns. As my grandmother would have said 'The gilt was very quickly off the gingerbread'. And despite the couple remaining married for over half a century I do wonder whether both parties came to ultimately regret their passionate affair of 1928/1929.

But that said I'm also aware that Arthur adored Annette. As mentioned he told my mother how glamorous and beautiful she was and how after she died in 1981 aged 69 years Dr Motley had made the afore-mentioned comment that Annette had reminded him of the film star Betty Davies.

To Study or to Work

With Arthur now living once again in Leith if he had returned to university he would have reverted back to travelling the two miles uphill from Leith Walk to Teviot Place to the university's medical school. From a cost angle as well as enjoying the exercise he would most probably have walked there most days during the week, similarly walking back home rather than taking one of the rattling trams that ran through the Edinburgh streets.

Photograph Willem van de Poll

But whether he had indeed returned to university or instead was more likely going off to work each day, as he walked out on those fresh and invigorating autumn and winter mornings through late 1930 and in to 1931 he would have had the time to reflect on his life.

And whilst tempered by the joy of being married to Annette and being the father of a girl who by February 1931 was approaching her first birthday, that happiness would have been overshadowed by his worries for his family's future well-being.

Having to take Anatomy into fourth year alongside the new academic year's studies would have been a fearsome challenge even if he had been able to focus all his energies and devote all his time to studying.

But instead there was the constant concern as to how he could support the family financially.

And whilst home would have brought him much fun and much joy and happiness it would have been a difficult place to be and not conducive to studying.

The baby would have cried and screamed at times – as babies do!

Annette would at times have felt 'trapped' with a baby to look after all the week-long and would have naturally been looking for some quiet time to herself.

And to help keep the family afloat, she may have had to look for some work too.

As mentioned it would have been very difficult for Arthur, a young Black man in Edinburgh what with its colour bars in some parts of the city to have found any work at all.

What a dilemma for the new couple.

It was a very worrying time indeed for them.

Was there any way out?

Was there an escape route?

Even if Arthur had able to continue with his studies both he and Annette must have begun to realise that Arthur wasn't now going to pass his medical examinations and qualify to become a doctor.

So what then?

The young couple must have asked themselves this question, time and time again.

What does our future together hold?

And when they asked this question their prospects must have appeared pretty bleak.

An Edinburgh Boy

Returning to America wasn't really an option.

Difficult and challenging as Edinburgh might be for a mixed race couple it would be as naught if they'd moved to America.

It's certainly not something Annette would have contemplated and Arthur had now slowly begun to adapt to being an Edinburgh boy.

In later years he spoke of his great love for the capital so it would be unsurprising to discover that whatever the circumstances, he and his new family's future definitely lay anywhere but here in Edinburgh - in the so called City of Enlightenment - The Precipitous City - Auld Reekie - the city of fogs and smogs caused by the smoke that emanated from the thousands of chimneys of the town dwellers as well as the city's famous long established breweries, but perhaps for a brief moment the thought of returning to America may just have passed through his mind.

So there we have it.

If he did continue into that new academic year through being offered a place by the Dean, Arthur Motley - still a young man - would have set out for university, but more likely work, at around eight o'clock on autumn and winter mornings emerging into the sea mists of the Port of Leith to walk up the long hill of Leith Walk to traverse Princes Street and on to the North Bridge and from there continue up the South Bridge to Chamber Street past the splendour of Scotland's national museum, it would have been to work.

South Bridge and Edinburgh University

By this time the city would have been coming alive with workers heading off to work and gentlemen heading into the city to their offices to the lawyers' offices and the insurance and the banking companies that littered the town's streets and broad avenues.

He would pass the creamery carts as well as the horse and cart's of St Cuthbert's Dairy as they delivered the daily milk to help nourish families across the city.

Photograph Willem van de Poll

There would be the shouts of the news vendors at the east end of Princes Street just down from The Scotsman Newspaper's office on the North Bridge.

At the top of Infirmary Street there might be a man out with his cart yelling and selling fruit and vegetables.

And with Edinburgh being a city of breweries particularly down at the foot of Holyrood, so much so that when Arthur crossed the North and then South Bridge not only would he have done so through Edinburgh's smogs but he would be aware of the sour smell of burning barley which often pervaded the air and the nostrils of the Old Town's adults and children.

And come the end of the day, as dusk and night began to slowly fall he would have made his way home, but this time it was an easier journey – it was all downhill as he returned to Leith passing the hostelries and the pubs that littered the city particularly in and around Nicholson Street including the famous Rutherford's Bar where Robert Louis Stevenson enjoyed a drink when he too was a student at the University of Edinburgh.

With their welcoming lights in the dark and the fogs they attracted
working men like moths to a flame. And as Arthur made his way
down Leith Walk he would pass pub after pub.

It must have been quite a contrast to that earlier summer of
eighteen months previously of 1929 when during the month of
August, Arthur and Annette may well have been amongst the
thousands of the city's astonished citizens who looked up in wonder
to the sky above to see a Graf Zeppelin airship sail over Calton Hill
and Edinburgh's Disgrace – an early forewarning of a decade later
when Britain would go to war against Germany – another of the key
junctures – the key periods in Arthur Motley's life, but that was still
a full ten years hence into an uncertain future before he eventually
managed to qualify as a doctor in 1939.

On those walks up and down Leith Walk he would have passed
the Playhouse Theatre which had opened the previous year in
1929.

But it wasn't so much a theatre and instead was one of the new
Super-Cinema's with a seating capacity of 3,000 customers.

With its design based on The Roxy in New York it would have
caught Arthur's eye and when it opened perhaps Arthur and
Annette managed along there to enjoy a film or two.

Similarly reflecting Arthur's life the cinema was going through a period of transition moving from silent films to the talkies – in 1927 The Jazz Singer had come out and no doubt it would have been screened at the new cinema and was the kind of film the couple may well have enjoyed together before the demands of marriage and parenthood kicked in very quickly after the new cinema had opened her doors for the first time and they thereafter had little time to spend alone together as a couple.

The End of a Dream

Life for Arthur was now very different to his three previous incarnations – a schoolboy in the humid subtropical climate of McAlester City: the year spent in Marshall Texas with its relatively mild winter; and then Lincoln University which whilst it could be similarly as cold as Edinburgh was a very different environment.

Compared to Edinburgh, his two years spent in Oxford Pennsylvania was but a golden memory - he had thrived within the university both enjoying the curriculum, making friends and being amongst his Black friends and a member of various societies and playing American Football for a successful team.

Looking back this had been a halcyon period in Arthur's young life with its nice balance of studying for a degree whilst having great fun enjoying fine friendships so it was no wonder he returned half a century later to re-join his former classmates one last time before each member bidded their fond farewells before disappearing for ever into the night air.

He had thrived academically and he was able to put Freddie, his pregnant earlier girlfriend from McAlester City firmly in the past, as well as Ethel and Frank to a certain extent.

But now, on those longish Edinburgh walks up and down between home and university or more likely to work, whilst he looked ahead to what might be a bleak future he couldn't but reflect on what he had left behind too, back in the land of his birth.

But this new academic year was to prove a stage too far.

Having sailed through his education back in America the first indication of the tough field he had come to hoe came in that very first year in Edinburgh between 1928 and 1929 when he struggled in his first year to pass his university examinations after a resit: this must surely have begun to sow the first seeds of doubt that he might fail: it was always going to be a distinct possibility - always on the near horizon - and at moments he would have had to contemplate a very different and alternative future for himself.

And whilst it might not be as a doctor, he was at least armed with a university degree from Lincoln University.

That was surely something.

A balm.

Surely it might open some doors to him.

In theory it didn't leave him totally bereft of opportunities.

Thus the failure of 1930 wouldn't have come as a complete surprise and perhaps not to Ethel either given her correspondence with the Dean where she indicated that Arthur might have to take some time out of the university to try to fund his studies and his way through life.

Ethel's comment and observations indicate she now has a greater understanding of the precariousness of Arthur's situation: she is being pragmatic but has certainly not given up hope – how could she after all the miles her beloved son had travelled in life and in so many different ways too.

A Year of Crisis

If 1930 had been a difficult year for Arthur in some respects 1931 was to prove even worse.

It was a year of crisis as our young protagonist now tries to desperately change the course of his life to find a new and different way forward.

By the middle of the spring of 1931 Mr A. E. James the Registrar at Lincoln University Pennsylvania, Arthur's alma mater, writes to the Dean of the University of Edinburgh, J. Lorrain Smith:

April 27, 1931.

Dean J. Lorrain Smith

School of Medicine,

Edinburgh University,

Edinburgh, Scotland

Dear Sir,

In September 1928 Arthur P. Motley of McAlester Oklahoma was I believe admitted to your Medical School. I am writing to inquire whether he is still in residence and also I should be interested to have a statement from you concerning the quality of the work he has done within your school.

Sincerely yours,

A. E. Jones

Registrar

It would have been highly unusual for the Dean of Lincoln University to have suddenly – completely out of the blue – to have taken up his pen to innocently inquire about one of his former students and decide to write to the Dean of the University of Edinburgh's Medical School with a vague inquiry.

We need to read between the lines of his letter.

I think that in some shape or fashion one could surmise that this is suggestive of emanating from his worried and concerned mother, Ethel, having not had any communication from Arthur since the previous autumn of 1930 when she discovered that he had not resat his examinations.

In trying to get an update on what was happening in her son's life and at the end of her tether she decided to contact Lincoln University to see whether through the established route of one university speaking to another about a student in common, to see whether they could elicit some information about Arthur's progress – or lack of progress - for a worried and concerned mother.

Mr A.E. Jones's letter is worded in such a form and suitably vague so as to not reveal any information about either Arthur, his family back home in McAlester City nor any estrangement between Arthur and his American family.

Instead, it is cleverly worded both in terms of asking open questions but also two specific questions.

First, is Arthur still studying at the University of Edinburgh – that Registrar Jones should even ask this question means that Ethel must have had some doubt as to whether as she indicated in her letter of the previous September 1930 that he may have to leave the school for a while: and in the intervening six month period Arthur has not been in contact during all that time.

And second, Ethel still holds out a candle that despite not sitting the Anatomy Examination the previous year back in October 1930 and his ongoing financial challenges that somehow Arthur had managed to return to his studies - finding a way to somehow pay his way through college by finding work whilst continuing to study.

It was a forlorn hope on her part.

But she was an optimistic individual and a determined one too, so she still held out a small candle of light in this period of darkness and despair.

Almost a month to the day later Mr A.E. Jones's receives a response from the University of Edinburgh's Dean: he writes back to Lincoln University:

26th May, 1931

The Registrar,

Lincoln University,

Chester County,

Pennsylvania,

U.S.A.

Dear Sir,

I am in receipt of your letter of 27th ult and in reply have to state that Mr Arthur P. Motley is not enrolled as a medical student in the University during the current Academical year. Since he enrolled the University he has passed the Second Professional Examination in Physiology only, but I understand that his failure to make progress has been due to financial difficulties.

Yours faithfully,

Dean

A Change of Direction

So, there we have it.

Rather than my imaginings of Arthur making his way to and from the university each day during the autumn and winter of 1930/31 to study he neither resat Anatomy, nor did he accept the opportunity to continue to study the subject again in October 1930 and neither did he take up the Dean's offer of going into his third professional year of study.

Arthur had simply left the university.

There would have been a degree of pragmatism in his decision.

Whilst he might have recognised the insurmountability of the burden of the studies awaiting him it would have been combined with the impossibility of the challenge of trying to study within a household with a young baby: but more than this, the primary motivation in his decision to so dramatically change course, would have been the need – nay the necessity - to go out to work to support his new family.

On the surface this would appear to be the first time that Arthur went out to work – at least in an adult capacity: as to whether he had part time jobs as a boy or a student back in America we simply don't know.

In the circumstances of the time many children in the America of 1900-1930, particularly African-American children, many of whom did work whether in farm work, as news-boys or even in the likes of the mining industry and of course this was where part of McAlester City's growth and fortune had been founded upon. I have no evidence for it but an instinctive part of me feels that Arthur might have been pampered to a certain extent by Ethel and didn't work. But I have no evidence for this – the call is a mix of the intellectual and the emotional.

But 1931 was a major crossroads in Arthur's life: and it wasn't one of those crossroads in life that only reveal themselves so to be so in later life. Instead, he will have been fully cognisant with what this meant and how in all probability – to all intents and purposes - it had ended his aspirations to become a doctor.

Not only had he been derailed, but to all intents and purposes his dream had come to an end.

And whilst he may have consoled himself with the highly unlikely notion that one day he might return to his studies there would have been great doubt in his mind too – after all, how could he ever find the monies and the where-with-all to ever return to the world of academia and be able to finance this, but his confidence in having the intellectual ability to pass these difficult and challenging examinations must surely have been dented and perhaps even crushed.

In his mind, privately, he must have mused that even with a good following wind, could he really do it?

But what is also clear is that he hadn't informed either Ethel nor Frank Motley of his decision and the change of direction.

But given Arthur's financial circumstances back in the autumn of 1930 and the family's inability to offer the necessary financial support, whilst it wouldn't have come as a complete surprise to Ethel and Frank, nevertheless they would have been disappointed.

As to why Arthur didn't inform them, well, who knows why.

Perhaps, like most of us he simply didn't wish to upset them and

instead keeping the bad news to himself and thus protecting his mother Ethel from the great disappointment.

After all if it had long been her dream for him since he was that talented bright little boy back home in McAlester City: the family had lived with their hopes and their dreams for so many years: now Arthur couldn't bear or wish to distress Ethel further.

So at this stage in Arthur Philip Motley's story we have no idea what he's been up to since the autumn of 1930. And, if he hadn't been at university what was he doing?

Season followed season – winter has been left behind and the spring of 1931 moved on to early summer.

The harsh Edinburgh winter - in several senses of the phrase - has been left far behind.

The capital is now moving toward its fine fresh green best.

Thousands of snowdrops and daffodils carpeted Princes Street Gardens and The Meadows thereafter to be replaced by spring crocuses and as we move into June, the fine and sweetly scented old Scots Roses were moving towards their best and it's here that we get our next indication as to what has been going on in Arthur's world.

It comes in the form of some new and fresh correspondence and provides an update on the revelation back in May in the Dean's letter to Lincoln University that Arthur had, to all intents and purposes given up on his studies at the University of Edinburgh.

Arthur - he is just like a Bird

In June 1931 Ethel wrote to the Dean of the University of Edinburgh.

Interestingly she opens it by referring to his letter of the 26th May 1930: as to whether Ethel is actually referring to his letter of the 27th May sent in response to Mr A. E. Jones's the Registrar at Lincoln University to which she has been forwarded a copy and simply got the date wrong by a day or whether the Dean had written similarly and separately to her on the day before, we don't know. But certainly by this stage she is now aware that Arthur hasn't returned to university.

And whilst not unexpected, still it must have come as devastating news to her.

In her hand-written letter - later transcribed - I assume by the university - into a typed form she writes:

McAlister,

June, 8th 1931.

Professor Sydney Smith,

Dear Dean,

Your letter of the 26th May was mine to day June 8th and I must say I was more than glad to hear from you, but I want to thank you for being so interested in my son. Well he is some-what discouraged because bad luck fell on our pathway, his father lost his job on October, 14th, 1931, (surely 1930?) and since that time money has not been plentiful with us. I regret very much I have just been sending him five dollars per week which I have. I am very sorry indeed things happened as they did. Now I think things will be a little brighter for me, at least I hope so I have sacrificed so much for my son to make him a great Doctor but it seems like it is in vain and sure have spent money, now will you please write me in words how much money it will be. I have tried to borrow money but have failed. I have one more person in mind and after I hear from you I'll go and see what I can do. It's nothing like asking, for the blessed Master said ask,. He has gone too far not to try and finish. I am living on a very meagre fare trying to send him money yes he is in Edinburgh. Well I ask a favour of you will you do the the best you can? Instead of sending the £3: 10/ per week to Arthur I would send it to you. My sincere desire is for my son to be a polished Doctor. When can he enrol? Explain it all to Me. Arthur he gives up to (too) quickly he is just like a bird. I sent him to Wiley College, Marshall Tex two terms and thee (three) Summers and Lincoln University in Philadelphia, P. Two terms and then over there. It seems to me he could of got some assistance. Excuse lengthy letter. Again I thank you.

Yours faithfully,

Ethel Motley

He is in this place studying so he says, I don't know.

Animal Diseases Research Association

Biochemical Laboratory

in Royal (Dick) Veterinary College

Edinburgh, SCOTLAND.

P.S. but for all of this year he has had me just to address his letters: - c/o American Express Co.

I am also writing Arthur and impressing on him to go and see you.

Many thanks. I'll wait for a reply from you.

Much left unsaid between the Leaves and the Lines

Ethel's letter to the Dean of the University of Edinburgh is the most powerful piece of correspondence and insight that we have into Arthur's life at the time - an insight as to how his mother had supported him over a period of time.

It says much, but also leaves much that is unsaid between the leaves and the lines of Ethel's poignant and very lovely letter.

From the afore-mentioned letters between Lincoln University and the University of Edinburgh, Ethel has now clearly been able to ascertain more about her son's situation: it also indicates that she has been in correspondence with Arthur too.

Not only has she discovered his non-attendance but she has discovered that he now has a connection with the Edinburgh mirror image of the medical faculty, that of its veterinary school which is similarly well regarded throughout the world.

And we now have a further insight into one of the contributory reasons for Arthur not returning to university back in the autumn – it was also for reasons of finance and the lack of monies.

When he needed cash more than ever, his father Frank had lost his job back in Oklahoma and much of the cash flow and bank transfers between McAlester City and Edinburgh had largely dried up.

Perhaps Frank, who had at around this stage was employed as a Retail Estate Manager had been one of the victims of The Great Crash of 1929 and its implications for millions of families across the land.

Ethel comments that all she can forward to Arthur is but five dollars a week suggests that during his first two years in Edinburgh she had been able to send him much more helping to fund his studies and living expenses, perhaps even fully.

Whilst her letter highlights her natural concern for Arthur it presents a revealing insight into him as an individual, with a rare – indeed perhaps the only recorded instance of (small) criticism. In doing so she uses the most lovely simile when she writes rather charmingly that *'Arthur he gives up to (too) quickly he is just like a bird.'* What wonderful concise and colourful language perfectly capturing and encapsulating her thoughts about her son in but a single line.

But, like much of Arthur's life there are mysteries within mysteries that I can only hazard a guess at.

Since back in the autumn of 1930 Ethel had been in contact with her son and been appraised of his situation, but I would suggest she hasn't been fully informed.

For example why did Arthur not wish any correspondence to be sent to his place of residence in either Fettes Row nor Leith Walk?

Was it because he didn't wish to let Ethel know that he had moved in case she asked him searching questions?

Was it so that Arthur's wife Annette was kept in the dark so to speak either in terms of his parents or that she (Ethel) was sending him monies each week?

Alternatively it might simply have been that during this period of uncertainty that he, Annette and the baby might have changed their address from Fettes Row to Leith Walk - and therefore he wanted Ethel's letters and more importantly her monies to go to a specific, constant and guaranteed address rather than going awry or astray in the post.

After passing Edinburgh's finest hotel, the North British, he would pass Waverley Station which would have been both noisy and smoky from the great steam engines that ferried carriages from all directions – it was only in 1928 that the world's most famous train - The Flying Scotsman – had made its record-breaking London to Edinburgh run – not to mention all the trains that ran north, south east and west as far as distant Cornwall.

The Flying Scotsman: below Princes Streeet Willem van de Poll

In visting the American Express Company's office Arthur would have walked up from Leith Walk and along the busy and vibrant Princes Street which was always thronged with citizens – hundreds and hundreds of women and men out shopping along the thoroughfare.

Arthur would have walked past the fine Edinburgh stores and buildings of W.H. Forsyth and Jenners, the Harrods of the north - to the far end – to Princes Street's West End where the fine, handsome and impressive American Express Company was located at 139-140 Princes Street to see what mail and wire had been sent from Ethel in far off Oklahoma.

JENNER'S Luncheon and Tea Rooms
pleasantly situated overlooking Princes Street

ARE THE MOST POPULAR IN EDINBURGH

Dainty and Varied Menu, combined with Refined Service

JENNER'S
Princes Street, EDINBURGH

As mentioned stepping into the fine interior of the company's offices would have been the nearest Arthur got to stepping back into America and he would hear the voices of those with a similar accent to himself if not of a similar colour.

A further mystery is Ethel's dissonance with this existing arrangement and her suggestion that the monies should instead be sent to the University of Edinburgh itself.

Why did she suggest this?

Was she was unhappy with Arthur - not so much squandering her largesse, but that she felt that any monies sent should now be used purely for the express purpose of funding his academic studies.

It also suggests she is unaware that he is married with a baby and that her monies are being used to supplement and keep his immediate family in Edinburgh afloat.

But, surely, if she knew - being a wife and a mother and having had children herself - she would have been understanding not wishing to deny her extended family her small contribution, but nevertheless, she would have faced a moral dilemma.

However, what she clearly knows and has known for a period of time is that back in October 1930 Arthur did not resit the Anatomy Examination and neither did he take up the offer to study Third Year Medica Metrics: instead he has been 'studying?' at the famous Royal Dick Veterinary College.

Clearly Arthur has had a major rethink.

Ethel has indicated that she had been in the habit of sending him $5 dollars or £3.50 each week.

Thus if we go back just over a year to when Annette Junior was born, although Arthur has said the reason he hadn't sat the Second Year Professional Examination was because he couldn't afford the fees, then this would have come as a surprise to Ethel back in America.

She would have assumed he had the bare necessary to continue living and studying as he had done so in the academic year 1928/1929.

It must have made her wonder what had happened – why were things now so very different come the following academic year 1929/1930?

What was he doing with the monies she sent?

It's on this basis that I don't think she was aware that Arthur was married and had a child; but she must have contemplated various different scenarios in her mind's eye.

Was he being misled?

Was he being diverted from his studies and focusing too much on leisure and pleasure?

There are no real clues in her letter to the Dean – she does write *'I am very sorry indeed things happened as they did.' but that may simply be that Arthur had given up studying at university, didn't sit the Second Professional Examination nor did he take up his place in third year.'*

Alternatively was she aware of the full story, but didn't wish to elaborate further in case it might work against Arthur and prejudice any help from the University of Edinburgh which might have been available and forthcoming to assist a foreign student.

She would not wish to do her son an unintentional or clumsy disfavour in the Dean's eyes which might result in something less than helpful – less favourable an outcome – something punitive. But instead, what she does, is allude to his changed circumstances in a subtle way and for all she knew the Dean was already fully cognisant of Arthur's changed circumstances.

Now that Arthur has reached the momentous decision back in the autumn of 1930 of giving up at least temporarily on becoming a doctor - that he doesn't have the capacity within his changed life circumstances - or because he instead wishes to turn to something new that he is better suited too, we don't know.

And neither do we know what precisely he is studying - is he simply a student or is there a paid dimension to this new venture?

And also how did this all happen – was there any liaison between the two schools – the medical fraternity and the veterinary fraternity?

But whatever happened in arriving at this dramatic change of direction it's an interesting turn of events in his life and not only is he going down a new road because it might offer the prospect of a brighter future for him and his family, but it might also enhance his job prospects too because we've already established how very difficult it would have been for a Black man to have found employment in the capital - but the academic world might be more promising – more enlightened – more accomodating - and less subject to prejudice and discrimination.

The Dark Ages

The next period in Arthur's life might be called The Lost Decade whereas the past year is one which has been lost and partly found.

From this period of The Dark Ages - from out of the darkness there comes a small light which helps to illuminate proceedings. And it's also the only correspondence on record from Arthur himself, but even here it leaves mysteries within mysteries.

From the record held at the University of Edinburgh there are two letters of interest. The first one is from Arthur addressed to Professor Sidney Smith the Dean of Medicine at the University of Edinburgh.

Apart from the letter giving an extraordinary insight into what he's been doing, the address alone is most interesting: he's clearly been based at the Royal Dick Veterinary College.

Animal Diseases Research Association

Biochemical Laboratories

In

Royal (Dick) Veterinary College

Edinburgh

October 6, 1931

Professor Sidney Smith

Dean of Medicine

University of Edinburgh,

Dear Sir:- Please permit me to transfer from the Faculty of Medicine of the University of Edinburgh, to the Faculty of Medicine in the Royal College of Physicians and Surgeons.

For the past school year I have been working with Dr. Dryers here in these laboratories. I have analysed the blood samples taken from normal animals, for, inorganic phosphorus, total phosphorus organic soil soluble phosphorus, and for the relative ensymic activity of the plasma phosphatase.

I also had the supreme privilege of being co-author of a paper, the subject of which is;- 'The Effect of Total Thyro-parathyroidectomy on the Plasma Phosphatase Level'. This operation was performed by Dr. Dryers. A goat was used for this experiment. This paper is now ready to go to press. I will be very glad to have the privilege of sending you a reprint of the same. This change to the Royal College will give me some time to work here in the laboratory. I will be very grateful to accept any advice you may have to offer.

Most Respectfully Yours

A.P. Motley

Three days later the Dean wrote back to Arthur:

9th October, 1931.

Mr A. P. Motley,

Animal Diseases Research Association,

Biomedical Laboratories

In

Royal (Dick) Veterinary College,

Edinburgh

Dear Sir,

I have your letter of the 6th inst. and in reply thereto have to state that the University has no objection to your transferring to the

School of Medicine of the Royal Colleges to work for the Qualification of the Scottish Conjoint Board.

I shall be very glad to have a reprint of your Paper when it is available.

Yours faithfully,

Dean.

A further three days after his letter to Arthur the Dean wrote to Arthur's mother, Ethel for probably the last time.

12th October 1931

Mrs Ethel Motley,

Box 628

McAlester,

Oklahoma,

U. S. A.

Dear Madam,

I have to inform you that your son, Arthur P. Motley, has given up study for the University Degrees. He intends now to work for the Qualification, L.R.C.P. , L.R.C.S. given by the Scottish Conjoint Board and for information regarding his work, you should in future write to the Dean of the School of Medicine, Royal College of Surgeons, Nicolson Street, Edinburgh.

Yours faithfully,

Dean.

So there we have it – the only example of a letter from the pen of Arthur Philip Motley aged around 25.

Part of the mystery has been solved but it leaves other questions unanswered.

In its way it's a most odd letter because Arthur is asking permission for something he doesn't actually require permission for and the mention of him offering the Dean a copy of an academic paper is odd too.

I'm unsure what Arthur hoped to gain from this correspondence – for example whether in some ways it would make up for his previous failure to sit the Anatomy examination of 1930.

The letter is couched in good manners and politeness which is unsurprising given the era and those involved, but some of the language or phraseology makes for slightly uncomfortable reading today reflecting Arthur's more subservient position particularly the 'most respectfully your's last sentence.

He didn't require the approval of the Dean – all that he needed to do was to inform the University of Edinburgh of his decision to withdraw from the course.

The Dean of course is aware of this and also isn't really interested in the academic paper but out of politeness says yes please forward me a copy – but overall the Dean's tone as in all his correspondence I find to be a little bit stuffy and at heart I don't find him to be truly caring and interested in the welfare of Arthur, but that may be an unfair summary.

But for me he always comes across as somewhat superior.

But he does write to Arthur's mother to bring her up to speed as to what Arthur's been doing – and indeed not been doing over the past year.

Arthur's obviously not been studying at the university and he's abandoned his medical studies, however on a more positive note he's not given up on his dream to become a doctor – he's become aware there's an alternative route open to him to proceed and perhaps to succeed – not only a different route but perhaps an easier one too and one which will allow him to more effectively balance studying with earning a living – because the other significant finding here is that he's found employment to work within a scientific environment at the Royal Dick Veterinary College within their animal research laboratories. It confirms too what I thought might be Arthur's best bet to find employment – within academia where there would have been less prejudice.

Royal Dick Veterinary College

And whilst the Dean writes to Ethel - to be fair to him he is proactive in bringing her up to speed - still I find the tone formal and almost as if he's now glad that in future that he won't be 'pestered' by her. But of course Ethel is already aware that Arthur's based at the Royal Dick Veterinary College but his departure from studying at the University of Edinburgh will still come as bad news to her.

The Lost Decade

There's now a significant gap in Arthur's Edinburgh life.

All we know is that five years later Arthur, Annette and Annette Junior now aged five and approaching starting primary school are still living in Edinburgh in 1935 where the U.S. Census records him as working in Edinburgh at the Royal Hospital Edinburgh as a medical intern.

But this in itself is an oddity because to be a medical intern would entail having passed a medical degree and to have qualified as a doctor - and of course we now know that Arthur had failed Medica Metrics and left the course.

So, what was he doing?

What we are certain of is that the family has now moved from Leith out to Colinton Mains Road circa 1935/36 to a brand new house on the fresh breezy southern boundary of the city.

That suggests that he has been in employment and now has the necessary resources to either rent the house or to even have taken out a mortgage to buy their first home – a dramatic change of fortune and circumstances, but perhaps over the previous five years the family have been counting the bawbees.

But as to his employment, all we have to go on is Ethel's letter of him being based at the Royal Dick Veterinary College.

Did he continue to work there or alternatively did he move to work at the Edinburgh Infirmary perhaps in the capacity of a medical technician or in a research postion?

Based on the census entry that may well have been the situation as opposed to being a medical intern.

And working within the world of medicine and medical work it maintained his interest, even developing some aspects of his knowledge and over the years in doing so, all the while he was wondering – could I somehow still qualify and become a doctor.

The Honorary Medical Officer

Alongside this we also know that he was something called an Honorary Medical Officer at the Colinton Mains First Aid Post.

And whilst this would most likely have been a voluntary thing – a community contribution – it too would have kept his hand in and maintained an ongoing interest in the world of medicine, similar to laboratory work or research work it utilised the knowledge base from his days at Lincoln and Edinburgh Universities.

But more than that he would have developed some practical skills.

He would also have found out just how much he enjoyed it – how satisfying it was to help people.

And not only would it have helped to nourish and keep alive his earlier dream, it would have given him both the confidence and the motivation to try one last time – to qualify as a doctor – only he now had to find a different way to achieve his ambition.

It's a Mystery

But as the decade of the 1930s moved to a close come 1940 a further mystery lies therein - Arthur is recorded in the 1940 United

States Census but denoted as being absent from the family home at 902 Monroe Avenue McAlester City, Oklahoma: his previous address in 1935 is given as Edinburgh and under the occupation category it states he's employed by the Edinburgh Royal Hospital (Infirmary) as a medical intern, but it records him as being single.

This is a rather odd entry as we know he's been married for a decade with a small family and yet within the census he is recorded as being single – unmarried – it's quite extraordinary!

Whilst it could just be a slip of the pen, alternatively this of course backs up the theory that Arthur has kept both his marriage to Annette, a young white Scots girl from a decade before and that he has a ten year old daughter – Annette Junior – hidden and a complete secret from his parents.

As described, those were the days when knowledge and information came slowly, thus Arthur was able to maintain a secret life which he had enjoyed in Scotland for a decade.

But when his father as the head of the household recorded his son Arthur as living in McAlester City, I wonder if this was influenced by the prospect of the Second World War, although it was something which America herself was still to enter in to: Frank may have thought that somehow it might help and assist Arthur in some shape or fashion perhaps offering a potentially safe place to return to offering greater safety.

But overall it does suggest the family still thinks he may return home again.

The U.S. Census provides us with further information in that Arthur's father Frank is now recorded as being aged 57 and employed by the church as a minister.

He had been educated to Sixth Grade whereas Ethel had been at school until Eighth Grade.

Those twenty years had seen significant changes in Frank's life, who back in 1920, had been recorded in that census as working as a Cleaner Operative, presumably at a (his) local laundry business.

Noticing that Ethel had enjoyed a longer period of education than her husband the Reverend Frank made me look at the 1930 U.S. Census and it revealed further information, providing an answer as to how Arthur had managed to support himself in his studies in Edinburgh between the years 1928 and 1930.

At this time, aged 47, Ethel is recorded as working as a secretary at the 'Lodge' whilst Frank is a Baptist minister.

From this I would intuit that Ethel has been sending most of the income from her job to support Arthur to help him to fulfil their dream of him becoming, as she so charmingly describes in her letter to the Dean of the University of Edinburgh '...a polished Doctor.'

But clearly by later in that year and perhaps as a result of The Great Crash, the Reverend Frank has lost his job on the 14th October, 1930, dramatically changing their life circumstances and situation in McAlester City – perhaps the couple are now full dependent on Ethel's work and her income as a secretary leading to her inability to forward any more than five dollars a week to Arthur.

A Ripple in the Pond

49. *George Square girls in the Thirties.*

Other than regular laudatory comments appearing about Dr Motley on the Oxgangs – A Pastime From Time Past Facebook page, Dr Motley's trail went slightly cold.

Also, I was pursuing other projects. However, on the 20th August 2020 a letter arrived through my post-box from North Yorkshire from 88 year old Mrs Betty Verrill.

Dear Peter Hoffmann,

Here is another 'ripple in the pond of memory.'

Annette Motley was at my school – George Square a.k.a. George Watson's Ladies' College. She was a year above me, well liked, I think, and popular due to her high-jump expertise! We had no playground, so lunchtimes were spent indoors dancing to records, doing gymnastics or playing musical instruments.

After telling my great-grandsons of my adventures in Dreghorn Woods in the 1930s and 1940s I went on the internet and found your fascinating writings.

I was never in Annette's house (had our own doctor in Colinton) but remember passing her gate and maybe we were walking over to the Braid Burn? There was entertainment there and we sat on tiered grass banks.

As soon as I read Annette's name I could picture her flying over the high jump at school. She wasn't particularly dark-skinned either – just a nice girl, one of us.

I left Scotland at 18 in 1950 (most reluctantly) for a Civil Service post in Surrey – a boring Surtax job – but that was where I met my husband David, a Yorkshireman, who died a week short of our 60th anniversary in 2016.

Kind regards.

Betty Verrill

Until five years earlier when Yvonne Hjerholm wrote about her step-mother, there was very little information available about Annette Junior other than some of her unhappiness and bad fortune in later years as described by Yvonne so Betty's letter coming out of the blue provided a small but very interesting insight into a happier time.

At this time Annette Junior was obviously an athletic and happy girl.

There are no pictures of Annette Junior that I'm aware of and unfortunately Yvonne is no longer at her previous address and I'm unable to contact her.

But Betty's letter gives us a snapshot - a small picture of her friend.

Betty remarks on Annette Junior's skin tone - *'She wasn't particularly dark-skinned either - just a nice girl, one of us.'* - may naturally and understandably rub some people up the wrong way - but she's not being prejudiced - all she's saying is that as it's likely the school was 99% white, was that Annette Junior didn't stand out as being Black - quite the contrary - she generally just looked like everyone else.

But in having a Black father I cannot but wonder how she really felt particularly as she grew older - what were her thoughts, reflections and attitudes.

Did it impact on her behaviour?

Was she reluctant to invite friends home?

At times life must have been difficult and challenging for her.

Children, never mind adults can be unthoughtful, unkind and cruel.

That Annette Junior had a Black father must have on occasion been a talking point and given the Edinburgh society of the time - an era when as Annette Junior moved toward the age of ten, there were still some colour bars in parts of the city meant that as the years passed it impacted upon her personality and her take on the world.

Within earlier blogs and vignettes on Dr Motley I referred to some of the vicissitudes that as a mixed race married couple from different backgrounds the couple may have suffered from, from prejudiced individuals so it was a small balm to hear something so very positive from Betty providing a small insight into happier more care-free times in Annette Junior's younger life at the time.

"The heights by great men reached and kept were not attained by sudden flight, but they while their companions slept, were toiling upward in the night."

Henry Wadsworth Longfellow

I wrote back to Betty and have included some of my response below for two reasons: first, it provides a useful up to date summary of Arthur Motley's story particularly between the decade 1928 to 1938; and second, it refers to how Arthur addressed the key issue in his life – how he finally succeeded in qualifying as a doctor eleven years after he first came to Scotland to study.

Dear Betty,

Many thanks for your letter and your memories of Annette Motley – what a very lovely surprise.

After receiving your letter it led me to undertake some further sleuthing leading to me unearthing one or two small pieces of additional information which helps complete some of Dr Motley's story.

As we've both remarked, when you throw a pebble into a pool you never quite know where the ripples will end up.

As previously written there wasn't a great deal of information on Dr Motley's daughter 'Annette Junior' other than some of her unhappiness and bad fortune in later years as described to me by her adopted daughter, Yvonne Herjtholm, so your letter provided a small insight into a happier time.

Within previous vignettes on Dr Motley I referred to some of the vicissitudes that as a mixed race married couple from different backgrounds the couple may have suffered from, from prejudiced individuals so it was a small balm to hear something so very positive, providing a small insight into happier more care-free times in Annette's younger life.

Twenty-four year old Arthur Philip (A.P.) Motley B.A. set out from New York and stepped upon Scotland's shores at Glasgow for presumably the first occasion on the 28th September 1928. He had travelled as a student on the Anchor Steamline ship 'Caledonia' – rather appropriate as he sought out a new life in Scotland to train as a doctor. But perhaps at that stage he had little intention of settling in Scotland and building a new life for himself and instead he would simply return to America. But as Harold Macmillan reputedly once said 'Events, dear boy, events'.

...Although he only moved to Edinburgh in the autumn of 1928, by the following year – aged around only twenty-two - in October 1929 - he married his wife Annette aged approximately eighteen. Come early the following year on the 5th of February 1930 their daughter Annette Junior was born which suggests Annette was already four months pregnant when they wed.

One would need the pen of a skilled and imaginative novelist to do the story justice but it can't but raise comparisons with A.P.'s illegitimate son Lewie born a few years earlier in 1925 when he would have been around eighteen having just left L'Overture High School McAlester Oklahoma.

Perhaps if he were to have married Freddie Royster back in McAlester City it would have prevented him from going into further education – one of those major crossroads in life – and if he had not done so and gone on that journey there would have been no Dr Motley in Oxgangs and the lives of thousands of his patients who knew and loved him, well our lives would have been very different from that 1925 decision.

Further to this and as I reflected on A.P's journey taken, there came a different twist in the road – one of those situations that was there – not hidden – but as far as I had been concerned, hidden in plain sight.

Because he had gone to the University of Edinburgh I had simply assumed that he had graduated from that esteemed institution – MB, ChB or MD. However, in fact he didn't graduate at all begging the question that he may have failed those ferociously tough and much feared exams.

I'm unaware of how many years he spent at the University of Edinburgh but from some of my earlier research we do know he was listed as being a medical intern at the Royal Hospital Edinburgh in 1935. However, an intern is normally someone who has completed a medical degree but is not yet able to practice, which if that premise is correct adds to the mystery – perhaps his B.A. degree allowed him to do so?

But what we do know (from The Medical Directory) is that he passed the L.M.S.S.A. (Licentiate in Medicine and Surgery of the Society of Apothecaries) examination in 1939 – a surprising five years later - which allowed him to thereafter practice medicine.

'The Society of Apothecaries, under a charter granted by King James, was authorised to license doctors in Britain. The Society does not, however, operate any medical schools. Rather, they conduct exams, and if the applicant passes the test, they are licensed to practice medicine.

Apparently, people who fail their university medical exams often took the Society of Apothecaries test.' And thus 'the LMSSA functioned as an alternative to the usual system and was frequently used by graduates of foreign medical schools who wished to practice in Britain, as well as by people who failed their exams at British universities. Apparently, there was little scope for retaking a failed exam.

The last Society of Apothecaries exam was held back in 1999 and the Society's legal authority to certify doctors was revoked in 2008. People already holding LMSSA's are allowed to continue to practice medicine.'

Peter Richards described it as non-university examinations as 'convenient insurance policies or late lifebelts.'

Going back to Dr Motley's period as an intern in 1935, he, Annette and Annette Junior were living at 275 Leith Walk. That period - 1928 to 1935 - begs such questions as to how the young A.P. was able to fund his travel to Scotland, the cost of studying here, living expenses, etc., etc.

Did he receive a scholarship?

I suspect not.

But looking back it must have been expensive and a challenge for him to support his young family - perhaps he had to work in part time jobs – a heavy burden when combined with onerous studies.

Between 1935 and 1939 the family moved out to the south of the city to Colinton Mains, set in the lea of the Pentland Hills, one of the newly developed areas of the city as Edinburgh began to spread her wings.

Their new home was at 356 Colinton Mains Road, one of the Gumley houses.

The family remained there until just before 1960 when he and Annette moved into the medical practice at McAlester Cottage which was listed as number 250 Oxgangs Road North in the 1960 Electoral Roll and as number 300 in the following Electoral Roll in 1965.

One further interesting snippet from The Medical Directory is that it lists him as having been the Honorary Medical Officer at Colinton Mains First Aid Post.

Without having the knowledge that reference begs further questions.

What exactly were First Aid Posts?

And what were Honorary Medical Officers?

Given that he had qualified in 1939 when he became fully qualified to practice medicine was that his starting date in this post or was it from before then?

Whatever, it paved the way for him to open his Oxgangs practice at McAlester Cottage, presumably after the Second World War.

I may be wrong, but the house – McAlester Cottage (clearly re-named by Dr Motley after he purchased it to remind him of his home and upbringing in America) - was designed by the architect A.A. Foot in 1927 for a J.C. Gibson Esq.

Passing the L.M.S.S.A enabled Dr Motley to join the army in 1941 - the R.A.M.C. (Royal Army Medical Corps).

He was appointed as a Lieutenant on the 27th September 1941 and whilst serving would have been a Captain.

He was awarded the War Medal 1939-1945 and the 1939-45 Star for operational service.

So, many thanks Betty for your 'ripple in the pond' which has helped to facilitate and add some further fascinating little snippets into the legendary and much loved Dr Motley's story and of his earlier journey through life including when he first stepped onto Scottish shores – of his subsequent marriage to Annette - and the birth of their daughter Annette Junior and giving a small insight into her teenage life – and also helping me realise that he didn't graduate from the University of Edinburgh.

I await to see what further ripples the update makes – I'm sure there must be more water to flow along the Braid Burn and under the bridge!

Once again, thank you for your letter.

Best wishes,

Peter

At the Last Gasp

So, Arthur is at last a doctor – Dr Arthur Philip Motley. But how did he get there?

I've alluded to that within the letter to Betty Verrill: Arthur had eventually qualified as a doctor through taking the somewhat unusual and unorthodox route of the L.S.S.M.A. examinations in 1939. Given he was now 35 years old and with the outbreak of the War it was very much at the last gasp.

As to whether this was through a period of self-study whilst he continued to work at the Edinburgh Royal Infirmary or whether it was by also combining this with some studies through the Society of Worshipful Apothecaries; the Royal College of Physicians; or the Royal College of Surgeons I don't know.

Royal Army Medical Corps

Back in 2012 I'm still working off the assumption that despite his U.S. War Record Card that as he's in the British Army rather than either the Royal (British) or American Navy which I'd wrongly assumed based upon Mother's story about him on board a ship docked in Cape Town, South Africa.

It's now the end of the decade of the 1930s and war has been declared.

Dr Motley goes on to become an army captain in the (British) Royal Army Medical Corps between the years 1940 and 1946.

The standard period of service in this unit was seven years which ties in with those dates.

When he joined up he would have needed to have trained for six months at RAMC Depot Crookham Camp Aldershot, but more of the War Years awaits.

Immediately after leaving the Army he would thereafter have sought out work so perhaps he joined a practice in Edinburgh or did he seize the opportunity to set up on his own in Oxgangs, which at the time was still ostensibly a farming community amongst the rapidly developing new housing developments in Colinton Mains?

I wondered too whether there was an element of pragmatism in that he recognised that because he was Black and because many people were prejudiced and discriminatory he acknowledged how difficult it would be for a local medical practice to appoint him so he realised he would instead have to set up his own practice.

Harold Motley

Three years passed between 2012 and 2015.

In late January of 2015, whilst sitting at the keyboard an e-mail winged its way through the air. It was from a Harold Motley. Things would never quite be the same ever again.

22nd January 2015

Hello Peter Hoffmann

Dr. Arthur P Motley is my Grandfather.

I am jumping up and down with joy.

I have been searching for my grandfather for quite awhile.

I have done Google searches before but all I would get would be old dudes from the 1600 and 1700s.

I did it today and up pops your blog.

I found a lot of unknown information about my grandfather.

Thank you.

As you might be able to tell I'm from the States.

My father Lewie Motley passed on in 2006.

He was born in McAlester Oklahoma.

In 1925 I think that was Dr Motley's senior year of High School. My Grandmother and Dr Motley were never married.

My father never talked about his father.

So I did not start searching for my grandfather until after my father passed.

As a teenager I got a chance to go to high school in McAlester Oklahoma in 1965 at L'Overture; the schools were segregated white only and Black schools until 1968.

Some of the teachers I had at L'Overture taught Dr Motley too, they were always talking about how smart he was.

Harold Motley – Dr Motley's grandson

While I was living in McAlester I got a chance to meet Dr Motley's mother my great grandmother and his adopted father Rev. Frank Motley.

I would like to find Dr Motley's descendants. It would be greatly appreciated for any information about his daughter you can give me. Peter thank you for the treasure of information about my grandfather. I attached a picture of myself to this email.

Harold Motley

A Dark Secret

Harold's e mail raised so many diferent questions.

It would appear that Dr Motley fathered a son, Lewie Motley, in his final year in high school in 1925.

I immediately thought of the amusing line in the Wiley College pen portrait - 'a lover of women'!

Dr Motley and Lewie's mother clearly never married.

However, it's interesting that Lewie and his son Harold both took the Motley name.

Was Dr Motley aware that he had a son? And if so did this influence him in moving a few years later in 1928 all the way to Edinburgh to study?

Lewie Motley and his wife and baby in happier times

After hearing from Harold I spoke to my mother about this astonishing new information.

She was unaware of this and said he never mentioned the subject. However, given Harold visited Dr Motley's parents in Oklahoma then he may well have been aware that he had a son and indeed a grandson too.

It's also interesting that the Reverend Frank Motley is referred to as Dr Motley's adopted father - I wonder therefore who Dr Motley's natural father was.

It's quite amazing what the blog had initiated throwing a stone into a pond and watching the ripples unfold.

Another Grandchild

Less than a month after hearing from Harold, on the 10th February 2015, another grandchild got in touch with me, but this time from Europe.

Hello Peter Hoffmann,

I was happy to find and read about my grandfather Dr Arthur Motley here on your blog! Amazing to read and see pictures of him. He was a wonderful grandpa. He taught me 'grandpa stick it up yo jumpa' 'I dene kene but canna whackum' He would test us again and again if we remembered who invented the telephone and the raincoat. He was very generous. His daughter Annette married a Norwegian man and they moved to Sweden and adopted me, my sister and brother. Annette died in 2000, 69 years old in London. She inherited all from her father but lost it all to men cheating it from her. After Annette and my father divorced she got involved with men of the lowest rank possible unfortunately for me and my sister. She had had a very unhappy upbringing though (in spite of such a wonderful grandpa in my eyes) and never found lasting love in her life due to having severe personal problems much caused by her own mother, Annette. Probably why you saw so little of them. His daughter Annette was a very artistic person, she worked back stage on some theatre when she met my dad. In my youth she designed clothes and painted on glass.

All the best.

Yvonne Hjertholm

Crikey - as they say, it never rains but it pours!

Out of the blue it turned out that not only did Dr Motley have a son and a grandson, but he also had three Norwegian grandchildren too who were adopted by Annette Junior and her husband at the time.

Yvonne's note to me raised a further aspect of Dr Motley's life giving a small but important insight into both his wife Annette and his daughter Annette Junior.

Yvonne more than hints that all was not well between mother and daughter which raises the question as to why this should have been the case.

Why did Annette Junior dislike her mother so and also why should her mother have made life so apparently hard for her?

How far back did this go?

Did it go all the way back to Annette Junior's difficult birth that almost cost her mother's life?

And that, despite it being no fault of her own or did she somehow hold it against Annette Junior that she had fallen pregnant with her and how that had altered the course of her life, not that it was Annette Junior's fault.

Or was it because she was white and Annette Junior was the child of a mixed marriage?

Or was it simply that she didn't approve of the course that Annete Junior's life had taken?

But certainly Yvonne seems to hint that Annette wasn't a 'good mother'.

Was she not cut out to be a mother – was she just too young back in 1930 when she was but 18 - or was she generally just an unpleasant individual?

Thereafter, Harold wrote an open letter back to Yvonne:

11th February 2015

Hello Yvonne,

Dr Arthur Motley is my/our grandfather. Your mother was my father's half sister. My father passed in 2006. So I guess that makes us first cousins, hello cousin I am so envious of you. I never had a chance to meet my grandfather, I would have love for him to quiz me too. I have been look for Dr Motley for a long time. I found out what happened to him by finding this blog. Can you contact me by email? at ndgrspcs@sbcglobal.net I'm so sorry to hear about what happened to your mother. I wish I could have met her too.

Hope to hear from you soon.

Harold Motley U.S.A.

22nd July 2015

Hello first cousin Harold.

How exciting with a cousin overseas!

And wonderful that the Motley family thrives still.

I got the surname Hjertholm, the name of a little village named after my father's family of farmers, who came from the westcoast of Norway.

I will contact you by mail. My mail is lexiaeldan@gmail.com

I certainly appreciated this blog and am curious about the book too on my grandfather.

I remember him as such a social person with lots of friends.

He used to bring me and my sister to the theatre to see a storyteller performance. I have a vague memory he was called Jimmy and was a friend of grandpa. So after the performance we went back stage to see him. That was an awesome memory.

All the best

Yvonne Hjertholm

After hearing from Harold and then Yvonne, two months later on the 20th April in the spring of 2015 a Vicky Mount got in touch with me.

Vicky too not only conveyed some interesting new information, but it also gave an insight into both Annette and Dr Motley and their later lives together including some very poignant photographs taken of the great man in hospital towards the end of hs life.

Dr Motley – a Vignette by Artist Vicky Mount

When I was twelve to seventeen I lived next door to Dr Motley in the Oxgangs area of Edinburgh. He was the first Black American to study in the late 1920s in Scotland and then set up a GP practice in the late 1940s. I remember him as a lovely, kind and jovial man. I regularly took his wee Jack Russell a walk up the Pentlands - a vicious little devil. On returning Dr Motley would give me a handful of sweets. My Mum, a district nurse, whom he called Angel' occasionally helped bath his frail and elderly wife.

When I was fifteen I did this drawing from a photograph of him. Also, on my wedding day we went to visit him in hospital. We turned up in full wedding gear and flowers for him. He couldn't come to the wedding so we took the wedding to him. He was very generous. He gave us £100 in an envelope before the wedding. I was so surprised. He died two months later aged 84. I'd like to thank my Mum for setting a great example and for never saying 'He's Black but he's very nice' in the way I've often heard down the years.'

Mrs Annette Motley

Annette Motley was only 69 when she died, so she wasn't old at the time. But in reading Vicky's vignette it's sad to read that she had become so frail and had to be looked after. It suggests that in later life that she had become unwell. She died on the 5th January 1981.

Their romance and their married life together had lasted over half a century from when they were married in 1929 – just over 51 years. Ironically, in the year they married, 1929, was the same year that Warriston Crematorium opened where Annette would be cremated half a century later.

Given that Dr Motley had only retired from practice just two and a half years previously and given Annette's ill health they were unable to enjoy a long retirement together which seems a shame after working for so many years and becoming relatively well off in their later years together.

Also, given Yvonne's earlier comments about her step-mother, Annette Junior's life and the schism between her and her parents, the couple wouldn't have even enjoyed the balm of their daughter and adopted grandchildren. For Annette and Dr Motley it seems a sad final few years together.

Late Summer 2020

After the exchange of letters with Mrs Betty Verrill once again the trail on Dr Motley goes slightly cold once again.

I had written a letter to the University of Edinburgh (see below) in the summer of 2020 seeking out any information which they might have about Arthur Motley, but outwith an initial acknowledgement followed by a more detailed response afterwards, as the months went by I'd forgotten all about it.

21st August 2021

Hi,

I wonder if you could please help me at all.

I was looking to update a book which includes a vignette on an Edinburgh doctor, Arthur Philip Motley.

He received his undergraduate degree from the great Black university Lincoln Pennsylvania in 1928. He thereafter arrived by ship from New York in September of that year to begin studying medicine in Edinburgh.

However in The Medical Directory whilst it lists this degree it also lists the L.M.S.S.A London 1939 qualification but there is no reference to a University of Edinburgh qualification such as the M.B. although there is a reference to R.C.S. Ed.

I wondered as to whether you might have a record as to whether Arthur successfully passed a University of Edinburgh qualification?

Thank you for any assistance which you may be able to provide.

Kind regards,

Peter Hoffmann

I received an acknowledgement from the University of Edinburgh that day:

Hi Peter,

Many thanks for providing this extra information, we shall check our matriculation records for any information on Arthur.

As you may be aware, the Centre for Research Collections has been closed for an extended period due to the Covid-19 outbreak. We have now reopened in a limited capacity and are starting to work through our backlog of enquiries. We shall add yours to the list and get back in touch when we have had the opportunity to complete further research. Our apologies for this delay.

Best wishes,

Daisy

CRC Library Assistant Centre for Research Collections.

Edinburgh University Library, George Square, Edinburgh, EH8 9LJ.

Toward the end of August I received an additional e-mail from the University of Edinburgh; this time from a Danielle Spittle: she wrote:

Friday, 21 August 2020

Dear Peter,

Thank you for your enquiry.

'R.C.S. Ed.' is the Royal College of Surgeons, Edinburgh. They are a separate institution from the University of Edinburgh and have their own records. You could try contacting them to see whether they have any information about Arthur. Edinburgh University only awarded MB ChB or MD qualifications at the time that Arthur would have studied, which aren't listed on his Medical Directory or Medical Register entries. So it looks like he didn't graduate from here. It is possible he could have studied here without graduating; if you think this might be a possibility then let us know and we can check our matriculation records to see if he appears there.

Best wishes, Danielle Spittle (CRC Library Assistant)

I replied to Danielle that same day:

Hi Danielle,

Many thanks for such a swift and helpful response. I think the fact that he undertook the L.M.S.S.A. qualification in 1939 may be indicative that he didn't graduate. I do know for certain that he attended the University of Edinburgh and it would be interesting to know what years he was in attendance. I've attached a record of when he may have started there.

Thank you again for any assistance.

Best, Peter

This was a promising, helpful and hopeful e mail: but in the months that followed nothing further was heard.

The Year of the Plague

We were now well into The Year of the Plague - the Covid-19 spring of 2020 had become summer, then autumn and now we were into early winter moving toward Yuletide and Christmas and New Year.

We had lived through weeks and months of lockdowns.

Then, just a week or so before Christmas my inbox pinged – and in it there was the most remarkable e mail from Danielle Spittle (CRC Library Assistant) at the University of Edinburgh with an astonishing 21 attachments from their records.

It was the most amazing little treasure trove and began to unravel and answer some of the questions I had long asked about Dr Motley, but of course they posed many new questions too. I had received new and lost pieces of the jigsaw picture, only frustratingly some of the pieces remained missing.

Yuletide 2020/21

Whilst I managed to skim read the attachments I had to set them aside; but it is from them that I have been able to refer to and

include in some of the vignettes above as used in telling his story.

They are remarkable because they include not just university correspondence but also hand-written letters from his mother Ethel Motley as well as a letter from Arthur himself.

Christmas and New Year came and went.

Our sons and their girlfriends had returned from the capital for the festive period.

Because of Covid-19 neither my wife nor I had seen our elder son for almost a year. So, it was very much family time – a time to be set aside – a break from work – to be together – to enjoy and celebrate wintertide – country living and country life – midwinter - to go out for invigorating walks – to play indoor games – and to eat and drink and to enjoy all the wonderful things that family gives you.

In accommodating a full household, the study – The Powerhouse – had been returned to a bedroom once again and the mainframe computer had been shut away into cold storage for over a fortnight.

I had had an unfortunate spell of ill-health too, so the Dr Motley Project – the working title at the time which was I Have a Dream, was put to one side.

With New Year done and dusted and the last remaining children taking a sleigh-ride down the A9 back to Edinburgh, the Christmas tree came down and the decorations were once more returned to the attic for another year.

The house was re-ordered, but with parents no longer quite as young and nimble as they once were – slowly - bookshelves were returned to the sitting room and once more The Power House – like the computer itself - slowly flickered back into life.

My ill-health remained. There were some occasional good days, but at best, they were mixed. But when I felt able to work on the project it was usually in small bursts.

The first task was to return to and properly read Danielle's fascinating e-mail of the 10th December 2020.

Dear Peter,

Back in August you sent us a request to research Arthur Philip Motley in our student records. Thank you for your patience in bearing with us while we worked our way through our backlog of enquiries. I have now had a chance to research your enquiry.

The record that you sent us looks like an entry from the UK Medical and Dental Students Register. It tells us that Arthur sat a preliminary exam with 'S. Univ. Ent. Bd.' (the Scottish Universities

Entrance Board) in July 1928. Passing this exam qualified him to study at the University.

Arthur began studying Medicine at the University of Edinburgh in October 1928, at the beginning of the 1928-29 academic year. We have a 2-page 'first matriculation' (enrolment) form written in his own hand from this time.

In Arthur's second year (1929-30) he didn't sit one of his exams, and it is unclear how much he studied in his third academic year (1930-31). In October 1931 he transferred over from the University to the Royal College of Physicians and Surgeons. From looking at his records it seems that this decision was due to a mixture of financial difficulties and a preference for doing more laboratory work.

We have his non-graduating record (8 pages). We also have 13 pages of correspondence between Arthur, the Dean of the Faculty of Medicine at the University Professor James Lorrain-Smith, Arthur's mother Ethel Motley, and the Registrar of Lincoln University, plus a couple of pages of notes about fees and exams.

I have taken photos of all of these records. There are too many pages to attach to one email, so I am going to send you them via the 'WeTransfer' service. Please look out for a separate email from 'WeTransfer' shortly: you may need to check your 'junk' folder, as WeTransfer emails sometimes end up in there. These were just quick snaps taken by me so are not high-enough quality to be reproduced in a book; however, you are welcome to use them for your own research or to quote from them. If you require high quality photos our professional photographers can do this for you at a cost of £8 per image (minimum order cost £15), but there is a delay for this service at the moment.

Best wishes, Danielle Spittle (CRC Library Assistant)

As advised by Danielle I wrote to the Royal College of Surgeons (RCS).

18th January 2021

Hi,

I wonder if you might be able to provide some assistance please. Over the years I've written one or two articles on Dr Arthur P. Motley a remarkable and legendary figure in the Oxgangs area:

he also features in a book that I've written on the community.Arthur Motley was brought up in the Deep South of America and sailed from New York in 1928 to study in and make a life for himself in Edinburgh over the following decades.

Further new information has been sent to me recently by the University of Edinburgh which has been very helpful. As part of this paper trail Arthur Motley transferred across to the Royal College of Physicians and Surgeons circa October 1931 to study under Professor Sydney Smith for the qualifications of L.R.C.P. and L.N.C.S. Danielle Spittle recommended I write to you seeking further later information on his career trajectory. I'm aware he finally qualified as a doctor in 1939 through the auspices of the L.M.S.S.A.

Any information which you could furnish me with would be very gratefully received.

Thank you.

Peter Hoffmann

19th January 2021

The following day I received a response from the RCS.

Dear Peter,

I have checked our records and am afraid Dr Arthur P. Motley did not have a connection with the Royal College of Surgeons of Edinburgh. I notice you have already been in contact with the University but you could also try the Royal College of Physicians of Edinburgh. When you say he "transferred across", do you mean from the University of Edinburgh?

It may be, if he was a student on the University of Edinburgh degree course, Arthur took some extra mural classes that were offered to students working towards the Scottish Triple Qualification (TQ) of the Scottish Royal Colleges. This was standard procedure for some University students at the time. However I'm afraid due to Scottish Government Covid-19 restrictions I am currently unable to check further class or examination records. I will certainly check those once we are able to work onsite at the College again, and will get back to you. I should note though that it is highly unlikely we would have information on his later career trajectory if he did not qualify with us.

I should mention I'm not aware that Sydney Smith taught on an official basis with the School of Medicine of the Royal Colleges, as I believe his teaching duties were associated only with the University where he was Dean, however I will also check this out for you as I could be wrong!

I notice you mention though that he eventually qualified under the LMSSA, and therefore the English Triple, so you should contact the following London-based medical colleges:

Society of Worshipful Apothecaries

Royal College of Physicians

Royal College of Surgeons

I'm sorry I cannot help further at the present time, but wish you luck with your ongoing research.

Best wishes,

Jacqueline

Dr. Jacqueline Cahif

College Archivist

20th January 2021

Dear Peter,

Just to follow up on my previous email, I have attached an article on the Triple Qualification by Helen Dingwall, which you may find of some help. It provides an excellent and succinct summary on the profile of students who attended the School of Medicine of the Royal Colleges to study for the TQ.

Best wishes,

Jacqueline

Three days later on the 23rd January 2021 I received an unexpected and very informative e mail. It didn't have the name of the person who had sent it, but I surmised it might be from Harold Motley who is based in California.

23rd January 2021

Hello Peter,

Here is some information on Dr Motley's Grandparents.

Paternal Grandparents; Brad Dinwiddie Bn 1837 and Malinda J Sanders Bn.?

Brad and Malinda were more than likely were enslaved I've found some information of Brad's enslavement. I believe that both were enslaved in Tennessee. Brad's father was William Jasper Dinwiddie Bn 5 Jan 1815 - D 13 Sep 1873. Brad's father William was European and Brad's enslaver.

Maternal Grandparents; Finley C Triplett Bn 1855 and Texanna Lee Bn 1840

I think Finley might have been a Free Person of Color because he went to college in 1871. Before the end of the Civil War, it was against the law for the enslaved to read or write or to be educated. It could be that he was enslaved too.

Texanna was more than likely enslaved.

Peter, I think that I found a couple of reasons why my grandfather never wanted to return to live in the USA. I'm sure both of these incidents affected him deeply when he was in his pre and teenage years. Leaving links below:

Tulsa Race Massacre

Tulsa is 146.45KM from McAlester: Dr. Motley was about 15-16 years old then.

Lynching of Laura and L.D. Nelson

Okemah is 86.9KM from McAlester: Dr. Motley was around 6 years old when this event happened.

These two events occurred close to McAlester but around this time in the USA, these types of events were happening all over the country.

23rd January 2021

I think Finley might have been a Free Person of Color because he went to college in 1871.

23rd January 2021

Before the end of the Civil War, it was against the law for the enslaved to read or write or to be educated in the south.

Oklahoma Land Rush of 1839

At precisely high noon, thousands of would-be settlers make a mad dash into the newly opened Oklahoma Territory to claim cheap land. On March 3, 1889, Harrison announced the government would open the 1.9 million-acre tract of Indian Territory for settlement precisely at noon on April 22, 1889

23rd January 2021

Hi,

Thanks for your very helpful e mails.

They're greatly appreciated and were a nice surprise on a Saturday afternoon here in the snowy Highlands of Scotland.

I'll drill into the links and give some thought to them.

But I'm sure they'll provide some interesting possible theories about how Arthur evolved over the next seven decades or so.

In the weeks ahead I'm keen to explore a number of different areas including his family history.

Apart from when he returned to Lincoln University Pennsylvania in 1983 aged 79 years for the 55th reunion of his former classmates from the graduate year 1928 I don't know if he ever previously returned to the United States before then.

And also how much contact he had with his mother Ethel and his (adoptive? – according to Harold Motley) – father Frank.

On the surface it seems to have been very little.

It therefore begs a number of fascinating questions as to who his natural father was.

From your helpful e mail his last name appears to have been Dinwiddie.

I wonder what happened to him, what his background was and the course of the rest of his life.

Did he decide not to marry Ethel or vice-versa?

Or did something happen to him?

Was Ethel's move to McAlester City a direct result of wishing to move far way – 130 miles to the north to a different state?

Had she met Frank Motley by this stage or did that happen later?

And when did she and Frank marry.

It will also be useful to find out when they both died.

I'm unsure if they had any children – perhaps Arthur was her only child which if he remained out of touch, must have been difficult for Ethel to bear.

With him being born in Clarksville Texas (birthplace of the great and iconic Tommie Smith) he and his mother Ethel must have moved to McAlester City at some stage but I'm unsure when.

I seem to recall too that his adoptive father was a minister at one stage but he lost whatever job he had in 1931 – perhaps as a result of The Great Depression. But I wonder how Ethel and Frank prospered in the years ahead.

It would also be useful to find out the name of the lady who was Harold's grandmother – where did she meet Arthur and when – was it when he was at Wiley (before attending Lincoln for two years he attended the great Black Wiley College – made famous in the film The Great Debaters), or when he lived in McAlester City or when he attended Lincoln University between 1926 and 1928?

And also the course of the rest of her life - if she ever married – the fact that her son was given the last name of Motley is interesting too. Did she have further children? After she fell pregnant was there ever any contact between her and Arthur Motley again? Two key questions in following this trail is whether Arthur Motley knew that he had fathered a son and whether he ever acknowledged this in the years and the decades ahead. On the surface I assume the answer is no to the latter.

If Dr Motley never returned to the States (apart from in 1983) I wonder if he remained in contact with Ethel and supported her in any way during the decades ahead from 1940, particularly given the sacrifices which she had made for him. I'm aware that when he studied in Edinburgh he didn't seem to write much to her at all between the years 1928 and 1931. There were some reasons for this, most of which I can only surmise but intend writing about further. Once again – thank you for getting in touch and I look forward to hearing from you again.

Best,

Peter (Hoffmann)

Tulsa Race Riots Harold Motley suggests that a main reason for Dr Motley moving from Oklahoma to Edinburgh Scotland was because of the infamous Tulsa Massacre of 1921 which occurred when Arthur was aged 14 and that it had a profound and powerful effect upon him. Certainly in the July 1921 issue of The Brownies' magazine there's a terse mention of it and it's also referred to in the August and September issues too.

By way of background the relatively newly formed state of Oklahoma (1907) was one where the political and social atmosphere over the racial divide was tense. By 1921, at least 31 people had been lynched in the newly formed state and of those, 26 were Black, and nearly all were men or boys.

It was only three years after the end of the First World War with many Black servicemen who had returned home after serving their country. Despite the American Civil War from 56 years earlier Civil Rights for African-Americans were lacking and the ghastly and reprehensible Klu-Klux Klan was resurgent and on the rise once again.

However despite this background, Tulsa, was a booming oil city, with a large number of affluent, educated and professional African-Americans.

The Tulsa Race Massacre took place between the 31st May and the 1st June 1921 when mobs of white people many of whom had been deputised and given weapons by the city officials attacked many of the Black residents and their businesses in the Greenwood District in Tulsa, Oklahoma.

It's an event of infamy - the single worst incident of racial violence in American history.

It was an attack upon what was at that time the wealthiest Black community in the United States.

More than 800 people were admitted to hospitals, and thousands of Black residents were interned for several days.

The official number of recorded deaths was 36 although a 2001 state commission confirm 39 individuals had died - 26 Black and 13 white citizens.

The touchpaper for the massacre was lit during the Memorial Day weekend after 19-year-old Dick Rowland who worked as a Black shoe-shiner, was accused of assaulting Sarah Page a 17-year-old white elevator operator at the nearby Drexel Building.

After Rowland was taken into custody rumours began to spread through the city that he was going to be lynched.

Hundreds of white men gathered around the jail where Rowland was being kept; to help protect him a group of around 75 Black men, some of whom were armed, arrived at the jail to help ensure that Rowland would receive proper justice and would not be physically harmed. The sheriff gave them an assurance and the group dispersed and began to leave the vicinity when allegedly one of the white men attempted to disarm one of the Black individuals.

A shot was fired and all hell was let loose with ten white men dead and two Black individuals.

As news spread throughout the city, mob violence exploded when white rioters rampaged through the Black neighbourhood that evening killing men and burning and looting stores and homes.

By the following day the National Guard imposed martial law, effectively ending the massacre.

Around 10,000 Black people were left homeless.

Many survivors left Tulsa, but for those who stayed the ill-event was conveniently forgotten by many of the town-people.

75 years later a bipartisan group in the state legislature authorised the formation of the Oklahoma Commission to Study the Tulsa Race Riot and the 2001 report concluded that the city had conspired with its white citizens and recommended a program of reparations to the survivors and to their descendants.

But this wasn't only happening in Tulsa as during the year 1921 at least 31 people had been lynched in the newly formed state; 26 of whom were Black; and nearly all of whom were men or boys.

With such goings on so close to home it was no wonder that 17 year old Arthur Motley was aware of the fragility of the society in which he lived.

4th February 2021

Peter, more information about Dr. Motley's relatives.

Dr. Motley's birth-father; Arthur Porter Dinwiddie birth 08 Aug1884 Clarksville, Red River, Texas, USA death 24 Sep1963 Dallas, Dallas, Texas, USA

Dr. Motley's mother; Ethel Della Triplett birth 12 Sep 1882 Clarksville, Red River Texas, USA death 3 Apr 1976 McAlester, Pittsburg, Oklahoma, USA

Dr. Motley's adopted father; Rev. Robert Frank Motley birth 03 Mar 1882 (maybe) Clarksville, Red River Texas, USA. death 28 Jul 1972 McAlester, Pittsburg, Oklahoma, USA

A Rolling Stone

Within Harold's e mail was a brother – a marriage – and a divorce.

Arthur Porter and Ethel were married on 17 Nov 1900 in Clarksville; they had two children, Harold Lee birth 07 Oct 1902, and Arthur P. birth 18 Jun 1904. My father named me after his uncle Harold. So far I haven't been able to find a divorce document. I had trouble learning Arthur Porter's birth date because every document I found had a different date. (It's the same for Rev. Motley.) From the documents I found on Arthur Porter he seems to be a rolling stone - he was always in a different location. Arthur Porter married Lucretia Amanda Beal b1886 d 1942. I couldn't find a marriage license but found them together in the 1930 census. No records of children. Arthur Porter died Sep 1963 in Dallas Texas at Parkland Memorial Hospital the same Hospital that President John F. Kennedy died in in Nov 1963.

Rev. Robert F. Motley and Ethel were married on 8 Jun 1909 in Hopkins, Grayson, Texas, USA. I found them, Robert, Ethel, Harold, and Arthur living together in McAlester in the 1910 census. I thought that I had found Rev. Motley's birth location and family in Alabama. A couple of months ago I found a document that may change who I thought Rev Motley was and where he's from. (I attach the document to e-mail.) I'm continuing the search to find Rev Motley's parents and birth location. I also attach a photo of Rev. Motley. I think that Rev. Motley was the only father Dr. Motley knew because Arthur Porter and Ethel were divorced shortly after Dr. Motley's birth.

My grandmother Freddie Royster and Dr. Motley were classmates in High School: they graduated in 1924 and I believe she was pregnant with my father that summer. There were a lot of animosities between the families when Dr. Motley left McAlester, but my grandmother would take my father to visit his grandmother Ethel so I'm sure that Ethel told him about his son.

I've been searching for documentation that Dr. Motley returned to the USA. I found a passenger and crew listing for a vessel arriving in New York on Nov. 14, 1959. I also found a travel document that Rev Motley travelled to Scotland on Apr. 29, 1955. I attached both documents.

Peter those two links were about how bad the conditions were in the U.S. for African-Americans when Dr. Motley grew up, I used those two links because they were in Oklahoma close to Dr. Motley's home town. These incidents were happening all over America in the South and in the North during Dr. Motley's growing years. I believe that Dr. Motley thought Scotland was more like heaven when comparing living conditions to the United States. I believe that's one of the reasons he decided to live in Scotland and did not return to live in the U.S

Harold

4th February 2021

Hi Harold,

I'd half assumed the earlier e mails were from you - great to hear from you and many thanks for some of the wonderful new additional material, much of which is very useful indeed - some fantastic detective work there by you - a *BIG WELL DONE!*

Some of it I'm familiar with but much of it is new - fantastic that you've identified that Ethel and Arthur Porter were married and subsequently divorced. I'd surmised, wrongly, that no marriage had taken place. Also well done on establishing the date of the Rev Frank and Ethel's marriage too. Similarly that's another part of the jigsaw completed in that Arthur and Freddie were classmates - I'd guessed they might be - oh, to have been a fly on the wall when some interesting discussions took place back in the day!

It's revelatory too that Dr Motley knew about his son, your dad, Lewie.

The additional information about the Rev Motley coming to Scotland is a wonderful new addition - it's given me something to think about. I couldn't quite work out before from a photograph that I'd come across whether he was white or not - it appears that he was which adds another additional twist to the story.

I'll get back to you with some further thoughts and questions. What I'm working on is starting to grow arms and legs and my intention now is to turn it into a small book - a bit larger than a monograph - really the story of a journey of discovery based around AP's life trajectory - the working title is 'I Have a Dream'. Maybe we could get Spike Lee interested in it - ha-ha!

As well as getting my head down to complete it I'm keen to speak to two or three people here in Scotland and will have to track them down as well as one of Annette Junior's Norwegian stepchildren.

I'm very keen to speak to you at some stage - I've asked one of my kids what he thinks might be the best and cheapest way to do so. But I think before I get round to that I would intend to send you a copy of the first working draft for you to comment upon because it will inevitably have some errors and gaps and allow you to input from your more knowledgeable insight from the other side of the Big Pond.

I am making good progress but the document is getting larger by the day. I do however think it could make for a good and interesting story with a larger audience and broad appeal.

Trust you're well.

Best,

Peter

Friday 5th February 2021

Hello Peter,

I wanted to send you this image of Rev. Motley that I had colorized. I'm my family's unofficial historian.

I am a novice genealogist, because of health conditions I have to do my genealogy searches on the internet. I'm hoping that I can soon figure out a way to travel to all of those country courthouses for information. I think Annette's adopted daughter's name is Yvonne, I would like to talk to her too.

Harold

5th February 2021

Hi Harold,

Thanks for your message. I'm sorry you're not keeping well - please look after yourself.

It would be wonderful if you could eventually get out and about for a grand tour around all those old courthouses - good luck with that - it's something for you to look forward to.

Thanks too for the attached photograph of Arthur's adoptive father, the Rev Frank R. Motley. He has a very strong presence. Although he's described as white there's a certain swarthy appearance to him – I wonder what his heritage might be.

He also looks like he's a very strong personality.

Do you think that life would have been challenging for him and Ethel at the time being a mixed marriage?

That he visited Arthur in Edinburgh for 3 months adds a wonderful new strand to the tale. He must have been so proud to see the transformation in the circumstances of the now Dr Arthur Motley and his son's day to day life. I wonder too if Ethel ever visited Edinburgh and also why she didn't accompany him in 1955. As you will have noticed I posted this new information about the Reverend Motley's visit to Edinburgh on the Oxgangs Facebook page although I'm not optimistic of getting any information back for this period, but it's always worth a try.

The tensions between the two families – Freddie's and Arthur's sounds interesting and important– do you have any further detail or information?

I wonder why Arthur went to Wiley College Marshall Texas for a year. Why was this the family's choice rather than a more local college. Was it to do with Freddie falling pregnant with Lewie?

There's some confusion about Arthur's date of birth – was it 1904 or the 1907 that Arthur would continue to use throughout his life – that's a mystery too! Certainly Ethel put the record straight, so to speak, in her affidavit in 1969, by saying it was 1904, but it means Arthur would have completed school aged 21 rather than 18.

Before he went to L'Ouverture High School – and at what age - did he attend a local Junior School before this?

With its connotations and radical name how much Black History was part of the L'Ouverture High School curriculum and syllabus? Dr Motley never struck me as being radical, but in his own quiet way, he perhaps was.

Also, it would be wonderful to hear of your memories of the school and just how that came about in you attending there.

Outwith School and education how do you think Arthur spent some of his leisure time when hanging around? What would the kids have done in the way of play? Or was it a case of part-time jobs, reading books and focusing on your studies? But because he went on to play American Football he perhaps spent some time outdoors and was quite athletic.

Also do we know if Freddie said anything in the decades and afterwards about Dr Motley?

I wonder how not marrying Freddie sat with the Motley family particularly with them being religious and how this sat in the community – an ongoing spectre? But that Freddie thereafter took your dad to visit Ethel there must have been some form of reconciliation between the two families and surely Arthur's subsequent life must have been a discussion point. And rather ironically if Arthur had gone on to marry Freddie, then Ethel wouldn't have 'lost' her son so to speak, perhaps only ever seeing him again on a single occasion in the late 1950s?

I wonder too in the age of greater affluence and communications whether Ethel and Arthur ever spoke to each other by telephone.

As Dr Motley became better off financially and as his career developed and he grew wealthier I wonder whether he helped his mother and father at all?

Before becoming a minister the Rev Frank Motley is at times listed as being employed at a laundry and as a Retail Estate Manager – I'm aware that around 1930 the family became much poorer – this could have been as a result of The Great Crash of 1929.

It would be interesting to try to recall your dad's memories – anything that he said about Dr Motley, his mum Freddie and of his life and upbringing at the time.

What was day to day life like in McAlester City throughout the four seasons of the year? I wonder what Ethel and Frank must have thought when Lewie was born and they came across him out playing, going to school, seeing him in the shops, at church, etc.

When Arthur returned each summer vacation between 1926 and 1928 from Wiley College and then Lincoln University, in such a small community no doubt his and Freddie's paths must have crossed – that too would have been interesting!

That Freddie chose the name surname Motley must have been awkward at times from number of different angles – an aspect of permanent and public shame for Ethel and Frank and all closely concerned within the McAlester community.

Given the small age difference one would have thought Arthur and Harold were close – do we know much about Harold's career and work – I wonder too if in later life they both kept in touch with each other.

A treasure trove would be if Ethel left any correspondence, photographs, graduation records, etc of Arthur. It seems a shame nothing exists. Sadly, I'm aware from my mother that after Dr Motley died that his daughter Annette Junior had a bonfire of such items.

A major question is to why Arthur chose to study in Edinburgh – one that I can only surmise. I wonder if there was an influence from Lincoln University. And also how much of an influence Ethel was in his choice of career. And also how the family managed to finance such a venture too.

Much for discussion!

Please look after yourself Harold and thanks again for the information.

Best,

Peter.

Reverend Frank Motley

Harold's e mails raised many different questions as well as helping to piece together some of the picture that was missing from the jigsaw.

That his father, the Reverend Frank R. Motley had travelled all the way from his home in McAlester City to visit his son, the now Dr Motley, at McAlester Cottage - a home from home so to speak - was a quite incredible moment in the story.

And that after travelling from so far away to see and stay with his son for three months was simply wonderful to come across, not to mention it answered some of the questions that I had posed earlier as to whether after setting sail to Scotland back in 1928 whether Dr Motley ever met his father again. He had indeed and each and every day throughout that Edinburgh spring and summer of 1955.

Reverend Frank Motley

That revelation in the contents of a travel document paints its own picture and tells us so much. If they had been separated and grown apart in earlier years Arthur and Frank were now very much reconciled.

Frank and Ethel's financial position had improved from over two decades earlier when he had lost his job 25 years previously.

As to whether Dr Motley was able to help with the cost of travel, well who knows. But certainly he would have been able to subsidise Frank's stay welcoming him into the bosom of the Edinburgh Motley family household and home at McAlester Cottage.

It would most probably have been the first occasion that Dr Motley's wife, Annette, had met her father-in-law and as spring moved toward summer they would have had every chance and opportunity to get to know each other.

They of course shared something in common – both Annette and the Reverend Frank were white and had married Black partners, albeit on different continents and in similar but different countries and societies.

It would also have given Frank a chance to meet with and bond with his granddaughter Annette Junior who by this time was 25 years old – a lot of water had flowed through the local Braid Burn as well as down the Mississippi River since she was born back in February 1930.

For both Annette and Annette Junior, given the length of Frank's stay and vacation they would have found out all sorts of things about Dr Motley's younger life and his boyhood and youth back in Oklahoma which they had never known before.

As to that Dr Motley had fathered a son – Lewie Motley – who was five years older than Annette Junior – and that she therefore had a half-brother rather than being an only child - I suspect this remained hushed up - across the dinner table there would have been a discreet silence on the matter

The Reverend Frank would have had to watch his P's and Q's to avoid any conversational slip or faux pas: I wonder just how much Dr Motley was on tenterhooks in case the subject of his unacknowledged son, Lewie Motley, was accidentally introduced into the conversation.

More positively, Frank must have enjoyed seeing how far in life his son had now come – and not just in terms of distance travelled, but how he was now the proud owner of a lovely house with an established and growing general practice which in matching the new flats and houses being built in the rapidly expanding Oxgangs could only similarly grow in size.

And whilst Dr Motley may have taken some vacation, Frank would have taken pride in and enjoyed witnessing his son provide medical and pastoral care to his local patients.

All the earlier sacrifices which he and Ethel had made had been worth it to now see how much Dr Motley had flourished and become such an integral part of a young and ever-growing new community – Oxgangs, set in the lea of the Pentland Hills.

New housing blocks of tenements were arising from the ground and becoming well established after ten years of building work by Edinburgh Corporation; but many new blocks were still to be erected, including our home at 6 Oxgangs Avenue. Indeed, when Frank visited the community it was still a sun-burnt field across from McAlester Cottage - three years later it, alongside other blocks of flats were built and immediately allocated out to young families including our own.

Frank would have felt a sense of pride, warmth and deep satisfaction seeing his son working closely at hand and will no doubt have written regular weekly letters to Ethel back home in McAlester City Oklahoma describing her beloved son's life here in Edinburgh.

And after all of Ethel's struggles and sacrifices it must have brought her uncalculatable pleasure simply to know that her son – her darling boy – was thriving and living a good life - a life very different to anything back home in the United States.

Frank would have been interested too in the City of Edinburgh – it was investing in and developing a new infrastructure and a new future for her sons and her daughters.

It was still only a decade since the end of the Second World War but the Corporation was moving thousands of her citizens who previously lived in older central Edinburgh who up until then had to share accommodation with their parents – now they were moved out to the southern parts of the city – young families now had the opportunity to grow up in new homes with indoor plumbing and great spaces to be outside playing in the fresh, healthy and airy parts of the capital well away from local industries and the unhealthy smogs of Auld Reekie.

The Kings' Doctor

A fascinating small aspect of Dr Motley's life, as retold to me recently by my mother here in February 2021, was the reminder that he had been the Kings Theatre doctor.

The Kings Theatre remains a well-established and greatly loved Edinburgh institution hosting regular plays, dramas, pantomimes and an occasional musical.

This role not only reflects Dr Motley's interest in entertainment but as part of this arrangement he would have received regular free tickets for shows so the family will have taken the Reverend Frank down to Tollcross regularly over the three months of his stay to enjoy some evening entertainment.

My mother went on to say that it was from this role and relationship that many of the house parties that Dr Motley hosted – when there was a stream of fancy cars lined up outside McAlester Cottage along Oxgangs Road North - emanated.

The world of entertainment was a more enlightened world – with less prejudice and discrimination – and those occasions with full houses after full houses so to speak must have been lovely and happy evenings. In facilitating such Saturday evenings Dr Motley would have met a motley crew of different individuals – many of whom were famous – what a riposte to the Edinburgh colour bars of earlier decades and what a wonderful example of social integration.

I'm sure those evenings brought great pleasure and insight to Frank about the life of his son – my what a contrast to life back home in the American South – and once again such stories and such observations and such revelations when conveyed across the Atlantic Ocean would have brought both wonderment and joy to Ethel's heart when she received such colourful epistles of such colourful episodes through the post to her home in McAlester.

And then come the following day – Sundays - the Reverend Frank would on occasion have travelled into the city to join a church service, perhaps a Baptist Church such as the one located on Queensferry Road.

But Colinton Mains Parish Church had newly opened the year

before in 1954 and it was but a pleasant five minute stroll down Oxgangs Road North from McAlester Cottage.

Walking in both directions would have offered Frank a pleasant interlude to reflect on the happiness and well-being of his son.

Three months was a long time for him to be away from his McAlester City ministry. I wonder if there was any opportunity for him to preach in one of Edinburgh's churches.

It would have been a revelation to the congregation.

And come the end of July 1955 when Frank returned across the Atlantic Ocean and then took the long train ride from New York to McAlester City with his head full of experiences from The Old World of Britain and Europe – an older world yes, but one which was much further along the road in terms of race relations, what must he have thought and how much of that experience in Oxgangs, Edinburgh, Scotland found its way into his Sunday sermons in McAlester.

When he returned home to Ethel she would have been so keen to glean as much information as she could from her husband – Frank would have responded – 'Ethel – your boy done good!'

As to why Ethel didn't feel able to join her husband on his visitation to their son in Scotland remains a mystery.

Was it too difficult for her to get time away from her work?

Was it because of health reasons?

We'll never know if she ever did visit Arthur, but I suspect she never left American soil.

She lived to a good old age so it wasn't for health reasons; perhaps it was simply for more pragmatic reasons not to do so – it just never happened.

But it's such a long period of time for a mother and son not to have met up again – by then it was over 25 years – a quarter of a century had passed since she had last cradled Arthur in her arms.

Photograph of 18 year-old Pamela Gibson backstage at the Lido Paris 1970 in the show Grand Prix

The Bluebell Girl

Pamela Dobson wrote: *'I often wondered how at the tender age of eight years I was told by Dr Motley to become a Bluebell Girl! Neither I nor my mother had ever heard of them but Dr Motley said that if I would grew tall enough and kept up my dancing training with Miss Patricia Brown I could audition for them when I was older. I always found it fascinating that it was our family doctor who put me on the road to my showbiz career, but now I understand. He obviously loved the entertainment world and may even had gone to see the spectacle whilst on holiday. As you know I did continue my dancing training and ten years later I was dancing as a Bluebell Girl on the Lido stage in Paris! Unfortunately by then we had moved house, changed doctor and had lost touch with him, but I will never forget it was thanks to Dr Motley and his entertainment knowledge that put me on my path to fulfil my dancing dreams. He was a wonderful doctor and I can still remember climbing up the three steps as a wee girl to the waiting*

room and wondering what the huge round grey stone in the corner
was used for! He brought a touch of the exotic to grey Edinburgh
and I will never forget him.'

There's a nice wee postscript to Pamela's story when she writes
further:

Postscript

*'I need to put the record straight! My mother kept a diary of me
when I was growing up and in it I have found a line which said 'Dr
Motley still raving on about her having a shot at the Bluebells!' This
was dated March 20th 1967. It proves he was always our doctor
even when we moved to Gracemount when I was 10 because in
1967 I was 15/16 so he must have been saying it for many years! It
just shows you what getting older does to your recollections and
memories.'*

Tie a Yellow Ribbon round the Old Oak Tree

1928 may not however have been the last occasion that Ethel would
ever cradle her boy in her loving arms.

Both Harold Motley and I had separately unearthed a further piece
of information that Dr Motley is listed on a 1959 passenger list for
a return visit to the United States.

He flies out from Prestwick Glasgow arriving in New York on the
14th November 1959.

It's only Dr Motley – so he isn't accompanied by either his wife or
his daughter.

I can't but wonder if he's on his way to visit his home in McAlester
City for perhaps the first occasion since he left there back in 1928
– a period of just over 30 years – three long adventurous decades.

In my heart my guess to that question is the answer yes. But my
head says no.

36. BOAC Boeing Stratocruiser

And that instead he was attending a medical conference or similar but, even if so, surely he couldn't travel this far without taking the opportunity to visit his mother, Ethel, for the first and indeed last occasion between 1928 and her death in 1976.

But in my imagination I like to think that he was on his way home to straddle for one last time, two worlds.

It's difficult to make out the date of the visa which was authorised back in Edinburgh – it may be the 11th October 1959, so the trip was a planned one. It's an unusual time of the year to travel. Stepping off the B.O.A.C. jet into a wintry New York, Dr Motley would have found the weather cold.

But of course McAlester City would have been warmer than either Edinburgh or New York – probably around 62 degrees Fahrenheit and there would still have been around nine hours of daylight to enjoy.

But in searching for a happy ending let's project ourselves into that imaginary world – that wonderful interlude for Arthur and Ethel to have spent together – the boy who had left home aged 24 and here he was returning to see his mother, now a man of 56 years and a qualified doctor.

Over those 30 years a lot of water had flowed across the Atlantic Ocean.

When Arthur left home there there wasn't a single grey hair in his head – and now, three decades later, both he and Ethel had an abundance of grey hairs.

They would have had much to talk about and much to share and there would have been hugs, embraces and kisses galore and much fun and laughter as they reminisced about the past and the wondrous journey and expedition and route of travel he had taken and what he had done and was making of his life.

Ethel would have been immensely proud of her son and his homecoming – Dr Arthur Philip Motley – just think of it - DR ARTHUR!

She would have been keen to take him out to meet her friends and the extended family and undoubtedly there would have been get-together's and small or even large parties.

Thanksgiving Day

One reason for Dr Motley selecting the date of travel is that it would have allowed him to join the extended family to celebrate Thanksgiving Day which was held on the 26th November 1959, being the fourth Thursday of the month.

The meal would have been a culinary trip for Arthur taking him back to his youth as the family gathered around the dinner table to tuck into the roast turkey and cranberry sauce; collard greens, macaroni and cheese, green beans, mashed potatoes, sweet potatoes mashed perhaps covered with marshmallows, corn, cornbread, yeast potato rolls, black eyed peas, rice, gravy, and potato salad. It conjures up Dickensian images and Arthur would have been the guest of honour – oh what an unforgettable memory for all of those who partook.

Arthur would have returned and revisited some of the haunts of his youth – where he first played – where he first went to school – he would have looked by L'Ouverture High School, still almost a decade away from desegregation – did he meet up with one or two former teachers.

I think he may have done so, including his friend the remarkable School Principal Dr Willa Strong who had been in his school class back in the early 1920s.

Much of the small town would have remained the same and he would easily have found his way around her streets. But much had changed too in terms of the shops and the local businesses.

And the town had grown by 50% since he left with the population moving toward 18,000 – when he left it hadn't quite reached 12,000 in size.

School Sweetheart

But amongst all the joys, the celebrations and the fun - of a local boy made good returning to his roots - would have been the spectre of his earlier relationship with Miss Freddie Royster, his school sweetheart with whom he had fathered a son, Lewie Motley, 35 years earlier.

That undoubtedly would have been a concern for Arthur and perhaps one reason why he may have been reluctant to travel home in the previous decades.

But perhaps now, almost 35 years later he felt it was relatively safe to do so, despite what Harold Motley his grandson said were some previous tensions between the two families – the Motleys and the Roysters.

Miss Freddie Royster and Arthur Motley circa 1921

Miss Freddie Royster

In 1940 when the U.S. Census was undertaken Freddie was still living at home at 1300 Jefferson in McAlester City. At this time she was the eldest of the four children still living there. So, 15 years after her relationship she remained unmarried - a long time. I wonder how much being an unmarried mother had affected her and impacted upon her: she was now the mother of a 14 year old son, Lewie.

Did it put her off future relationships?

Did it put potential suitors off her too?

Freddie's father - Fred - whom she was clearly named after - rented their home at $5 dollars a month, roughly $100 dollars in today's monies.

It was a large household consisting of ten individuals with three generations including a niece, Opal, of similar age to Lewie and also a nephew lived there too.

It was Freddie's mother who completed the census form on behalf of the family.

Freddie's father was born in Mississippi and her mother was born in Arkansas whilst Freddie and her siblings were born in Oklahoma.

So, at the age 31, Freddie was the oldest of that generation of children within the household, but there was a third generation too including her son Lewie.

Freddie's father was 61 and at the time her mother was 59. He was employed as a janitor at a public school – I wonder whether it was L'Ouverture High School. His salary was $520 dollars a year.

The census worker recorded Freddie's occupation as a maid employed in a private home. It was a full time job – around 35 hours each week and in the previous year, 1939, she earned $156 ($2,964 in today's dollars) and worked 52 weeks of the year. Her younger sister by two years, Naomi, was similarly employed as a maid but she earned $260 dollars a year – considerably more than Freddie.

One of the advantages of large inter-generational families living together under the one roof is that it is helpful in terms of childcare allowing Freddie to work full-time.

However, by 1946 Freddie's world had moved on and she was now married to a James Homer Hale in Sebastian, Arkansas. Her father Fred died three years later and her mother, Emma, five years later in 1951.

What is interesting though is Freddie appears to have had a daughter, a Jean Hale, in 1932, presumably by her future husband.

Jean is also living within the Royster household and thus at that time eight years old.

She's therefore a half-sister to Lewie Motley and thus it appears that Freddie has had another child out of wedlock, but not marrying James until 1946 – a long gap in years and in terms of their ongoing relationship.

Freddie would live until 1973 whilst James wouldn't die until 1978.

Freddie Royster in later years

Even with the passing of the years that common link between Arthur Philip Motley and Freddie Royster would never completely vanish and disappear and whilst Freddie and Lewie may only have passed through the busy Dr Motley's thoughts occasionally, surely a week wouldn't have gone by that Freddie didn't think of their affair back in the early 1920s.

And that she didn't re-marry until 1946 did she still hold a candle for Arthur Motley – who knows, but remember that in the census of 1940, Arthur Motley was recorded as being single!

I'm unaware how long Dr Motley stayed over in his home country in November 1959, but would surmise that by early December he will have travelled back to Edinburgh.

That trip would have brought him mixed feelings.

He would have enjoyed returning home one last time to see his mother Ethel after all those years apart: it gave him the chance to meet up with former friends and classmates and to return to old haunts as well as such things as the diet of his youth – a change from

Scottish foodstuffs. He would have enjoyed a little bit of sunshine too.

But I suspect that he will have realised the world had moved on and that his life was now firmly back in Edinburgh and he would have been keen to get back to work to continue to develop his ever growing and expanding practice and over-seeing the welfare of his patients as well as returning home for Christmas 1959 a few weeks before the decade of the Swinging Sixties.

But a small footnote is that we are of course aware that he did indeed return to the United States one last time, in 1983 – five years after his retirement and two years after the death of his wife Annette and but five years before his own death.

But by then his family back in McAlester City were dead – his brother Harold had died in 1971; the Reverend Frank had died the following year in 1972; and his beloved mother Ethel who had been so supportive of him had died in 1976 - all gone now, so there may have been no final visitation to McAlester City.

Two Worlds

By then I wonder how he felt – Arthur Philip Motley, caught between two worlds, so to speak.

After retiring from the practice five years earlier in the summer of 1978 he lived a much quieter life – did he feel that nowadays he was no longer at the epi-centre of Oxgangs life but neither would he have been at home in McAlester City either.

In 1983 did he go for one last visit back to McAlester City for a final stroll down the streets of his youth – a final contemplative old man's slow walk down East Monroe Avenue stopping by number 902 for a final moment – to reflect on how this is where it all began – it was here that I set out 60 years before on the most wondrous journey.

And then he turned around.

He took a return flight home to Edinburgh where he would quietly pass out the remaining five years of his life.

11th February 2021

Hi Betty,

The Motley Family

I trust you're well what with all the sub-zero temperatures just now not to mention the ongoing Year of the Plague. Here in the Highlands we've had snow on the ground since Boxing Day.

I've been making good progress on a small book on Dr Motley which I hope to finish by late spring and was keen to inquire if you have any further memories of Annette Junior or indeed the family too.

In particular I was keen to know about the years that both you and Annette Junior spent at school at George Square – would that have been both primary and secondary?

I wonder too on the Motley's choice of school – did Annette's mum have a link there at all? Was it expensive to attend and also how would both you and Annette Junior have travelled there and back each day – by tram?

I'm aware that in later years Annette was quite artistic and perhaps that sensibility was first developed at the school. Did you ever hear or meet her in later years when you were back home in Edinburgh visiting your parents at all?

Between approximately 1936 and 1939 and prior to him qualifying as a doctor, Arthur Motley worked as the Honorary Medical Officer at the Colinton Mains First Aid Post – do you have any recall of such branches – I assume this was prior to a GP practice being established within the area.

Last week my mother told me how much Annette Junior loved parties and shopping too – on one occasion, rather like Miss Havisham, she wore her new party dress for a whole fortnight!

Thank you for any assistance or anything that comes to mind. By the way I put through a Facebook Friends Request to you.

Take care in this cold winter – on the brighter side, March is but a fortnight or so away!

Best wishes,

Peter

I Have a Dream - Nye Bevan

As I continued with my somewhat scatter-gun approach, flitting Dali-clock-like between the years and the decades one very interesting piece of new information came to light.

I had assumed that after Arthur's war service he had come home to Colinton Mains Road and opened his general practice there.

However, in the intervening period, he was actually an Edinburgh GP working for a short period of time at a surgery at Albert Cottage Gorgie Road – or possibly he had actually opened the small practice himself.

Once again this was one of those surprising pieces of further information that occasionally comes through the ether.

This would have been immediately before the establishment of the NHS in 1947

As to NHS registered practices there must have been some competition to secure one of the new practices to be approved by the Lothian Health Board because my mother said that on occasion Dr Motley was quite gleeful in that he obtained the right to practice there and that Dr Neil (well-known in later decades for his beautiful Duddingston Village garden adjacent to the famous Duddingston Loch) had lost out.

And of course Dr Neil had very strong attachments to the area as his brother operated the butcher shop and the grocery at Colinton Mains - all part of Dr Motley's new patch!

But what a thrill that must have been to be given the opportunity to develop his own Oxgangs practice from scratch.

Initially he did this from his home at Colinton Mains Road, but when what became McAlester Cottage came up for sale he rightly identified it as being perfectly positioned in the Oxgangs area and able to prospectively serve Colinton Mains, Caiystane, Swanston and as far as Firrhill – opening its doors for the very first occasion was another big moment – another large and brave step in Dr Motley's life.

Thus, it was no wonder that around eight years later he was happy, pleased and proud to be able to share what he was beginning to develop and achieve with his father in that early summer of 1955. Ethel's sacrifice and his fortitude had won through – he had won the day - Dr Arthur P. Motley was on his way to becoming a local legend and in that highest and most loved of all roles or positions – that of a family doctor.

The War Years

After qualifying in 1939 and passing his L.M.S.S.A. exams in London shortly before developing his own practice in Oxgangs, an external force was about to impact upon Arthur and millions of people throughout the world – Britain had declared war on Germany.

They say it's an ill-wind that blows no good, but for Arthur there was one positive outcome from Neville Chamberlain's announcement on the 3rd September 1939 that Britain was at war with Germany.

The War was about to affect the trajectory of the now Dr rather than Mr Arthur Philip Motley's life.

With him being so very recently qualified and inexperienced the War provided him with the opportunity to practice - to 'experiment' – to learn on the job so to speak - on young Forces' personnel over the course of four or five years and all at a very fast pace.

Whilst it may sound crude, having young and fit men to administer to would have been a useful learning ground and he would have had back-up too in terms of access to medical staff with far more experience than him – after all he had only recently qualified in the year that the War began – 1939 – and by the following year, 1940, he was part of the Royal Army Medical Corps - the R.A.M.C.

One aspect of his new expertise as recorded in The Medical Directory was that he was experienced in venereolgy!

In his capacity as a medical officer he could now learn on the job and develop his skills and knowledge as well as his bedside manner, especially as his patients would be mainly white. And it was from that experience that gave him the confidence that whilst in some parts of Edinburgh a colour bar remained, he would realise that it wasn't a complete barrier to achieve his dream to become an Edinburgh doctor.

We have very little information of the newly qualified Dr Motley's time in the R.A.M.C. over the next five years or so other than he was appointed as a Lieutenant on the 27th September 1941 and whilst serving would have been made a Captain (Regular Army Emergency Commission). He was awarded the War Medal 1939-1945 and also the 1939-45 Star for operational service.

The War Medal was awarded to all full time service personnel who had completed at least 28 days of service. The Star was awarded for operational service.

What is interesting is that his record is on a U.S. World War II draft card, not a British one: he remained an American citizen and not British. However, what we can garner from the card are two further points.

First of all, his point of contact is not his wife Annette in Edinburgh, but instead, his mother, Ethel – Mrs R.F. Motley back at 902 East Monroe Avenue McAlester City Oklahoma.

Once again this is suggestive that neither his mother nor his father were aware that Arthur, aged 33 – at least according to the record card – actually 36 - was married.

But in terms of his war service it denotes that his address is 13 General Hospital British Middle East Forces, so he is in all likelihood now abroad. That it doesn't state a specific location is for reasons of security.

Therefore not long after qualifying as a doctor, but with some limited first aid practical experience garnered from working in earlier years as the Honorary Medical Officer at the Colinton Mains First Aid Post, Dr Motley was conscripted into the Army.

Aged 36 – not young for joining the army - and no doubt he would have lost a lot of general fitness since he last played American Football back at Lincoln University Pennsylvania over 13 years previously, so alongside all the other dramatic changes, the new lifestyle would have come as a bit of a cultural shock to him.

Unlike many soldiers he was not only twice the age of many of the new recruits, but he was married, he was a father, he was American and he was Black.

That would have made him stand out.

But as is the way of Forces' humour it would have stood him in good stead for the future after the War not only preparing himself for a future medical career but in dealing with the joshing and joking that would have gone on – army humour – his mates wouldn't have been averse to giving him an un-PC nickname – but he would also have learnt that behind this, there was no often no real ill-will or malice toward him – instead he was one of the boys and it would have further developed his skills to ride the punches and win others over with his sense of good humour as well as his kindness and gentleness too.

In 1941 he would have taken the long train journey from Edinburgh down to Aldershot to begin his medical training. Even today that journey takes around ten hours but back in 1941 it would have taken a great deal longer as the great steam engine puffed its way southwards from Scotland's capital.

Did Annette Motley and their daughter now aged 11 and about to start secondary school the following year see him off at Waverley Station or did they instead say their goodbyes earlier that autumn morning back at Colinton Mains Road just as Annette Junior set out for school.

It would have been a very worrying time for the three of them.

It would have been very scary for Dr Motley, but also for the two Annettes not knowing whether they would ever see their husband and father again – theoretically, that September morning of 1941 could have been their last time spent together.

But instead we of course know that Dr Motley fortunately survived that terrible period in world history, but those were pivotal years for Annette Junior – when her father left Edinburgh she was but 11 years old; when his tenure in the Army ended she was aged around 16 - a key period in her life and one where most of the parenting duties fell upon her mother Annette.

In its own way this must have impacted upon each of the different relationships within the family and does beg questions as to some of the information which Yvonne Herjholm provided decades later relating that the Annettes had a poor relationship with each other.

But come the autumn of 1941 when Dr Motley set off on that long train journey it was moving toward the end of what had been an incredibly tough year for Britain testing her resilience to the full, particularly in the southern capital of London.

The Blitz – German for lightning – only ended in the spring and the May of that year: a million houses in the capital had been damaged – a very heavy toll. Over that earlier eight month period over 40,000 civilians had been killed.

Fortunately, on British soil there was now a slight reprieve as Hitler's attention transferred to the Eastern Front and Operation

Barbarossa. But when Dr Motley set off on that fresh autumn morning he would have had no idea as to where he might be posted.

When Dr Motley joined the R.A.M.C. because it's the autumn of 1941 we're aware America had not yet entered the Second World War not doing so until the 8th December 1941 when it declared war on Japan and then three days later on the 11th December 1941 it declared war on Germany. And therefore strictly speaking, as an American citizen, Dr Motley could have left his Forces' tenure for a further few months not joining up until the end of the year or indeed into the following year, 1942.

On his arrival at the Royal Army Medical Corps Boyce Barracks, near Aldershot, Dr Motley joined the other new recruits for training, discipline, marching, PE and lectures. Clothing, kit and equipment were issued and he would have been given a service number.

On the completion of training the new recruits were offered the privilege of a weekend pass to travel home after duty – from Friday evening through until Sunday night, but given how long that journey back and forth to Scotland would have taken and the difficulty of coordinating such a train journey I think it's unlikely that Dr Motley would have been able to take advantage of this, tempting as it would have been.

Whilst he would have been missing his wife and daughter, he will now also have gotten into a new pattern and to disturb that for but a few hours together would have been a tough call to make and disruptive too. And certainly for some soldiers who when they did report back to barracks some were told not to bother unpacking and instead were informed they were about to embark to begin their commissions.

Based on Dr Motley's U.S. World War II Service card we can assume that he was thereafter sent off to join the team at 13 General Hospital British Middle East Forces.

There were over one hundred such hospitals and number 13 was initially established at Tidworth Park and Leeds Malmesbury, however by the time Dr Motley joined the unit they had moved out six months earlier to the British Military Hospital in Suez.

Whilst Dr Motley would have initially had no idea where he was being sent to it's most likely he would have sailed in a converted troop ship with thousands of other soldiers on board alongside dozens of doctors from the R.A.M.C. as well as dozens of nurses too. As their destination was Suez it would be via the Cape of Good Hope and then on to Egypt.

Small tugs would have assisted the boat out of dock and as the ship set sail away from England's shores, bands may well have seen them off as well as cheers from the remaining docked ships.

Sailing beyond the River Mersey of The Beatles and Gerry and the Pacemaker pop groups fame, England and Britain would slowly and gradually fade into the distance.

The troop ship was supported from the enemy by accompanying destroyers and a fighter escort flew overhead too.

Qualifying as he did as a doctor in London in 1939 not only would alter the course of the rest of Arthur Philip Motley's life but it may also have helped save his life too.

If he hadn't passed the L.M.S.S.A. exams he otherwise might have found himself being conscripted and having to go off to fight the Germans rather than undertaking medical duties.

The sea journey itself would have taken around two months so alongside the previous training at Aldershot he would have got to know many more of his colleagues on board and made new friendships.

I'm unsure whether Dr Motley was a good passenger or not, but certainly I know that in later years as his newly founded Oxgangs practice developed and thrived he began to take regular cruises with his wife and I believe they enjoyed these trips very much. Indeed it was from one such trip that he became friendly with the world renowned thriller writer Ngaio Marsh who asked his permission to include him in one of her novels – a thriller which featured a ship's doctor!

On such a long journey there would have been occasions when there was more than just a gentle sea-spray especially when the ship sailed through the North Atlantic Ocean.

Being the Forces they would have got into a new daily routine which apart from enjoying three square meals a day would have involved some drill work but outwith that there would have been plenty of time to try to keep fit and much leisure time to perhaps draft a letter home to loved ones, spend some time reading or studying or just lounging on deck enjoying the sunshine.

The food was good – better than back home, but water was scarce – a bit ironic with millions of gallons of the stuff just below the ship, so there were no baths: as to whether they could rig up some home-made showers who knows, but they arrived in Egypt rather smelly.

During the night so as not to attract enemy vessels or German aircraft there would have been a blackout in operation.

Growing up in a country where there was still segregation in place Dr Motley would have come across a different type of segregation on board ship, with officers enjoying better conditions than the common soldier.

The ship kept up a steady pace at between 16 and 21 knots.

For most of the time he would have had to wear his life-jacket probably a Kapok which some soldiers used as a pillow.

Being on board a ship that makes steady progress over the sea would have given Dr Motley much time for reflection although based on my experience of him, I'm unsure whether that was a significant part of his nature – I don't think he was the philosophic or reflective type.

But he would have worried not just about his own safety but also about the safety of his wife and daughter back home in Edinburgh.

Although Edinburgh wasn't at the heart of German bombing the way for example Clydebank, Glasgow or Coventry or Liverpool was, nevertheless it had been subject to irregular bombing from the start of the War in 1939.

Indeed whilst he was stationed in Suez, as late as 1943 and only a few miles south of the Motley family home at Colinton Mains Road – both Annette's may have heard the sound of the engines of an aircraft overhead on that foggy Oxgangs evening of 24 March 1943, of a four-man German crew including Oberstleutnant Fritz Förster had earlier embarked on a mission to bomb Leith Docks aimed at disrupting wartime naval traffic in and out of the busy port.

Their Junker JU 88 had earlier left an airstrip near Paris and travelled up the Dutch North Sea coast before turning north-west towards the Firth of Forth. On their approach the crew failed to locate its target and decided to jettison their incendiary payload across farmland outside Edinburgh. But as they made their way south across the Pentlands, their plane struggled to clear the summit of Hare Hill and crashed into the hillside. Mr Förster and the other three crew were killed and the wreckage was scattered over a half-mile radius.

When Lieutenant Motley was on deck during hot days under a glowing warm sun or in the evenings when he might glance up to the heavens and to the stars and to the moon, there must have been times when he thought of his wife and daughter back in Edinburgh, Scotland and whether he might ever see them again; and if he did what would he do when he returned to secure a future for them all.

He must surely have thought too about his mother and father, Ethel and Frank, half way across the globe in Oklahoma. He recalled his boyhood and his youth and just how far he had sailed in life, but now he didn't know whether his future journey would be either long or short.

As the troop ship made its steady progress south, by the time the boat reached the north-west coast of Africa the men were issued with Forces' tropical kit.

Imagining Dr Motley in such attire brings a smile to my face.

As I remarked and recalled in my introductory essay I say what a snappy dresser he was what with his fine suits, shirts and ties, but I don't think tropical kit would have flattered him!

Suez would not have been the first and only port of call and en-route the ship will have docked in other ports and countries.

Sundays may have been the most delineated day of the week when a chaplain took a service on board: whether Dr Motley attended those services I'm unsure but given the precariousness of life at that time if I were to hazard a guess, I'd say yes.

The journey to Suez was via the Cape of Good Hope.

I've rationalised this for two reasons - firstly because the Germans and the Italians commanded the Mediterranean and secondly because of the story he told my mother of how he couldn't go ashore in South Africa for fear of being lynched: for a while I'd slightly doubted the validity of this story but I now believe the opposite and that this would have been the only occasion he was ever in the vicinity and the port of Cape Town.

It also answers two earlier puzzles. When I'd kicked off his story I had wondered whether he had been employed or commissioned as a ship's doctor and thus in the Royal Navy which of course cast further doubt, but I now realise the occasion of his tale arose from when the troop ship was transporting members of His Majesty's Services en-route to Suez. Some of the troops of course would have embarked for duty in this part of the continent.

After leaving Cape Town and circling the Cape of Good Hope the ship headed north passing the opening to the Red Sea and then onward to enter the Gulf of Suez.

The Land of the Pharoahs

Egypt was of course a completely different world for Dr Motley and his comrades. It was hot and the skies were a clear blue and the dramatic landscape featured brown hills and golden yellow deserts.

Suez Harbour was a literal and metaphorical minefield. It would have been appropriately guarded from the Germans but again and in borrowing from Arthur's name it would have featured a motley array of other ships at anchor as well as sunken ships which were currently blocking the canal as a passageway, whilst on t'other side it was under the control of the Germans ably supported by the Italians.

So approximately two months after finding his sea legs Dr Arthur Motley stepped on to dry land and ashore at Port Tewfik to begin his active war-time service.

Stepping ashore Dr Motley would have been met by the cacophony of another world with very different sights and sounds – an exotic new world.

The local people – mainly boys and men would be trying to earn a dollar or two by trying to inveigle the disembarking passengers into buying some of their local wares whether fruits such as oranges which would have been a very welcome and refreshing alongside trinkets and the usual touristy type items.

Goodbyes would have been made to the ship's crew with both them and the troops wishing each other bon voyage.

But it would have been a wake-up call for the boys and girls from the R.A.M.C. what with the hot and debilitating conditions making them very thirsty and there were great containers of tea on the quayside, a welcome sight for many.

And whilst Egypt wasn't part of the British Empire it was a British Protectorate so in some respects and despite it being the middle of the War, the Union Jack would have been flying welcoming them, a home from home so to speak, perhaps giving the R.A.M.C. a small degree of comfort.

Dr Motley would have shared a tent with up to half a dozen other medical officers all fervently hoping to be able to sleep under the brown canvas.

If the officers didn't use the kit given to them on board the ship they would have been allocated new kit – the standard khaki shorts, drill shirt, desert boots all topped off with the topi hat: once again this attire wouldn't have flattered Dr Motley at all.

Each officer would also be allocated a fly whisk too to help combat the ever-present flies and bugs - another disadvantage of working in hot climes compared to cool Edinburgh.

But at least in arriving in the autumn of 1941 Lieutenant Motley was able to avoid some of the searing heat of summer.

But it was a very different world what with the constant sand that would often swirl around and get everywhere.

Very swiftly the medical staff were put to work, not just in attending to injuries and illness but undertaking preventative work too in the form of administering yellow fever vaccinations to the troops.

And of course being a medical officer didn't mean you weren't under threat from the enemy and there were occasions when bombs fell.

Suez itself, whilst being a northern sea port in Egypt is a large city.

It's of course most famous for its canal and a decade later in the mid 1950s was at the centre of an eventful episode in British modern history and regarded as a low point.

But the first thing Dr Motley would have noticed was the climate – what a change from cool, wet and windy Edinburgh.

When he arrived there in September 1941 it was moving toward the start of the cooler, dry and mostly clear winter season with warm to hot temperatures but as the year moved deeper into 1942 and in the future years ahead the summer temperatures would be hot, humid and arid.

Growing up in McAlester City Oklahoma I'm sure this is one aspect of his war experience that Arthur would have enjoyed and he would have coped better with the conditions than many of his fellow doctors.

Indeed, such was the heat many of the British officers often slept outside at night under mosquito nets.

Like many of the staff he may well have spent the whole period living under canvas rather than living in a building.

For sleeping purposes those were smaller tents whilst for dining purposes there were larger marquees.

Each camp tended to have water towers, cook houses, toilet blocks and some even had an open air cinema.

Being commissioned within a predominantly white army Dr Motley would have got to know his colleagues well sharing mostly everything with them. Once again that experience would have stood him in good stead in the years and the decades ahead and his confidence would have grown knowing that he could successfully integrate within British society.

Yes, no doubt he would have been given such nicknames as the appalling and unimaginative 'Darkie' or 'Sambo' but he would have also realised this was less about discrimination and prejudice and instead he was simply one of the boys, most of whom would have had nicknames and the mickey taken out of them at one time or another. In some respects it was a very un-PC term of acceptance.

He would also have had to endure some of the vicissitudes of life out in Egypt including catching diarrhoea from the insanitary conditions and the poor quality of some of the water.

As to where he was specifically based we don't know but it may have been at one of the Medical Inspection Rooms or the Medical First Aid Posts. Each of these had prescribed roles.

A Baptism of Fire and Brimstone

Dr Motley's first year in Suez tied in with its most intense involvement in World War 2.

Much of the city's prominence stems of course from the Suez Canal allowing ships to bypass sailing and circumventing the Horn of Africa, instead travelling from the Mediterranean or North Atlantic to the Indian Ocean. A ship travelling from the United Kingdom to India could expect to save around two weeks travel time by using the canal.

When World War II broke out the enemy Axis had sent troops to North Africa in 1940 to capture the canal.

The fighting in North Africa went back and forth with neither side able to vanquish the other.

In the summer of 1942 – Dr Motley's first summer in Egypt – the Axis was poised to break through with an offensive launched in May including the Battle of Gazala and Battle of Bir Hakeim.

On the 13th June 1942 known as 'Black Saturday' the enemy inflicted a heavy defeat on British armoured divisions. On the 21st June 1942 Tobruk was captured by Axis Forces and a week later Mersa Matruh, Egypt fell to General Rommel and by the end of the month, on the 30th June the Axis Forces reached El Alamein and attacked the Allied defences on American Independence Day – the 4th July – the First Battle of El Alamein thus began with the Eighth Army launching a series of attacks; but by the end of the month General Auchinleck called off offensive activities to allow the Eighth Army to regroup and resupply.

August 1942

The Allied lines held and the following month, August 1942, Montgomery was appointed commander of the British Eighth Army and on the 23rd October 1942 – a year after Dr Motley had arrived in Suez – Montgomery launched a major offensive from El Alamein which forced the Axis to retreat.

And then come the 8th to the 10th November Operation Torch landed Anglo-American troops in French North Africa (Morocco and Algeria) cutting off the Axis Forces in Tunisia.

By the following early summer, on the 13th May 1943 the Axis Forces in North Africa surrendered.

So Dr Motley's period in Suez – that first 18 months coincided with when the war was at its zenith so he was incredibly busy and he would have gained an extraordinary and considerable intensive experience in dealing with badly injured troops and men.

But arriving in the autumn of 1941 would have allowed him the time to settle in somewhat and become aware of what was expected of him and to grow in confidence before that first and intensive summer and for the course of another year he was stretched to the limit having to work all hours of the day and the night to provide medical attention to hundreds of different patients.

He came across men suffering from terrible injuries some of whom would have died on his watch, but many others whom he helped to mend and repair so that they could be nursed back to health and go on to live a good life after the War.

For a newly qualified doctor it was a baptism of fire and apart from all the practical experience he was able to gain it would have impacted upon him psychologically too.

I wonder how much that influenced his generally sunny nature and optimistic persona and disposition – having been amidst the horrors and terrible sights of war, when he came back to Oxgangs to begin his practice within a young, vibrant new community made him determined to both grasp and help to ensure a better future for all – he had moved from hell to heaven and that he intended making the best of the rest of his life. And like many others, having survived the War thanks to the sacrifices of millions of others he was going to salute their efforts by living life to the full.

At quieter moments in the Suez day or in the evenings when he went off duty he would have thought of his wife and daughter back home at Colinton Mains Road. Undoubtedly he would have written to them both.

The air mail letters used by the Forces measured slightly less in size than 5 by 7 inches. On each of the three sides Dr Motley would have been able to write colourful letters with news and descriptions of his life in a very different world from Auld Reekie. But the rule of thumb was that Forces should only write about private and family matters.

At this stage in the War it was probably ordinary letters and in addition he would also have had an allocation of one green envelope each week. The green letter wasn't censored by the Unit Officers but would most certainly have been by Base Censors.

Censorship was of course a necessity to prevent secret important information falling into the hands of the enemy. And of course it was better that neither family nor friends had such information – as the famous saw runs *'Loose lips sink ships'*.

By 1943 and two years after Dr Motley had arrived in Egypt he would have used air-letters and air-graphs – the Army Form W3077 which was a sheet of paper that folded in half and then in half again. The front was lined for name and address and required a threepenny (old money) stamp. The back was blank and the inside pages were for correspondence and nothing could be enclosed.

The air graph was a page set out with the recipient's address, positioned so it fitted the envelope space, the sender's address and a space for communication with the form being sent to the Army Post Office, photographed on film, reduced in size then dispatched by air to Britain. It was then printed on to a small letter-form, enveloped and put in the ordinary post to be sent on to Colinton Mains Edinburgh. But whilst that sounds efficient and speedy most often it might take a month to arrive in Annette's hands.

I suspect Dr Motley spent all of his war service in Egypt and that experience would have made him realise that he was now an accepted part of British society perhaps tempering his concern that even whilst on board a British ship it prevented him from going ashore on to South African soil to enjoy some local entertainment for fear of 'being lynched'

But still there may have been an ongoing conflict in his mind that never quite left him tying in with Harold Motley's comment about the Tulsa Massacre and how he believes this influenced Dr Motley to remain in Edinburgh rather than to return to McAlester City.

Come the end of the War – now Captain Arthur Philip Motley - his time in the British Army came to an end.

And whilst the Suez Canal itself remained important to the British – it had been of vital interest to the British Empire before the War and then perhaps even more important afterwards because of oil whilst a passage to India became slightly less important with India gaining independence in 1947, but before that in 1945 there was a General Election and to the surprise of many Clement Attlee would become the Prime Minister replacing Churchill and the new Labour government would shortly afterwards implement the new NHS.

Thus amidst all the uncertainties and havoc and massive changes within the world, in an odd way they helped Dr Motley on his onward journey.

He had qualified as a doctor at the commencement of the War, he had received the most intensive practical experience imaginable for its duration and now at the end of it, Britain was going to create a

National Health Service of which Dr Arthur Philip Motley could become an integral part.

And of course, very fortunately and happily for us all Dr Motley had survived the War being demobbed in 1946.

He was now a qualified doctor with five years of intensive experience which would stand in him in good stead – not just in terms of the normal day to day ailments that come in the direction of family doctors but also at the more extreme end that most doctors would normally rarely ever come across in decades of work – for most general practitioners they spend all their working life within the confines of a more peaceful world, whereas Dr Motley had been given a life-time's experiences squeezed into just a few years just after he had qualified to practice.

Demob Happy

So, in his demob suit Dr Arthur Philip Motley returned to Colinton Mains Edinburgh set in the lea of the Pentland Hills.

So, what now?

He had to both adapt to and help to create a new family life for himself, for his 16 year old daughter who would have been on the verge of leaving 'George Square' – George Watson's Ladies College (School) and also his wife Annette.

As with all Forces personnel returning after spending years apart from their families it was a particularly challenging time for all involved taking a period of transition and adaption.

Each party had got used to living apart in different circumstances and the nature of their ongoing relationships would have changed and altered with the passage of time.

Each of them were now different people.

At the top of Dr Motley's to do list would have been to find a job to support his family.

This was still just before the launch of the NHS so it was still an era when people were reluctant to visit a doctor because of the prohibitive cost involved. As to when Dr Motley first began to hear about the prospective the proposed new National Health Service in the United Kingdom, who knows.

TACKLING THE FIRST GIANT

"WANT is only one of the five giants on the road of reconstruction" — The Beveridge Report.

But at some stage during the War he would have become aware of The Beveridge Report of 1942 with the economist William Beveridge's vision of a post-war Welfare State to banish from Britain the evils of the Five Giants – want, ignorance, squalor, idleness and disease.

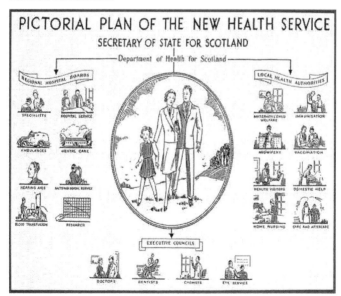

PICTORIAL PLAN OF THE NEW HEALTH SERVICE

After the War the NHS came into being on the 5th July 1948 – with the official "vesting" day of the National Health Service across the UK, although in Scotland the service was set up by a separate Act passed in 1947. Thus it's around this time that Dr Motley was able to apply to successfully set up his new practice in the Oxgangs area.

A year after returning from the War the Colinton Mains Surgery list of patients would have grown and it was from this basis he determined to secure the local health board's approval to practice as an NHS practice.

What an exciting moment for him – what a challenge.

But he was now in a good position to do so. He had learned much from his tenure in the R.A.M.C. developing his skills and his confidence had grown.

He was aged 43 or 44 so at the peak of his abilities and his skills if not his overall knowledge which would continue to grow and develop over the years ahead, learning both from his successes and his failures.

But whilst it was an exciting time in Dr Motley's life it must have been particularly satisfying in terms of his career and he would have enjoyed the contrast with life just a few years earlier during the War – this was his first tenure after qualifying.

He was living and practising within a very young part of Edinburgh surrounded by many young families all of whom were optimistic and hopeful after six long years of war. Oxgangs, Colinton Mains and Firrhill was a grand place to be.

YOUR HEALTH *Service*

HOW IT WILL WORK IN SCOTLAND

And now for the first time, everyone in Britain had free access to a family doctor, to prescription drugs, to glasses and to dentures.

And whilst hospitals would mostly carry on with their normal daily routines looking after their patients, the key difference for the new general practices, pharmacies, opticians and dental surgeries was coping with the flood or torrent of demand from patients who previously could not afford treatment or essential appliances.

May we retain what is fine and beautiful in the old system and carry those features into the New One

Open for Business

At first glance it would seem that he may not have been discharged until around 1946, but there is some conflicting information in that even as late as the 1947 Electoral Register it only records Annette as living at Colinton Mains Road: this may simply be a matter of timing in gathering the information during 1946.

But what we do have from the 1946 telephone directory is the extraordinary information that Dr A.P. Motley is listed at 356 Colinton Mains Road but underneath this entry is the additional listing of a Branch Surgery at Albert Cottage Gorgie Road Edinburgh. Just think about it – a branch surgery! He hadn't hung around!

To operate two surgeries meant he staggered his hours each day or only opened the branch surgery on a couple of days each week.

The branch may only have been run by Dr Motley for around a year or so because by the following year it's no longer listed within the phone book and of course this correlates with the advent of the NHS.

But on reflection I wonder if Dr Motley first set up his practice at Colinton Mains Road immediately on qualifying in 1939. He would only have been in practice for less than two years before going off to War joining the R.A.M.C.

But on his return, business so to speak may have been quiet and with the monies which he had managed to save up he opened up a second surgery to help to generate a further income.

The Gate-Keeper

With Dr Motley re-opening the practice at 356 Colinton Mains Road in 1946 it was still of course the family home and had been for a decade.

However when it first opened in 1939 Annette Junior was only 9 years old – now she's sweet sixteen.

As the list of patients grew and the increasing demands were made upon the practice he would have quickly realised he needed to accommodate them within better and larger premises and when what became McAlester Cottage came up for sale he grabbed the opportunity to purchase the building which would thereafter double up as both the new family home as well as becoming the new surgery. It would appear that he bought the house in around 1948.

Those were heady days for Dr Motley – he had come back home safe and well from the War – he had re-opened Colinton Mains Road as a surgery and swiftly opened a branch surgery too – now he had decided to focus on a single practice and taking advantage of the NHS had bought the finest house in the local area - and in the coming years he developed a glowing reputation with his patients creating lifetime relationships. What a transformation.

He was ever-helpful, but his wife Annette was perhaps and understandably less so.

At times she became the gate-keeper and my mother said that when patients knocked on the door or rang the bell when Dr Motley was off-duty, she could be gruff and unhelpful.

But of course family doctors at that time were often never really off duty.

Mother said to me that on one occasion when Annette Motley was sending her on her way, Dr Motley was behind her on the doorstep silently gesturing to her intimating that Mother should instead go round to the side door to the practice and he would see her for a consultation.

On another occasion when my father had been working on a fishing trawler and we had far too much fish to know what to do with – we didn't have a fridge never mind a freezer – and Mother wanted to gift some of the fish to the Motleys she was initially 'greeted' by Annette's fearsome manner, before Annette realised she was on the receiving end of a gift and her manner turned to one of gratitude.

But in this new era of free treatment patients were now more likely to visit the doctor, although within the Oxgangs area that was somewhat tempered with a predominantly young population who were generally fit and healthy perhaps allowing Dr Motley to gradually cope with the increasing demand as more and more new flats were built in the area.

A few years afterwards prescription charges – at a shilling - were introduced in 1952.

Five years later our flat at 6 Oxgangs Avenue was built and we moved in towards the end of the decade.

Vaccines were of course administered at the surgery and for many patients this would have been their first introduction to Dr Motley.

As described Dr Shepherd became his partner for a period of time taking up residence at Dr Motley's former home at Colinton Mains Road and then as the years passed, locums might be employed too before the introduction and addition of lady practitioners such as Dr Sharon Gilmour.

17th February 2021

Hi Vicky,

I trust you're well.

I wonder if you might be able to please assist me at all.

I'm working on a small book on Dr Motley and because of some of the interesting information you sent me six years ago I thought I should get back in touch to see if I could tap into some of your memories of the days when you lived next door to him at Caiystane.

Essentially I'm looking to discover information or stories around half a dozen areas or so – his childhood in McAlester City: his schooldays; his time at college; his early days when he first moved to Edinburgh; family life with Annette and his daughter; the early days when he first set up his practice putting his name above the door; and then his social life with his wife.

Also I know you drew that lovely portrait of him in his Army uniform – did he ever speak to you about his time in the War in the RAMC and his experiences there?

When he sadly died do you know what became of any of his possessions in terms of photographs etc? I assume it was Annette Junior who came back to take care of such things.

Thank you for any assistance. I'm hopeful we may be able to spark off each other in adding some key stories in doing justice to a remarkable life.

Best wishes,

Peter (Hoffmann)

The Apple of my Eye

Adopting a Dali folded clock-like structure has its advantages particularly when combined with a scatter-gun approach to research. This evening, the 20th February 2021, very late in to the project, I came across an interesting piece of new information.

When Dr Motley's daughter, Annette Junior was aged 21 it transpires she travelled from the United Kingdom to the United States to live there for almost two years.

Annette Junior sailed from the port of Southampton on the 18th October 1951 on the ship the R.M.S. Caronia which took a week to cross the Atlantic Ocean docking at New York a week later on the 25th October 1951.

The Cunard ship was new and this was only her third and indeed last transatlantic trip as thereafter she became a cruise ship operating between New York and the Caribbean which gives a flavour of what a fine ship she was: for Annette Junior being aboard the *Green Goddess* would only have added to her pleasure and excitement as to what lay ahead.

She's single and has five pieces of luggage with her – a substantial amount suggesting she's there for the long haul.

Her destination is given as 478 Grand Concourse, Bronx, New York. I may be wrong but I would surmise that this is to take up residence in an apartment there.

The Bronx is adjacent to and was strongly influenced by Manhattan styles and tastes and some of the range of Art Deco buildings were constructed only five years before Annette Junior stepped in to the area for the first occasion in mid autumn.

When she stepped out each day she would have enjoyed the sense of style of the buildings with their curving walls and the vertical and horizontal patterns of the brickwork not of course to mention the sheer excitement of coming to live in New York – The Big Apple.

I surmise that she came to live in America because she didn't return to British shores until just over two years later when she sailed from New York to Liverpool this time on the M.V. Britannic which sailed on the 5th November 1953 just as the weather in the city is beginning to get much cooler.

The very act of Dr Motley being able to facilitate his daughter going to live in the United States is a sign of his increasing prosperity as there can be little doubt that he funded the trip and her ongoing living expenses. At the time he had now been working as a doctor for around five years after the War and running his own general practice.

Annette Junior was the apple of his eye.

My mother told me that as the 'only child' (forgetting about Lewie Motley back in the United States) she had been spoiled.

On one occasion she had so loved her new party dress she kept it on for a fortnight – shades of Miss Havisham!

However, Mother went on to say that Dr Motley was quite shrewd when dealing with her wants and wishes – by way of example, when she was young, if he wanted her to buy a certain pair of shoes he would suggest the other pair, knowing that she would be contrary and therefore say she instead wanted the other pair instead – reverse psychology!

Yvonne Hjerholm, Annette Junior's adopted daughter said that her mother was quite artistic, so I have no doubt that Annette Junior would have thrived in and loved being in the New York of the early 1950s enjoying the whole buzz of living there – the sights and the sounds – and in terms of the arts New York was gradually displacing Paris as the centre of the art world if not the world of fashion.

Annette Junior was just 21 with her whole life in front of her: but what a thrill – what a treat to be going to live in The Big Apple at the age of 21.

There was less traffic in the city then making it a more pleasant environment to walk about in allowing her to take in all of the city's sensual delights.

After the War the United Nations was situated in the city and alongside taking in all the famous spots – The Statue of Liberty, Central Park, The Museum of Modern Art, Times Square, etc. she would also have the time to visit Broadway to take in some shows.

It was the town that never slept so at all times of the day and the night she would see and experience the vibrancy of the city.

All life was here.

Lorries were piled high with boxes of deliveries.

She would come across policemen using public phones to call in to their local stations.

She would ride the subway.

And on the packed streets she would come across an array of colourful individuals rigged out perhaps in a cowboy suit playing a guitar to publicise a store – and oh the stores!

With her keen interest in fashion it would have been a joy to visit the shops and to treat herself.

But she would also see disparities between those who have and those who have not and those in between.

Many Black people were employed in low level jobs.

Many were unemployed.

She wouldn't be able to travel along a sidewalk without coming across a shoe-shine boy, a job seemingly dominated by Black people - the old and the young.

She would come across the homeless and the dispossessed too.

And during the day in winter and in to the evenings she might come across Black people without a roof over their heads sitting on old orange boxes whilst warming their hands over open-fired braziers all set within the theatrical background and the wealth of lit up hotels such as The Waldorf or The Astoria and the giant signs which flashed out giant adverts for Pepsi Cola.

The men – mainly white men - some of whom would be attired in two piece suits and at this time still wearing Fedora hats, but six years after the end of the War fashion styles were changing too and certainly come the spring and the summer fewer and fewer men continued to wear head-wear.

But of course Annette Junior would have been much more interested in what the women were wearing and how the styles might contrast with back home in Edinburgh. And whilst dress lengths may have been broadly – forgive the pun – similar - the coats and the hats were much brighter in colour than in dour old Scotland.

The winters would have been tough for Annette Junior – certainly harsher and colder and with more snow than she was used to back in Oxgangs Edinburgh whilst the summers were far warmer and during August the heat and the humidity was extreme.

Eateries and restaurants abounded assaulting your senses – outdoor salesmen would be shouting out selling their wares whilst at some of the clothing shops the owners would stand atop boxes cajoling and encouraging potential customers to seek out a bargain. And whilst she simply passed such shops by she may have enjoyed visiting the local record stores.

Annette Junior's trip to New York makes me speculate on a number of things.

Firstly, she has visited the United States several years before her father, Dr Motley did in 1959. When he did visit it was over a quarter of a century after he had left home back in 1928.

A second key issue was whether she ever visited her grandparents in McAlester City in far off Oklahoma. In normal circumstances I would have taken this as an absolute given, but as her father had been recorded in the U.S. Census of 1940 as being single who knows.

However, given that the Reverend Frank Motley would visit Scotland for three months a few years later in 1955, I might surmise that she did indeed.

But that of course raises further questions – in doing so, did she and her half-brother Lewie Motley ever meet in McAlester City - did their paths inadvertently cross – was she made aware of his existence? I assume that on her visit to the town she would have stayed over with Ethel and Frank – was it a subject that was ever raised – given the sensitivity and the circumstances, perhaps not.

Coming across Annette Junior's sojourn to the States also suggests that when her grandfather the Reverend Frank Motley did come to stay at McAlester Cottage in Oxgangs she would already have known him by then.

But the third and most pertinent aspect and the one which I have no information on is why did she choose go to New York to live?

Was it to study or was it to live, to find out whether she might be able to create a new life for herself and leave Oxgangs behind – after all, we know she is an American citizen.

It's difficult to say.

If she had stayed in New York for a further year – three years rather than two - we may have assumed she was studying there taking an undergraduate degree – alternatively she may already have graduated back in the United Kingdom and this was her reward for her efforts: but then again, perhaps she was about to undertake a postgraduate course.

But my instinct on this, is that was something long promised to her when she reached the age of 21 – and that she had travelled there, seeking out a job, looking to begin a new life - only it didn't quite work out for her.

She is recorded on the passenger list on her return to the United Kingdom to Liverpool where it states it's indefinitely.

Annette Junior had left United Kingdom shores with five pieces of luggage and great hope and excitement in her heart: two years later she similarly returned with five items of luggage feeling who knows what – disapointed? - but her adventure had come to an end.

I find a poignant sadness in her story – a story of dashed hopes. She had sailed out on a new cruise liner which could acommodate 580 First Class passengers and 350 Cabin and she returned on the New York to Liverpool M.V. Britannic - a boat built in 1929.

We know that according to the Electoral Register she is recorded as living back home at McAlester Cottage until 1957 but by 1958 she is no longer at this address which ties in with my mother saying she doesn't recall ever seeing Annette Junior and we moved to Oxgangs in 1958.

But after all the excitement of living in New York for two years it must have been a retrograde step to return to live in grey Oxgangs for the next four years or so to where felt quite restricted compared to the relative freedom which she enjoyed in the city that never sleeps.

And of course she was now a woman aged between 23 and 27.

The years between 1951 and 1953 were the happiest period of her life: in comparison, everything thereafter was a disappointment

21st February 2021

Another day and another update.

On getting hold of a different, hand-written version of the R.M.S. Catriona's passenger list sailing on the 18th October 1951 arriving on the 25th it describes Annette as a student and also that her stay of residence is to be permanent.

Two things.

First, by permanent, this is actually defined as being for more than a year.

And second, it describes her as a student so perhaps she went to New York to study rather than to work.

By way of final postscript I also managed to find her burial notice.

Annette Junior died in January 2000, the same age as her mother, Annette, aged 69 years.

She was buried in a Roman Catholic burial ground in Harrow near London with the service conducted by a priest, so another turn in the road in that at some stage in her later life she converted to Roman Catholicism.

Her home address is recorded as 226 Pinner Road Harrow.

And one final thing - as to whether it is her or not there is a record of an Annette Motley marrying a Mr S. Jones in Solihull Warwickshire in January 1964. Certainly her name is an uncommon one and at the time she would have been aged 34, so who knows.

Betty Verrill and Rosa Parks

I did write a further time to Mrs Betty Verrill in North Yorkshire.

She responded that she didn't have much further to add to her earlier letter to me but she did say that because Annette Junior was in the class above her she had little to do with her.

She went on to say that unfortunately Annette Junior's name

doesn't appear in any of the school re-union booklets nor at any of the reunions such as the 50th anniversary celebrations.

Betty was at 'George Square' school between Easter 1937 until the summer of 1949 so she enjoyed both a primary and a secondary education at George Watson's Ladies College.

Betty went on to say that it was her grandfather, a James Lyall Hunter, a Shetland descendent who paid all her school fees throughout the years. This wouldn't have been an insubstantial amount of monies and Dr Motley must have similarly invested in Annette Junior.

Betty recalled travelling from Colinton and Oxgangs – 'known as Colinton Mains' to school each day by the S.M.T. (or Balerno) bus or Corporation bus. She said she had to change trams at Tollcross – 'quite dangerous for a wee 5 year old' – as the 9 and 10 went down Lothian Road to Princes Street and how Annette Junior would get the 23 all the way from Firrhill and then up Lauriston Place: she said the tram fare was 1d (one penny) - 2 1/2d (two and a half pennies) for adults.

Betty's memories are helpful because it gives an insight into Annette Junior's similar route of travel each day and when she goes on to write about looking out at all the young 'city men' queuing at the bus stop at Colinton Mains how amusing she found them all identically dressed with their little moustaches and like babies sucking on their empty pipes!

Rosa Parks

Once Betty reached the age of 13 she doesn't recall ever seeing Annette Junior again, but she goes on to tell an illuminating and revealing story into the Edinburgh of the era. Betty was on a bus or a tram: there were three or four well-dressed older ladies standing in the aisle and further up there was an empty seat next to a Black man. Betty said she was only a kid but marched straight down saying 'excuse me-excuse me-excuse me' and sat next to the man. Betty said how even at such a young age she found such prejudice shocking.

The Golden Years

After all the years and decades of struggle Dr Motley's practice went from success to success.

He had worked hard and assiduously during the late 1940s to establish it and developed it further throughout the 1950s and the practice grew and expanded.

As the 1950s moved into the 1960s he was at the peak of his powers.

In giving a flavour of those halcyon decades and the context and the environment within which Dr Motley was working is best summed up by the Prime Minister, Mr Harold Macmillan, when he told the electorate that they had never had it so good.

His comments were partly based on the progress made in implementing the Beveridge Report and tackling the five evils of want; ignorance; disease; squalor; and idleness.

The Oxgangs World of Dr Motley

The young families who moved into our stair, the newly built 6 Oxgangs Avenue in 1958 were direct beneficiaries of what men had gone to war for and the new vision of a country fit for them to live in afterwards.

There were 16 adults and 25 children living there, probably given the nature of this new young community atypical of the other local flats in the area.

Generally the families who lived in The Stair at number 6 lived in harmony.

Yes, there was occasional friction, but it was very mild and occasional.

All the families were good neighbours.

The culture was a happy one which probably reflected the optimism of the 1960s.

Compared to the housing which had existed a decade earlier, the modern flats and new housing schemes with their indoor loos and open coal fires were great places to live and bring up young families.

Children played safely. There were formal playgrounds, sports pitches and tennis courts; and we could easily go off for youthful adventures to Redford Burn, the Army's polo fields and Braidburn Valley all of which were on our doorsteps.

And one hundred yards away was Dr Motley's surgery and Mr Russell the dentist at Oxgangs Road North.

There was a new school with the beautiful title of Hunters Tryst

which was set in lovely spacious grounds with large playgrounds, a small wood and football pitches.

It was a period of stability.

Families were generally happy.

Despite the daily grind and drudgery, mums and dads enjoyed the novelty of parenthood. Women were mainly the homemakers, men were the breadwinners. Access to employment was relatively easy. No one was well off and each household could be described as working class.

At The Stair, no one owned a car, however people weren't desperately poor either, even if Child Benefit made the difference between eating or not.

The Stair reflected the changing decades.

If the 1970s were about strife, then some of the new inhabitants were not as neighbourly. The 1980s of Mrs Thatcher led to families buying their own houses. The 1990s were a period of growth, better wages and no doubt those now at number 6 will have enjoyed foreign holidays and car ownership. By the Noughties the impact of the recession could be seen when I paid a visit to Oxgangs where The Stair was looking a little neglected - hardly surprising given it was fifty years since it was built.

In giving an insight into the lives and the lifestyles of Dr Motley's patients this could best be exemplified by focusing on our immediate neighbours.

Next door to us at 6/1 Oxgangs Avenue lived Dougal Swanson (6/1) who worked as a shop assistant at James Aitkenhead's Grocery shop and then as a stock-keeper at Brown Brothers Engineering Company. As for my father Ken (6/2), well, Mother gave up counting at thirty, the number of jobs he had been employed in - assistant cinema manager; stock clerk; lorry driver for George Bain's delivering meat to butchers' shops in Edinburgh and the Borders and also as a long distance driver for John Bryce Transport. However he had also been a Chief Officer in the merchant navy, training at the renowned Edinburgh company, Ben Line. His qualification was probably the equivalent of a degree in physics or maths, however those were before the days of NVQs so he found he could not use transferable management skills to gain better employment. The other issue was that being an alcoholic made it difficult for him to hold down a job for any length of time.

Mr Stewart (6/3) was a policeman and like many others in that line of work kept himself to himself, a complete distance from any other neighbour in The Stair. George Hogg (6/4) was a joiner. George was part of a small cooperative of skilled tradesmen who in later years built their own houses toward Oxgangs Green. Eric Smith (6/5) worked as a general helper at Marks and Spencer. This was a secure job; previously he may have been a bus driver, but his wife, Mary, didn't like him working shifts.

Charles Blades (6/6) worked for many years at Ferranti's where he was a personal assistant to Basil de Ferranti. He regularly accompanied him to meetings in London. Whilst in the Army Charles had initially trained as a doctor but late on in the course dropped out. Like my father, he too was an alcoholic. This prevented him reaching his full potential. This condition blighted the lives of both families. Dougal, Ken and Charles were clearly bright individuals and incredibly Charles' father was Lord Blades, the respected judge and appointed the Solicitor General for Scotland at the end of the war in 1945. But at times in the late 1960s and the early 1970s Dr Motley helped to facilitate treatment for both Charles and Ken at the Andrew Duncan Clinic for alchoholics.

Charlie Hanlon (6/7) worked for many years at the Uniroyal Rubber Mill which superseded the North British Company - a steady and secure job for many years. He worked shifts. Sometimes Hilda would hang out the top floor sitting room window and chastise the kids down below for being too loud and 'keeping my Charlie awake when he's on the night shift!' I liked the way Charlie brought home a Friday treat of chocolate bars for his four sons, Michael; Boo-Boo; Colin; and Alan. If you'll forgive the pun, it was a sweet thing to do. Meanwhile, Mr Duffy (6/8) was a general labourer and scaffy in later years; previously he may have worked elsewhere but that change may have been brought about because I think he lost his driving license.

Let it Be and the Elephant in the Room

One particular shop that a few of us from The Stair used to frequent back in the 1960s was Robbs' Electrical and Radio Shop at Morningside Road. Douglas Blades could write a better and more knowledgeable article on Robbs than me - it was here that he used to buy his large collection of American records and have cognoscente discussions with the staff - he was far in advance of most of us, albeit older.

The main reason for my visits was to buy a Top Twenty record single, but occasionally it was to buy an item which was quite new to me - it was called a stylus. When I think how switched on kids are today re: computers, iPhones, et al I have to smile at my innocence.

Our first record player at 6/2 Oxgangs Avenue was a portable record player that when it was packed away looked like a small suitcase. It was daft really, because in most households it was set up permanently, however if you chose to close it down after play, particularly if there was little space in your bedroom, it was useful and compact. I guess the concept behind it was that you could take it with you to visit friends to play records together.

I got my first one from Mum's catalogue. It was a very happy day when it arrived - at that moment 20 weeks of payments weren't a concern; and after all I had my paper money from Baird's Newsagent's for delivering morning newspapers as well as The Edinburgh Evening News in the afternoons.

My first introduction to the intricacies of the stylus was when something went wrong - the record wasn't playing properly.

'Have you tried out the stylus, Peter?'

'The what?'

'The stylus - the needle - you'll find it located under the arm - it comes out! You'll get one at Robbs - Neep!'

I seem to recall the styluses came in different sizes and brands, because I had to return the first one I bought - initially it was a little tricky to fit, but once I had done it I felt quite proud of myself - like a proper technician - a real man!

The first record that I bought was in 1967 was Scott Mackenzie's

San Francisco. It remains a haunting track taking

people back in time. Another record I bought was Peter Sarstedt's *Frozen Orange Juice* which I remember playing relentlessly on a jukebox in a cafe in Grantown-on-Spey on a holiday with my grandparents.

During the late spring of 1969 we'd been visiting my father who had hospitalised himself in liaison with Dr Motley for another six week spell at the Andrew Duncan Clinic to try to get himself back on the wagon after he'd been on a bender.

Visiting him was difficult, but we were supportive, particularly my mother.

Those daily visits were made easier by playing table tennis in the hospital's games room - it was great fun to do something as a family - it was something which we could all join in and participate as a family - good competition and several laughs - but wasn't it incredibly ironic that it took such a visitation to such a place to facilitate such a rare happening!

I've never thought about that irony until typing this vignette. Over a decade ago I bought a table tennis table and we all played out in the garden from the spring through to the autumn - even my wife the non-sporty Alison and my brother Iain Hoffmann on his regular visitations. It's given much fun over the years and the occasional argument!

On reflection was there something in my subconscious - was the decision less about free will?

After Mother, Anne Hoffmann Jr and Iain Hoffmann and I visited the hospital we used to stand outside Robbs' Electrical Shop awaiting the dear old Number 16 Bus to take us home.

I'd enjoy looking in Robbs' window at all their goods.

And it was on the way down for such a hospital visitation that I had nipped in to Robbs' to buy *Get Back* by The Beatles. Their record label featuring a large apple was good enough to eat - the novel design captured my imagination.

Let It Be by The Beatles must have been on the go around this time too.

Leaving the hospital was always bitter-sweet.

As a boy a part of me was glad to get away from the hospital and the people in there and also from my father, but I also felt very guilty too and a sorrowfulness descended as we strolled along Miller Crescent, turning to wave to my father as he receded into the background.

And when the broken hearted people living in the world agree
There will be an answer, let it be
For though they may be parted, there is still a chance that they will see
There will be an answer, let it be
Let it be, let it be, let it be, let it be
There will be an answer, let it be
Let it be, let it be, let it be, let it be
Whisper words of wisdom, let it be
Let it be, let it be, let it be, let it be

Whisper words of wisdom, let it be

McCartney/Lennon

Charles Blades's eldest daughter reflected on her father too saying: *'My own father spent periods in the Andrew Duncan although I'm not sure that his were voluntary. I wonder if Charles and Ken were ever there at the same time and shared therapy sessions. Now there's a thought.*

It was nice to hear that you visited Ken as a family, in support. Well done Anne Snr. I assume that my mother visited Charles but we were not included in such visits or informed. In our family alcoholism was the secret curse. It was the elephant in the room that was off limits for discussion. We used to play a game - hunt the bottle - a search and destroy mission, as if that would do the trick! The naivety.

The strange thing was that we did not witness my father drinking. I remember Mr Hogg having the odd beer and being appalled that he could be so blatant about it all. Again the naivety. My father drank in secret of course because there was so much fuss otherwise. He could conceal the drinking but not the effects. Helen could detect the drunk at 50 paces! He could drown his sorrows and our finances at The Good Companions but he could not avoid coming home to the repercussions of his behaviour.'

I got back to Liz responsing about the openness versus concealment issue which was an interesting point revealing something of the era.

Out-with the general principle of trying to be open and transparent I am unclear of my own motivation for being open about my father, Ken Hoffmann.

But one aspect of any consultation with Dr Motley was that there was no embarrassment involved – alchoholism like any subject could be discussed with him quite easily.

However, at the time it was not something which I have ever really spoke about amongst friends or colleagues at all.

But in more recent years when Fiona Blades (6/6 Oxgangs Avenue) and I met up we've been able to be quite open - there's been no embarrassment.

But all that Liz says of the Blades family's experience with Charles we at 6/2 could empathise and identify with; looking back if we had only been more open with each other as kids it may have lessened the burden.

Helen Blades and Anne Hoffmann Snr were articulate and open with each other, particularly for the time and the existing mores and values.

But it's understandable why it was kept secretive, particularly when you are living cheek by jowl within the confines of a small community, amongst eight families in The Stair.

To understand our reasons perhaps begins with what motivates people - acceptance and the need for approval; the avoidance of rejection; status and the need for social prestige as well as the period in which it took place.

I hated the embarrassment when I might have some pals in the house and totally out of the blue my father turned up drunk and unnaturally good natured and effusive.

I'd try to usher my friends out of the house quickly before they might notice; the down side of that was that his mood would then transform to Mr Hyde when I would be on the end of some sarcastic and cutting remarks and looks which would then, more often than not, move beyond mental abuse.

Another embarrassing incident was him coming into the classroom at Hunters Tryst to ask for the house key - he was drunk and his breeks were held up with a piece of string. I'm actually laughing at that particular memory, but it wasn't funny at the time!

Like 6/6 we didn't really see him drinking at home at all - it was all hidden from view.

Ditto on the bottles, indeed, I once couldn't sleep properly because a bottle of vodka had been planked under my pillow, but I was too terrified to mention it!

Andrew Duncan

I'm unaware whether other families in The Stair knew that Charles and Ken were alcoholics; my impression is that it was kept quite well hidden, but perhaps I'm being a little naive?

Liz responded *'As for the alcoholism, it was very much the post war era. My father had not dealt with his life pre-war, let alone post-war. He just stepped up his drinking to cope - I believe there was an element of post-traumatic stress not dealt with - but it wasn't dealt with in any of the services was it? Still today soldiers return from*

Afghanistan etc, wives have to cope as best they can, children suffer etc. Thus I think there is very much a universal aspect to it.'

Looking back I don't recall either being on the end of any social disdain or receiving any social empathy.

I always felt that at times I had a special relationship with Helen Blades, so perhaps there's an inherent contradiction there, but I'm only surmising.

But undoubtedly it was the wives who suffered most - Helen Blades and Anne Hoffmann, but my mother was always supported by Dr Motley whether in facilitating my father going into the Andrew Duncan Clinic for a period or even as someone for my mother to talk to.

Aye Working

And as for the women and the wives they were in many ways not dissimilar to when Ethel Motley was running the household in McAlester City during the 1920s - Oxgangs in the 1950s and 1960s was in some respects really not so very different.

If two words could best describe the women in The Stair and all the surrounding stairs, flats and houses in Oxgangs the words would be 'Aye working'. Never mind Stephen Covey's bestselling management books, the women at The Stair could have shown him a trick or two.

Mrs Helen Blades cleaning The Stair

They had to deploy wonderful management skills - ingenuity; stamina; resilience; and character in raising their families and running their households with few time saving aids; not to mention making ends meet with very little money.

During the calendar year the work didn't vary overly much. But winter was the busiest or the hardest of the four seasons and summer, perhaps the easiest. Breakfast might have to be made for husbands before they headed off to work. Certainly, at 6/1 Dougal Swanson was provided with a cooked breakfast of bacon and egg each morning. From each household the younger children would have to be raised from bed and dressed for school. In the dark months of December, January and February the day might begin with the fire ashes being cleared out. However, to keep costs down, the fire would not be lit until much later in the day. At 6/2, Anne, Iain and I would be given breakfast - mainly tea and toast, something which we were soon taking responsibility for ourselves. And on a Sunday morning, we were encouraged to do a fry up of sorts. Without a washing machine, washings were time consuming. Doing a washing by hand, followed by putting the clothes through the wringer or mangle, was killer work, even before the drag of having to hang it up at the washing green in the warmer, sunnier months. Who needed a gym or to go jogging! But if there were other mums out at least there might be a little respite, when they could enjoy a quick chinwag.

In the winter, clothes needed to be dried inside - no mean feat in a small flat without central heating. And whilst back in the 1960s we had fewer clothes and there was perhaps a lot less washing done, imagine what life was like at each household in The Stair which averaged five in size, never mind the large Blades family household with around nine individuals - talk about Sisyphus. It must have been like a Chinese Laundry, washing and drying on an industrial scale. For much of the time such repetitive work was sheer drudgery with few thanks or appreciation. Some families used the washing green, others didn't.

Mrs Hanlon had a washing out on most days. Mrs Swanson and Mother also regularly hung their washing out to dry; no doubt some interesting conversations took place there. There was a rota for each Stair however because some families didn't use the washing green at all there was an arrangement whereby the regulars had all week access to The Stair's allocated section.

For example Helen Blades didn't use the washing green.

When Fiona Blades, Mother and I met up back in 2012 we concluded the reason for this might have been that it would have been so time consuming having to go down three floors with a heavy pile of washing and then all the way back up the stairs, not to mention dashing in and out if the weather changed and the rain came on.

Certainly if a mother had a washing hanging out to dry and the rain suddenly came on and she happened to be elsewhere at the shops, because of the sense of community, one of the other mothers in The Stair might take their washing in for them.

And if there was a sudden and an almighty downpour of rain and we children were about it was always great fun for us to run out to the washing green and give Mother a hand.

In the winter or when it was raining, the washing had to be dried indoors on the pulley.

Looking back it was a rather clever invention and design - if you couldn't hang the washing out the back at the washing green then instead it could be hung up to dry on the pulley indoors. Whilst the theory was splendid, in practice it had its drawbacks.

Between 1958 and 1972 there was no central heating in each flat; instead there was only a small coal fire in the living room.

Large items such as sheets would often have to be hung up around the fire to dry, but a member of the family always had to stand guard, in case the sheet became singed.

The other items of clothing would be hung up on the pulley which was located on the kitchen ceiling to allow any drips to fall onto the linoleum floor.

Because the pulley was affixed to the ceiling you had to untie and lower the rope to enable the frame to come down, before then pulling the rope to raise it back up. Now whilst it was an ingenious device because the flats were quite small and space was limited it had its drawbacks too. Being able to haul the clothes up above meant it took up no floor space.

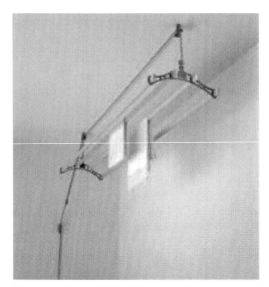

However, the two drawbacks were that it must have taken days for the clothes to dry. And more significantly any cooking smells would impregnate the clothes - a major drawback. Looking back I guess the hall or bathroom would have been better locations for the pulley, especially as for many years we could only afford to have linoleum on these floors - indeed only the living room (sitting room) had a carpet.

However, being creatures of habit and devoid of lateral thinking, our family never considered relocating it. Thereafter, housework needed to be undertaken, ironing done and lunch made for the young children at home during the week.

Groceries too had to be bought in. Without fridges, this often meant daily visits to the shops. And come the evening, tea or dinner needed to be prepared and served.

Then you needed to take your share to wash and clean The Stair too.

It was only into the evening that women might be able to put their feet up and relax in front of the television, but even then they might multi-task doing some sewing and mending or knitting all the while.

As we grew older, Anne, Iain and I shared some of the burden, particularly after our parents divorced in 1971 and Mother went out to work in the Civil Service.

We tidied the house; made the fire; did the messages; and washed, dried and put away the dishes.

We took a certain pride in having the place looking ship shape for our mother arriving home at tea time.

Home was a much more relaxed place to be as the three of us were growing older too.

During the 1960s there was considerable stereotyping.

Whilst men had to be seen to go out to undertake economic work, women did all of the repetitive household chores.

Most men would rather be seen dead than be seen hanging out the washing.

As one might expect, this was another example of Father being different.

He was quite happy to be seen on the washing green.

Running a ship's tough Merchant Navy crew or playing fullback at rugby, the bold Ken didn't need to prove his machismo.

I seem to recall Mr Bowman (4/6) also hung up the washing too, but they were rarities. Mr Bowman was a fit bloke who used to play football for an amateur team and would even be seen going out jogging which was unheard of at the time and for which you might be the subject of derision - how things change.

Today whether I arrive in the capital early in the morning or very late at night, the streets are dotted with joggers, the majority of whom I'm delighted to see are women.

Such a radical cultural change from the 1960s - perhaps the housework burden is at last being shared.

Or not!

That stair microcosm provides a useful flavour of the overall Oxgangs environment which grew and grew as a community particularly as more and more houses were developed and built including the three giant skyscraper 15 storey tower blocks at Firrhill – The Village in the Sky - many of whom became patients of Dr Motley.

A Fictional Hero Too

Despite the volume of work, Dr Motley, with the addition of new partners was able to enjoy an occasional holiday away and as my mother mentioned both he and Annette enjoyed taking cruises.

And it was on one such occasion during the mid 1960s that whilst on board a cruise ship he met and became friendly with the world renowned author Ngaio Marsh who asked for his approval to include him in one of her detective novels, *Clutch of Constables* which was published in 1968 so we might assume the cruise took place the year before in 1967.

The novel as usual features the detective, Roderick Alleyn of Scotland Yard: his wife who's a celebrity painter - Agatha Troy - on a whim - takes a canal cruise on the MV Zodiac through 'Constable' country.

Included amongst the passengers and of course suspects are a literary lepidopterist; a pair of gushing American tourists; a sporting Australian clergyman; a London slum landlord and of course 'Dr Motley' but transposed to being an exotic and distinguished surgeon of Afro-Caribbean origin, to whom Troy is greatly attracted, and who is the subject of overt racism from several of the passengers on board.

Within the context of Two Worlds and the theme of racism it's interesting how regularly this theme features within Marsh's books where coloured people are sympathetically portrayed.

The 1970s

And then as the years passed the first major change which would begin to impact upon Dr Motley's practice along with all the other such Scottish practices was in 1972 with the establishment of fifteen new health boards with a view to making the NHS more efficient with the provisions in the Act finally introduced in 1974.

The new health boards took over many of the health responsibilities of local authorities.

It heralded the start of a new culture in the health service where managers took more key decisions and the involvement of the public was reduced.

And it's perhaps around this time that Dr Motley may have first turned some of his thoughts toward retiral - after all, in 1974 he was actually 70 years old rather than the 67 years recorded as based in his matriculation record at his alma mater.

In giving a flavour of his day to day work during this last decade of his professional life could best be given by some comments from some of his patients as well as extracts from my journals for the years 1971 to when Dr Motley retired in 1978. I was aged between 14 and 22.

The View from t'other Side of the Consulting Table

In being able to appreciate and get an insight into those golden years this can be appreciated from the other side of the consulting table so to speak: herewith a small selection of comments from just a few of Dr Motley's former patients

PsyGeo Thanks for remembering Dr Motley. He did his best to help my mum. That trip to the cottage was a regular one with me in tow. We lived at 34 Oxgangs Avenue in the mid 70s/early 80s so far away now and a mostly unhappy time but made me who I am. Contact me if you'd like to see some pics.

John McDonaugh What I remember most about McAlester Cottage Surgery was the curling stones for some reason as they fascinated me. As a youngster it felt like every time I went to see him I'd end up in hospital. One time visiting him due to a comment at school that my eyes were yellow all he said to me was to go home get Mum to pack a bag for you as an ambulance would be picking me up in twenty minutes not knowing what was wrong. I ended up in the City Hospital with Jaundice quarantined for fourteen days then another fourteen after that feeding squirrels digestive biscuits from my hand. Three weeks later after my release then going back to see Dr Motley as my nose would not stop bleeding; he said go home get a bag ready an ambulance will be there in twenty minutes - yes back to the City Hospital to have my nose cauterised - a simple routine but because the bleed had been so heavy I needed blood. Having said all that he was a kindly gentleman who would ask about all the family before asking you what was wrong. Another Oxgangs stalwart in the pictures was the Rev. Orr often seen walking the streets visiting his parishioners. Again a gentleman.

Peter Curran My late dad was a telephone engineer with the GPO as it was at the time. He used to park his van at Fairmilehead Telephone Exchange which is next to the Charwood Restaurant on Buckstone Terrace. He would occasionally take me there after he finished work to walk around the exchange. There were lots of cable racks and Strowger switches making a lot of noise clicking and banging. On this day he asked if I wanted to go I was excitedly tying my laces then stood up and hit the my head on the snib of the front door. I immediately split my head open. I rand own the road to the doctor's surgery. I can't remember if it was with Mum or Dad. Dr Motley immediately put a couple of stitches in with what appeared to be a carpet needle without any drugs! I was carted off to hospital to get it sorted. I had to go back every couple of days to get the wound cleaned up. I remember it being very painful every time. I wore bandages on my head like a turban for a couple of weeks. I now have a very visible scar on my head and if any pressure is put on it, it can be quite sore. Apart from that I always liked Dr Motley. He always commented on how tall I was.

Neil Mc Gilvray My family was originally from Oxgangs Farm Gardens but we moved to Oxgangs House when I was six so my brother Stephen and I had been back up to the Gardens playing with our friends so on the way back home we crossed the road at the bus stop outside the dentist's and across the field when somehow I cut my leg on a broken bottle for some reason unknown to me. Stephen picked me up - he could have only have been about ten years old carried me all the way home to Oxgangs House to be told by Mrs Brannan next door to take me back to the doctors: this memory will never leave me Dr Motley decided I needed stitches so without any pain relief proceeded to start stitching me up; as I screamed the place down he said with that big smile of his it's okay - only two hundred more – lol! I burst the stitches within a few days and I've still got the scar today.

Pamela Dobson I was told as Dr Motley delivered one of the Ravizza children that the baby had been in his Black doctor's bag which he carried everywhere when visiting patients. I remember watching him leave the house and my Mum saying 'Ah good, the baby is here'. I never doubted for a moment!

Peter Hoffmann Wonderful story Pamela - who needed a stork in Oxgangs!

Maureen Henderson-Lowe said 'Dr Motley came to see my sister at Christmas - a house call was never a problem, unlike nowadays; she got a petite typewriter from Santa and he typed her a letter on it. I don't think she got a prescription, but she loved it!'

Tom H. Cosgrove I remember when I was about 4 I was taken to see the Dr but not Dr Motley. I still remember turning to my mum as we left the building - I stopped her, drew myself up to my full height and as I wiggled my finger at her I said " Don't you ever do that again it's Dr Motley who is my doctor!!!" Then stomped off home.

Maggie Broatch I remember I talked to him before I took up my nursing career in 1974. I remember him talking about being from America and how better it was over here.

Harry Chamberlain My over-riding thought about this man is that it never entered my head that he was a Black man. He was just someone who was going to make me feel better. The scar I have on my right thumb always brings back memories of the treatment he gave me for the cause of that scar (Electrocution). In later years I have strong reasons to be glad that immigrants reached our island. My life was saved by a surgeon who's ancestry is very likely not initially British.

Richard Cropper My Mother had some sort of deep vein thrombosis going on as a side effect of the contraceptive pill whilst my younger brother had a yeast allergy which AP did his best with but was getting nowhere. In both cases I think it was Dr.McDougall if memory serves me correctly who sorted both out. In reading the various comments in all your blogs Peter I am curious to know - if indeed anyone has a definitive number - is that during APs tenure in Oxgangs & Colinton Mains - just how many babies did he deliver over the years? It must be in the hundreds surely.

Pat-Paddy Corry My mother was devastated when she had to leave the surgery as we were living too far away. When I was 17 and went to live in the States he came to the flat and had a long chat with me about the difficulties I might face. How good you and your family were to him. I remember tea at Jenners being a very special treat, sitting near a window to see the view. More often it was a film and high tea at the Playhouse. Remember I am talking about the 1950s! We must have been seeing Dr Motley before your flats were built! We saw Dr Motley from the very early 50s. I remember my mother looking at all the building going on and saying how clever he had been settling there. His practice must have grown tremendously.

Peter Hoffmann Yes, I think you're right Pat in that he appears to have got rid of the small branch practice at Gorgie Road circa 1947 perhaps recognising the potential, but serendipity too moving to Colinton Mains circa 1936. The NHS general practices were paid on a capitation basis so yes it would have become lucrative - a long way and a long journey from his recent ancestors working in the cotton fields in The Deep South.

Pat-Paddy Corry (front) at Duddingston Camp

Pat-Paddy Corry Thank you for bringing him back to me. Did you know that our connection with him started in Duddingston Camp? (Note the Duddingston Camp was one of the camps in Edinburgh that provided temporary housing for the homeless who were not eligible for Council Housing, following the end of World War 2.) When we came from Auchtermuchty to Edinburgh in 1947, we had to stay in Duddingston Camp in a hut. You didn't get a whole hut. As a family of four we got 2/3 (two-thirds) and a mother and her daughter got the rest bricked off of course. We had cold water, electricity and communal baths and toilets. It was awful for my mother but I loved it. There was acres of grass to play on, trees to climb and loads of children to play with. But we were viewed with horror. At school I was the only one from the camp to get in. I was initially resented or pitied until I proved myself. I cut my foot badly one evening. The National Health Service had just started and people were thrilled to see me set off for a free doctor's visit. My foot was stitched and a little later the doctor committed suicide. His wife couldn't come to terms with her husband not working privately any more and having to deal with the riff-raff. I thought it was my fault, going from the camp to his house in the evening. I don't know how my mother got hold of Doctor Motley but he came to the Camp for a house visit. My mother and sister had lots of health problems. I remember following him out and asking him to please not kill himself. I'll never forget the look on his face. He told me that not only would he not kill himself, he'd come back to torment me. He gave me a sweet he had in his pocket - they were still rationed - and we parted with laughter. We moved soon after to a respectable address where we had to play on the street, and he remained our doctor until, I think, the late 60s or early 70s when he no longer could cope with patients so far away. My mother never did find another doctor she liked. It was always a case of: *"Well, he's not Dr Motley."*

Peter Hoffmann Thanks for this Pat - I must add this to Two Worlds - fascinating and so interesting that he was the Camp's doctor.

Pat-Paddy Corry I don't know if he was the Camp's doctor or whether my mother managed to get hold of him privately. She went to work for the Tory Party. That's how I got into Portobello School. We also got the flat in Montgomery Street after two years in the Camp and I was still able to stay at the same school even though I was miles out of the area. A lot of strings were pulled. I think Dr Motley only came to us. He was very brave because of his colour. There was no-one of colour in the Camp and he was the first black man I ever met. So I am sure he was not the Camp doctor and came out of area. Montgomery Street was totally different - a complete mixture of nationalities and colour. Sorry to disappoint you. Perhaps in those days, he didn't have so many patients (pre 1950) and was willing to travel. As far as I know we didn't visit him until we went to Montgomery Street. I'm so sorry if I confused you.

Peter Hoffmann No not at all Pat - all very helpful and interesting helping to give a more rounded picture of his life - I'm greatly enjoying reading your memories of him.

Pat-Paddy Corry Please note my father's little garden (see below) where he grew a few flowers so I could take them to the teacher like other children.

Pat-Paddy Corry I now remember a second visit to the Camp by Dr Motley. He came to see my mother. When he was leaving, my father was shouting at my sister and me. He went back into the hut and told my mother to get out of bed as Dad wasn't fit to look after us. It was a bit unfair to my dad who did shout a bit but never laid a hand on us unless Mum stood over us and made him. He then made a big show of it and I knew I had to cry but he never hurt me.

Peter Hoffmann Thanks for the clarification - I'd assumed it was your mother. As Jessie Kesson might remark, from a number of different angles, such a fascinating insight into 'another time, another place' indeed, another world.

A Patient's Journal

Within Two Worlds on occasion I've remarked that I didn't consider Dr Motley to be by nature an overly reflective individual making it easier for him not to think about his family back in McAlester City or of abandoning his childhood sweetheart Miss Freddie Royster and their son, Lewie Motley. That was of course enhanced by the nature of his work whereby he would have been very busy indeed never quite knowing what the day might reveal including emergencies. In addition to seeing his patients there would be all the note-taking and records which required to be kept up to date. In giving just a microcosm of what might be involved herewith is a patient's journal – my own - and someone who was young and fit, never mind a more elderly individual requiring more visitations and treatment. The extracts also include one or two references to some other individuals from The Stair including Helen Blades and my mother.

26th **February 1971** I didn't go into Boroughmuir first thing; in fact I didn't go in at all. I went across to Dr Motley's first thing about my headaches but had to wait absolutely ages in the waiting room. It was a bit of a drag but in a strange way better than being at school. Dr Motley was his usual cheery happy go lucky helpful self. I'm very fond of him. Anyway I decided not to bother going in to Boroughmuir; any excuse will do. I have a ream of excuses - it's Friday; I've missed most of the morning; I could save on dinner money etc. etc. I suspect that subconsciously I'd already made my mind up before hand and just took advantage of the delay.

22nd April 1971 Crikey I was asked to attend the doctor's and was told I've got hepatitis - what's that all about. It wasn't Dr Motley but the other doctor. I don't know what it is but can you really get it off drinking a couple of cans of Sweetheart Stout? Anyway I've now got a ready-made excuse (as if I needed one) for skiving off Boroughmuir. I put it behind me and wandered up to Oxgangs Broadway to tuck into some chocolate and chips. John went to the bank along with Mum; she took a half day. A different sort of a Thursday. Aye you might say that again.

23rd April 1971 I was off school – AGAIN - with this diagnosis of hepatitis it means I've got medical permission to be off school. I've never needed an excuse before so when I've got a ready-made one. Meanwhile on the home-front John went home to Aberdeen to visit his relations. I spent a good part of the day playing records; to be honest it was generally a pretty boring day probably slightly worse than being in at Boroughmuir - the only plus is it's a safe haven with no unpleasant surprises. In the evening I watched the telly including The Champions which is an interesting programme. I find myself quite drawn to it with the crew's enhanced senses and powers.

6th May 1971 Well what can I say? After me putting in a full day and such a good shift at Boroughmuir yesterday I didn't bother going in at all today. I had to go across to the doctor's about this hepatitis thing so of course I had a ready-made excuse. It turns out I don't have it at all; it seems the doctor got my medical records mixed up with the old man's - crazy. After school came out Anne and I tided up the whole house. I then settled back with some crisps and Globe Sun Kool Kola. In the early evening there was a big bunch of us out playing Singles. I then came in to watch a good Z Cars episode - the theme tune's good. I can hardly wait to get Iain his Chopper on Saturday.

24th May 1971 I went to the Royal Infirmary Hospital this morning. It's part of my annual appointments after I ended up in hospital twice in recent years with extreme pains in my side which they never got to the bottom of. The last time was a year ago after competing for Boroughmuir in a triangular athletics match against George Watsons and Daniel Stewart's at Myreside. I got home after nine o'clock and before I knew it I was whisked off to the Royal. Anyway I had blood taken and felt all dizzy and had to lie down afterwards until I recovered. It was a horrible feeling. I don't like feeling unwell. Once I began to slowly recover a wee bit I wandered up to Ward 32 to visit Sister Turner who looked after me so well when I was in the men's ward twice before; I had a good wee blether with her.

2nd July 1971 Today was the last day of the school summer term but hardly relevant for me as I'm permanently AWOL enjoying holiday life. So whilst my pals went off to Firrhill School I busied myself with my new second-hand typewriter and happily "typed" away. Once Firrhill got out in the early afternoon I played with Les. My bragging about living the life of Huckleberry Finn and escaping any punishment from the school authorities over either the skiving or the accident in Biology when I accidentally fused the school lights has come back to haunt me as a further shock awaited me and what shite timing too just at the start of the school summer holidays. I had been asked to go across to the doctor's and he said that it might help me if I went to see a child physic...pycheicatris...psychiatrist – it's difficult to spell. Anyway I suppose it could have been worse and happened yesterday on my birthday. On a positive note it perhaps shows that Boroughmuir is at last showing an interest in my welfare.

26th July 1971 In the morning I took the number 27 bus up to Forrest Road and went to the hospital for my appointment. It went fine and was pretty uneventful.

1ˢᵗ February 1972 Miss Beattie our Maths teacher encourages us to read *The Scotsman* each day. She says if we did this for a whole year we would come on a bundle. Her paper lies at the side of her desk and I noticed today's headline said that none of the families of the thirteen shot dead in Londonderry were members of the IRA. Iain was off Firrhill School today. The doctor says he has asthma; what a shame.

5th June 1972 (Age 15) Note to Self - Hospital I went up to the Royal Infirmary for my regular appointments to monitor the excruciating pain I had in my side two years ago that landed me in hospital for three weeks. It went okay and I didn't collapse after the blood test this time. Need I say I just stayed off school so no Boroughmuir for me today. I'm already beginning to feel Boroughmuir's part of another life. When I got home I did some work on Iain's Raleigh Chopper. I've done some good maintenance work on it out in the back shed and it's going sweetly. After tea I went down to Meadowbank to coach Walker's training but wasn't running too well. I came home via Rissi's where I picked up some chips and Globe Red Kola. I'm looking forward to watching the new BBC series called Athlete which begins tonight at

11.20 p.m. Ron Pickering is doing the series but what will be brilliant is tonight's programme features the great coach John Anderson from Meadowbank and the brilliant Edinburgh athlete David Jenkins and Avril Halliday who is married to Don Halliday.

15th February 1973 Gaga gave me a lift all the way out to work. I had a fall out with Roy this morning and then just to rub it in I finished last at 'Scrabble' with a meagre (good word!) 23 points. My leg was hurting like hell and sitting down for most of the day wasn't really helping it at all. Also in the afternoon I was feeling quite sickly. So much so that Tommy Allan gave me a lift up to Oxgangs at teatime and I went to see Dr Motley. It turns out that Monday's bad fall on the ice (when I badly gashed my knee) has caused the leg to turn septic. He put a dressing on it. After seeing the doctor I went down to Meadowbank but not to train. Olympic hurdler Dave Wilson is back training; he's such a nice down to earth bloke with no airs and graces. On the big world front Ali beat Bugner on points. With not training I was back home by 8.30 p.m. to catch Robert Louis Stevenson's Weir of Hermiston on BBC 2; it was really very good indeed.

2nd May 1973 It wasn't too bad a day at work and in fact it passed quite quickly. Tommy Allan gave me a lift up to Oxgangs in his little Wolsely 1500; it's a dinky wee car. I wish I was old enough to drive and could drive such a beautiful car. I went to the doctor's to see him again about my leg. I looked into Mum's and she told me she is going to buy me a pair of trousers. I travelled straight down to Meadowbank for a time trial over 350 metres and was happy to beat Derek Smith. I bought the new Athletics in Scotland magazine; Dougie is selling it on behalf of the publisher George Sutherland who lives round the corner at Durham Square. My name should have been in it but wasn't. I'm watching Liza Minnelli in 'Liza with a Z' and also the 5 a side football so it's a good night for the telly.

25th May 1973 Hurrah! I got my cassette tape recorder this morning. It looks great! I nipped along to the chemist, Duncan McCallum at Comiston Road to buy some batteries. There was a not bad looking girl working in the shop. I went up to Oxgangs to Dr Motley's to get some iron tablets.

4th June 1973 I went back up to the hospital for one of my six monthly checks; I got my tests including a blood test and promptly passed out – again! I felt absolutely rotten. It was a horrible feeling. I came home and rested all afternoon watching Holiday73 with Cliff Mitchelmore in France featuring horse drawn caravans followed by a wee episode of Huckleberry Hound on in the background. I bought a pair of sunglasses. Dougie gave me a lift down to Pinkie Musselburgh. I ran okay winning the 100 metres. I was talking away with the Pitreavie boys. I got a lift back home.

27th **August 1973** I was off today – it was a Bank Holiday. It was tremendous not to have to go in – you really appreciate such a holiday when you're a worker. In the morning I went out to Oxgangs. Iain and Mum were both off today. I went over to see Dr Motley; I should have taken the sick line he offered me. I sat on the couch in the afternoon watching the Bank Holiday Athletics from Crystal Palace; it was the second day of the UK v Hungary match. Brendan Foster set a new world record for the two miles. With millions watching it's made him a household name.

31st August 1973 I had to get up at the usual time this morning so that I could go out to visit the doctor but at least I got a run out to Oxgangs with Gaga. It was a rotten cold windy wet day with more than a hint of autumn. Iain and Anne came down to Porty with Gaga after he finished work at the shop; Anne is staying the night. I went up to Meadowbank to play table tennis with Paul. On the way up I bumped into Keith Ridley on the bus. We had a pretty good game. After my chips I enjoyed another episode of the very amusing Clochmerle with the Baroness declaring war on the mayor for the insults dished out to her son!

4th September 1973 Oh well back to work again at the office. I worked really hard and got all my invoices finished. It was really hot all day. I had a big argument with the woman at the comp (comptometer). I took a 23 bus tonight from the terminus at Balcarres Street but it took absolutely ages. I was running rubbishly this evening. Mum is away to hospital today for her operation so Iain and Anne are staying with us at Durham Road.

15th October 1973 As autumn progresses the Edinburgh weather is getting colder and colder each morning. The journey to work at Thomas Graham & Son along Balcarres Street is no fun and the miserable wind tunnel only exaggerates it. As I stride along to work the westerly wind cuts straight through me like a knife. I've been offered the job at S.C.K. at seventeen pounds a week plus their offices are nearer to Meadowbank so it should be a no-brainer. It's almost double what I'm getting here at Graham's but I want to speak to Mr Rogan the manager to see if I can use it as a bargaining tool. He was away all day so I've kept the opposition on hold. Being offered the post has increased my confidence and sense of self-worth. Also it's made me more hopeful optimistic and positive about the future. It's another wee step on the ladder to getting on in life and starting to overcome my unfortunate start to post-school life. A year on from leaving Boroughmuir School I've got a Scottish title to my name and the prospect of a reasonable wage. It's a start. At lunchtime I won 23p across at the Heating Department at cards. After work I went up to Oxgangs to the doctor. He's sending me for an X-ray. I had my tea. My feet are absolutely killing me – blisters!

15th November 1973 Ah well the week's wearing on nicely. I started wearing a suit to work today. At nine o'clock I phoned Mum's office but she wasn't there today. Mr Lowe was telling me that one of John's cousins had been killed. I won a bit at gambling at lunchtime. The doctor told me that my back was all right. Anne is staying the weekend at Porty. This evening we were training around the stadium.

21st November 1973 I decided that if I am going to stay off all week I'll have to get a sick line so I went out to Morningside first thing with Gaga in the car. However by mistake I got on a number 15 – I misread it for a 16 – and had to run down from Fairmilehead to Oxgangs to the surgery. Dr Motley gave me a sick line – good lad. Afterwards I looked in to 6/2 – Mum was at home – it's her last day after her operation before she returns to work tomorrow. I had to get down to Meadowbank at six this evening. I did quite a good session. I came home and had fish and chips. Nana and John have fallen out with each other.

3rd December 1973 I got up at nine o'clock. After breakfast I went up to the hospital. I wasn't too popular for refusing to take the blood test. Having collapsed the past few times ending up feeling awful I just didn't want to experience that horrible feeling again. He's also sending a note to Doctor Motley to stop giving me iron tablets. I got most of the remaining Christmas presents this afternoon so I'm well organised. Gaga gave me a lift up to

Meadowbank. I forgot my money. I did a pretty good session tonight.

13th December 1973 It wasn't bad at work especially as it passed quickly. Willie beat me twice at chess today – back to the drawing board! At night Tommy Allan drove me up to Oxgangs because I'd received a call at Thomas Graham & Sons to be told that I should visit the doctor. (Note: He shortly thereafter took off for New Zealand because of his incompetence?) When I called round he told me that I had a diseased liver and that I wasn't fit for hard training! So that's pretty worrying. I of course was pretty worried about this and Coach Walker said he'd accompany me to see the doctor next week. When I got home to Porty everyone was just going off to bed. (Note: Later on Mother and I surmised perhaps the doctor had got my notes mixed up with Father who is an alcoholic.)

14th December 1973 Nana phoned me at work during the morning to tell me that Mum went to Dad's about my visit to the doctor's; she'd been very upset at work and had to be sent home. The afternoon was a bit boring. At five o'clock Gaga ran us along to Pentland House to pick up Aunt Heather and the Christmas tree. Wee Anne is down to go the stone club. I went up to Meadowbank to do my weights session and came home at half nine.

18th December 1973 I must have picked up a bug as I was up twice during the night with diarrhoea not to mention five times this morning! Nana phoned Graham's to say I wouldn't manage in to work. Fortunately by lunch time I felt better and Gaga ran me out to Colinton to meet up with Bill. We went to see the doctor together. The news was really good and I can restart training a.o.k. - immediately. What a fiasco it's been. At night I celebrated by buying a new Meadowbank Sports Centre membership. After the training session I had a good chat with Coach Walker before coming home. Earlier Paul and I had a bit of a laugh with me ending up bursting his balloon! I also gave Dougie McLean the dance tickets money. I'm really looking forward to the Edinburgh Athletic Club Christmas Eve Dance; it should be one of the highlights of the year.

19th December 1973 I got up to Oxgangs at just after eight o'clock. Mum and I went to the hospital. The young doctor was quite nice.

I'm also allowed to take 'Pollitabs.' I went down to 14 Dean Park Street to Nana Hoffmann's with the Christmas presents for Dad, Bett and Roddy. In the evening I was up at Dougie's for a minute. It started raining I was very tired when I went training this evening. I had a good chat with Bill. I'm going to ILLEGIBLE sometime for tests.

26th December 1973 Boxing Day (Holiday except in Scotland) It was quite funny. Nana had thought that I was off my work today and didn't awaken me. So I didn't get up until ten o'clock. I phoned up Paul and we decided to go to see Magnum Force with Chris Cole. It was pretty good. Afterwards I went out to Oxgangs to the doctor and he has signed me off until next Thursday. I decided to just stay overnight at Oxgangs. I ran down to the phone at Colinton Mains and phoned Gaga to let them know. The Two Ronnies Old Fashioned Christmas Mystery was very funny. After The Good Old Days Mum and I sat up late watching the ghost story for Christmas – it was called 'The Exorcism.' As usual a good annual treat.

18th March 1974 I was up early and went out to Dr Motley's. He says it's okay for me to start training again after being off with bronchitis.

19th March 1974 I was about to head off to work but after breakfast Nana said I should stay away from Graham's as my throat is still very sore. Mid-morning I walked down to Portobello Library and took out two books on athletics as I'm now trying to coach myself. In the afternoon Mum phoned to say Dad was in the Royal Edinburgh Hospital Andrew Duncan Clinic (for alcoholics) so Gaga and I travelled out to Morningside to collect his clothes and we returned them to Nana's at 14 Dean Park Street Stockbridge.

24th March 1974 We made the long overnight journey back from Cosford in the clapped out bus. Dave Hislop and I were walking around a quiet Glasgow at 6.30 a.m. on a Sunday morning whilst awaiting the Glasgow girls being picked up by their parents. Back in the capital I took Scrubs and Derek Innes home for breakfast. I did a relaxed session at Meadowbank. However I was barking away and the cough was so bad that David Jenkins came over and advised me to go to bed for four days. Later in the day the cough got worse and I felt so unwell that I travelled out to Oxgangs to see the doctor. He says I've got bronchitis and gave me a penicillin injection. I passed out. Quite a weekend but worth running to get that first AAAs medal.

15th May 1974 In the evening I went back to the doctor about my bronchitis which has got even worse; he gave me antibiotics. On the way home from Oxgangs to Porty I went in to see the Meadowbank manager Mr Bull about a summer holiday job; another positive wee step. So a poor day on the athletics front but perhaps a rich day to look back on one day; the day my future took a turn for the better.

25th June 1974 My letter invite for Oslo (to make my debut for the Scottish team) arrived in the post. As I was having my tea at Oxgangs I took the letter out to show Anne and Iain. After we'd eaten we went down to visit Mum at the Astley Ainslie Hospital; she looked very pale.

5th November 1974 I signed on at The Dole but there was no Miss Henderson there to see me. Some bad news – Bill phoned me to say he's got jaundice so he will have to self-isolate perhaps not being back to Meadowbank for two months. Mum was on the telephone too as was the hospital saying I'm not to take iron supplements any longer. Heather was off work with a cold so we got in an ice cream treat for the four of us. In the evening I trained with Norrie Gregor putting in some good work.

14th June 1976 The world at least my wee world went slightly mad this morning. Ironically when the news broke I was sitting in of all places the doctor's surgery (injured after racing on Saturday and Sunday). The receptionist came through and announced to the packed waiting room that I'd just been selected for the Olympic team! Grandma Jo had phoned up the surgery with the news. Like Lazarus it seemed to bring many of the patients to life as they came up to congratulate me. Dr Motley is always happy but he seemed particularly so this morning at my good news and was genuinely delighted. He was also regaling me with tales of his own career in American Football as well as saying how if I ever wanted to go to Oklahoma University he could arrange a scholarship for me. He's also going to arrange for a collection to be taken at the surgery. Well after that it was all a bit of a blur. I looked in to 6/2 Oxgangs Avenue to give Mum the good news. The press had been on the phone to Porty all morning indeed the phone never stopped ringing all day; Josephine did her best to field the calls. In the afternoon I met various photographers up at Meadowbank where I did some 'practice starts'. Brian Meek from the Daily Express was on the blower and Harry Pincott wants to do a profile for Friday's Scotsman as well as a myriad of other newspapers.

8th September 1976 A game of golf on Porty Golf Course in the rain before going out to Pentland Community Centre where I was presented with monies raised at Dr Motley's surgery towards my training expenses. Afterwards I travelled down to pick up Ruth and gave her a lift home!

17th December 1976 Doreen en-route from East Lothian picked me up in her Triumph Spitfire at Milton Road Crossroads which is handy - a lift straight to the door at Claremont Crescent for our work at the Scottish Council of Social Service. I had an hour and a half for lunch so went for a stroll around the shops. My left Achilles tendon is so sore I'm unable to train. At 5:45 p.m. I phoned Dad and have arranged to meet him tomorrow. I went out to the doctor and was very tense when I received me jag on de bum! After in the evening I saw the physiotherapist Bill Cummings at Meadowbank Sports Centre about the Achilles. He says it's just tight. Ruthie phoned me at ten o'clock for twenty minutes. She was baby-sitting in a largee house saying she felt quite scared.

13th June 1977 Because of this damn cold no work or training today. After a visit to the doctor Ruthie and I went out to West Linton and Carlops to the Allan Ramsay Hotel for a light meal and drink - a really nice evening.

20th April 1978 It was raining and misty here in Dundee. I whizzed down to Edinburgh looking into Mum's for lunch and then dropped her off at the Western General Hospital where she was going in to visit poor Helen Blades.

18th July 1978 I'm absolutely scunnered; I awoke this morning feeling wiped out with a temperature and a very sore throat. I don't know where the fuck I picked that up but it's completely floored me. Most worrying is we're due to fly out to Canada for the Commonwealth Games in a few days' time. Of all the times but is it really unexpected given the lost weeks every year since I started training five years ago. The worrying thing is how very slow I am at shaking these infections off - it usually takes me around ten days. I phoned the doctor but couldn't get an appointment until later. I ended up going in to work at my summer holiday job with Edinburgh Corporation; that was a big mistake as I felt pretty rough. I've been given some antibiotics - oxytetracycline and also a throat spray. I sat in feeling miserable. Later on Diana the goddess of love and hunting dropped by to see me.

28th August 1973 I was contemplating not going in to work this morning. At lunchtime my back was killing me so I had to go to the doctor who signed me off for a week. Mum goes in to the hospital next Tuesday for her operation. I went up to Meadowbank early this evening and took the kids' session. I couldn't train so all I did was ten miles jogging round the track very slowly – 40 laps – not bad. Good night Retep.

30th August 1977 After yesterday's international against West Germany Alan Dainton dropped me off at East Croydon Station to catch the train to Gatwick Airport. Unfortunately I had to hang around for four hours. I gave Diana the goddess of love and hunting a ring to let her know I'd be arriving at four o'clock. I didn't feel too good but managed to finish my book on the flight. On arrival in Edinburgh the rain was absolutely teeming down. Diana was there to meet me and we took the airport bus back. As Will was out running Jo to the Edinburgh Sketching Club we had to take shelter in the old greenhouse. In the evening I felt worse; a sore stomach; I was sick. Late on the doctor was called out. I've a rumbling appendix. End of the season: REST!

31st August 1977 After the doctor left things went from bad to worse. At 2.00 a.m. I was feeling terribly sick and was to be found lying on the bathroom floor wishing that terrible feeling would go away. I forced myself to get up and took a couple of tablets managing to sleep until 7.30 a.m. I visited the doctor who gave me a line for Leith Hospital; they decided I should remain in for the night. I spent most of the time reading a fine book from their library - ironically it was Brian Glanville's The Olympian. It's a funny old world. But it's not.

5th September 1977 After dropping Will off at his wee part-time job I took the dog to Portobello Park for a good run about. I took care of all my correspondence including my grant form now that I've decided to study at Dundee. Early afternoon I went out to the doctor's-sister for an allergy jag. I've just finished studying some Economics and Maths - I'm keen! As well as writing my journals. I feel happy! Late on I took the dog back out to the park; it's been very windy all day. Late on I watched a Michael Caine film Pulp. It was about a writer being asked to immortalise someone's life. Is that what these journals are about? Discuss!

16th September 1977 After being in at Dr Motley's I parked the car outside the Hermitage of Braid and went for a run through it and up and around the Braid Hills.

3rd October 1977 Whilst out at the doctor's I popped in to see Mum and John. Once back to Porty I painted the rhones making not too bad a job of them. At lunchtime I joined Bill for an hour of squash. I taped some Neil Diamond. Ruthie phoned – she's a wee bit depressed. I went up to meet her at a pub for a chat and then sat with her in the car in a rain-soaked Arthurs Seat car park. Later I went along to Bill's meeting – impressive.

24th September 1977 This week's cold turned to something worse. An inauspicious start to first year and to my venture into middle distance training and aiming for next year's Commonwealth and European Championships. I dropped Will off at his wee part-time butchering job and then Ruthie in town before driving out to Dr Motley's to get some anti-biotics. It's made it impossible to either train or to study.

25th November 1977 Because of my sore throat I went out to Oxgangs to visit the doctor and also called in to see Mother; she was in a cheerful mood. A lovely surprise – Ruthie turned up. As usual Dr Motley was in an excellent mood - what a cheerful persona; we were both laughing and chuckling away. He's such a character and a tonic. If you could only bottle his positive attitude to life and prescribe it to everyone then all would be well with the world. Driving through the Queen's Park Ruth and I were staggered at the beauty of the morning. On a fresh cold morning the scenery was stunning; the sun shone on Arthurs Seat bathing the hill in a warm and soft yellow winter glow; Duddingston Loch was as still as a millpond. Holyrood Park hasn't really changed much since Robert Louis Stevenson used to visit the park a century ago. Ruth and I visited John Macpherson. He's an old bachelor and a former maths teacher at Boroughmuir. Last summer he contacted me out of the blue and kindly offered me his golf clubs; because of old age he can no longer play at Prestonfield. He showed us an old photograph album from the 1920s with a lot of pictures of him hiking; there were also a few photographs of Dad who looked remarkably like me. We stayed there until four o'clock when Ruth had to go off to work at Safeways. I dropped in to Denis's for a rub; he'd received a letter from Roger in Paris; he's doing fine and aiming for the indoors. Homeward bound for a wee bit telly and some studying. No training to report again but detailed below from a younger me back in 1973 complaining 'I wasn't running too well.'

3rd February 1978 I visited the doctor and he gave me a nasal spray for my cold. With me having Dad's Opel Kadette Josephine and I took a wee tootle down to Stow. It was a very pleasant drive down through the snow covered Borders landscape. I suspect the Lauder road may have been blocked as there was some thick ice.

10th February 1978 I was out at Dr Motley's.

3rd March 1978 When Josephine awoke me this morning I was still very tired. There was a letter from Dr Motley. I went out to see him; he'd received some further correspondence from J. D. Martin at Oklahoma University but there's still nothing concrete.

10th April 1978 At 4 p.m. I went in to see Helen Blades at the Royal Infirmary; she's dying of cancer; the news came as a shock. Despite having to see so many visitors she was delighted to see me. Knowing I wouldn't see her again as I was leaving I kissed her; she hugged me tight and tried to hold back her tears. It was very sad. She was such a big influence on me when I was growing up at The Stair. She had such a magnetic personality; the nearest person I could compare her to is John Anderson. You always wanted to help her out; when I received the slightest modicum of praise from Helen I would be on cloud 9 for the rest of the week. I'll never forget how one sunny summer's afternoon when Helen; Marion; Mum and lots of the kids were out in our back garden and I was a wee boy showing off by sprinting round and round the block she said I'd run in the Commonwealth Games one day and how her eldest daughter Liz quite rightly but sniffily said Don't be silly Mummy. Well let's prove Helen right! Helen's passing is going to leave an enormous gap in the lives of her six girls and Douglas. Afterwards I gave one of her visitors a lift back to Craiglockhart. She was a pleasant middle class woman but was trying to pair me off with her daughter. Iain showed me his quadrophonic stereo - whatever that is!

21st July 1978 Despite my cold I decided to go out for a run, had a shower at Meadowbank and a relaxed few hours at home before going out to Oxgangs to Dr Motley's. It's probably the last occasion I'll see him as a patient as he is retiring at the end of this month.

24ᵗʰ October 1978 I played the Interflora man early this morn delivering a single rose to Ruth. I'd intended driving up to Dundee but spur of the moment changed my mind at the Maybury Roundabout feeling that despite a full on day of lectures and seminars I couldn't miss Helen Blades's funeral. I swung round by Oxgangs and drove everyone down to the funeral service at Charlotte Chapel. After the burial we went to Liz's (Blades the eldest of six daughters) house for a tea. Twas very sad circumstances, but it was lovely to see Douglas and all the girls again, reminding me of many happy old times.

2nd September 1983 I felt pretty grubby this morning – mainly me stomach – I phoned the doctor but there was no appointment until after the weekend on Monday. The receptionist wouldn't even consider an appointment. She was pretty offhand with a poor manner – changed days from when we just turned up at Dr Motley's surgery. It remained uncomfortable all day.

27th November 1983 It's Sunday evening and I'm sitting here reading Edna O'Brien's *The Girl With The Green Eyes*: it makes me realise just how much I would like to write such a lovely book too – it just flows along. Each time I pick it up I look forward to dipping into it wishing to savour the moment. These past 10 to 20 days I've been drifting along with my life. Yes, I've found a job. But at a measly £3600 a year. But as for the rest of my life, well it's a disaster. I've a hedonist approach to life and living, but I experience occasional feelings of dissonance without any goals to drive myself forward and to discipline myself. Lounging around doing as I please makes me feel fat and ugly. The days have been flying past and I've not taken any real exercise living as others do – each morning I awake with the desire to do something – to start afresh but I never do. Mañana! What do I want to do with the rest of my life? Where are my dreams? What are my dreams? I enjoy writing – I enjoy reading – I enjoy training – but to work spending my evenings in a Wimpy Bar? Who knows, but at £5000 perhaps I should accept that post rather than the Scottish Episcopal Church at £1400 less. And I can all the while look for something else.

Anyway come tomorrow – Monday morning – I'll get my act together and decide the better way forward. Elizabeth and I spent a good part of the evening laughing playing in bed until ten o'clock when she kicked me out to go out to Caiystane to Dr Motley's for a reference. That was the second occasion – earlier she'd kicked me out the bed for farting. Once out at Oxgangs I saw Iain who's fed up of life with K. He's stayed there overnight and will return back to Wester Hailes tomorrow or perhaps Tuesday. Dr Motley kindly typed out a reference for me but in doing so he essentially lacks imagination and flair and powers of description - essentially it's a factual CV rather than doing what a reference should do - favourably commenting upon one's positive characteristics and traits: when I gently tried to steer him in that direction he was quite dogmatic not really listening – he just doesn't get it! Later on I watched a video at Les's – The Wanderers – enjoyable rubbish. I got home late afternoon.

16th January 1984 Oh and Dr Motley is a little better – good.

26th May 1988 Mum was telling me that Mr (Charles) Blades our former neighbour at 6/6 Oxgangs Avenue had died before Christmas after spending his last days in the Grassmarket – hellish! When I was heading off to Boroughmuir School in the morning I recall how smartly dressed he used to be standing at the Oxgangs bus stop outside Dr Motley's with his briefcase heading down to Ferranti's. So very poignant to hear. At one time in his life he wasn't far off from qualifying as a doctor. Mum used to get on well with him often taking the same number 4 bus together to work.

20th November 1989 I've taken today (Monday) off work – the first holiday since I took up the new post. Elizabeth and I were away for the weekend to Dingwall. Despite picking up a heavy cold I enjoyed myself. Wyvis and wife made us very welcome and of course fed us well. Ann Ross stayed overnight on the Saturday. There was some good conversation and plenty of laughs. It was also amusing watching Wyvis and wife occasionally spark. On the Saturday we visited Jackie and her boys in Ullapool. Olly has been unwell. I telephoned both Jo and Mum today. Mum was saying that Dr Motley had died ten days ago. He was such an amazing character and a lovely man. I believe it was him that gifted me the £100 cheque when I was selected for the Olympic team back in 1976.

Out of Left Field

After the freezing winter of 2020/21 I was met by the welcome sweet sound of the birds singing and the light starting to stretch out - March and spring in Scotland had indeed arrived.

And with it I intended bringing down the curtain on Dr Motley's story when on the 5th March, 2021 a final e mail pinged in my in-box.

It was from Harold Motley from all the miles distant from across the Atlantic Ocean to sunny California.

Harold had responded to many of the questions which I had posed to him the previous month.

Within the e mail were some interesting pieces of information and reflections including one last major surprise – one last secret - one jaw-dropping and very sad and poignant item about the second shadowy and hidden figure within Dr Motley's story, his brother Harold.

It came out of left field, a bolt from the blue - I'll leave you, the reader, to read Harold's e mail below:

I personally believe that Frank (Motley) was Black; I only found one document that said he was white; all the others list him as being Black.

It was against the law for whites and Blacks to marry until 1967.

If Frank was white and claimed he was Black it was to allow him to marry Ethel.

I don't think that Ethel ever visited Edinburgh.

It was only very recently that I found out that Frank visited; I haven't found out the reason why yet.

From my personal experience, the animosity from the Roysters seems to be directed at Rev. Motley: the custom of the times where if you got someone pregnant you married them.

I believe that Rev. Motley shipped Arthur out of town to keep him from marrying Freddie.

L'Ouverture was a segregated school until the class of 1968. The old school 1908-1932 was a two-storied building that had kindergarten to senior grade classes in one building.

The school's books, desks and equipment were hand-me-downs (used) from the white schools.

The school taught European, United States, Black, Native American History and the Haitian Revolution was covered in the school's curriculum.

L'Ouverture was the first segregated school that I attended. All the schools in Oakland California (hometown) were integrated, Oakland is known for its diversity. Oakland has large schools and large classrooms, with less hands-on attention from teachers. L'Ouverture was the opposite – a small school and small classes.

The school had the feel of a family school, everyone knew everyone: a couple of the faculty taught my grandfather Dr Motley and they were always reminding me of how intelligent he was.

The principal of the school, Dr Willa Strong, was in Dr Motley's class of 1924.

L'Ouverture may have been poor in texts books, equipment, and funding but the faulty made up for it by stressing the importance of getting an education.

I went to the new school, the 1964-1965 school year.

The school was an "L" shaped building with the "L" laying on its side; the foot of the L was the elementary school, the next 1/3 up from the foot of the L was the middle school and the top of the L was the high school.

My parents sent my older brother Marlon and me (by bus) to visit relatives for the summer in McAlester, the schools in Oklahoma started almost 2 months before the schools in Oakland so my brother and I started school at L'Ouverture, we both enjoyed going and wanted to stay.

When the schools in California started, my parents brought my brother Marlon back home and left me to stay.

I think Arthur did some of the same things I did when I was in McAlester, playing basketball in the mornings before noon in the summertime because the weather was hot and humid by the afternoon.

I believe that I read that his nickname at Lincoln University was "Hoops" - for playing basketball. McAlester had an adult-supervised Teen Center that had Friday night teen dances.

I went fishing a couple of times with friends and sometimes just visit and hung out with friends.

Arthur and his friends would have played games that didn't require equipment or they made their own toys or equipment.

Every summer McAlester has a major golf tournament with a large demand for caddies - perhaps Arthur worked the tournaments.

For me, it was my first paying job, $3.50 for 9 holes. (1964)

I believe that the Royster family avoided Rev. Motley, with their animosity directed towards him.

Freddie married James H. Hale in 1946: they had three children and they lived on a farm in Krebs just outside of McAlester Oklahoma, so they had very little contact with the Motleys.

I'm not sure that Freddie knew that Dr Motley was in Scotland

In public, I believe that they, the Roysters and the Motleys were civil to each other.

I'm not sure that Freddie took my father to visit the Motleys: he spent a lot of time with his aunts and uncle, Freddie's four sisters and brother, but one of them may have taken him to visit Ethel.

I believe that Freddie's youngest sister Emma knew about Dr Motley, she's the one that had the picture of Arthur and Freddie as teenagers.

One of the old customs here is "that children should not be in adults' business"

If they knew that you were listening to family matters they would stop and send you out of the room.

Most of my information about the family is second-hand information from my mother.

I don't think that Rev. Motley and Ethel had a phone, although perhaps later in their life.

I believe that Ethel's family, as well as Ethel, were financially stable.

I'm sure that if they needed any financial assistants Dr Motley was there to help if she needed it.

I don't believe that Dr Motley ever returned to McAlester after he left the U.S.

I'm still searching for documentation. I know that he didn't attend his mother's funeral

My father never really talked about his father (Dr Motley), now while I'm thinking about it my father never met his father.

I feel that my father thought of himself more as a Royster than a Motley.

As a child, my father spent time with his aunts - Freddie's sisters - there might have been issues with my dad reminding Freddie of Arthur.

I was around 15 years old when I met Arthur's mother, Ethel.

I remember knocking on the door and she asked who is it?

I had forgotten that her oldest son was named Harold Motley when I told her my name I could hear that she was really getting excited - I had to tell her that I was Bo' Motley's son (Bo' was my father's (Lewie) nickname).

I was about a foot taller than her.

She invited me in and we sat down and talked: she was mostly asking questions about my family.

The Rev. Motley was there and I remembered that he was blind.

I could only stay about an hour because I needed a ride back to my grandmother's home in Krebs Oklahoma.

I now regret not visiting Ethel again and spending more time with them.

I was young and uncomfortable being around older people.

If I could do it over I have a million questions to ask them.

Ethel was a sweet, gentle, and intelligent little lady; she remembered all my brother's and sister's birthdays (8) and she would send us birthday cards with a dollar in them.

When Arthur was a boy the day-to-day life was laid back and easy-going: they had men with horse-drawn carts selling produce and grocery items in the spring and the summer and in the winter most things were shutdown.

It was hard for me to get used to four-seasons with me being from California and its two seasons - sunny and rainy.

The thing that worried me the most about Oklahoma weather was the thunder, lightning, and tornadoes.

My father never talked about the Motleys.

I am sure that when Ethel and Frank saw my father they treated him like the grandson that he was.

I haven't found any information that Arthur returned home during summer breaks.

I believe that Rev. Motley was influencing Arthur to not return home to prevent any issues.

I've just remembered that Clarksville is half the way between McAlester and Wiley College.

Arthur has relatives in Clarksville, with his birth father being from there.

The custom here in the U.S. is for the birth mother to give the baby the father's last name, married or not, the only reason they wouldn't, was if they disliked the father and didn't want to deal with him they would instead have used their maiden name.

The shame in this country goes to the unwed mother, thus the main reason for the Roysters' animosity towards the Rev. Motley.

There is another custom, it's called a "shotgun wedding" where they force the expecting mother and father to marry, to save face for the unwed mother's family.

Negro Is Charged In Child's Death

ATOKA—Sept. 5.—(A')—H a r o l d Motley, 33-year-old Negro, former school teacher, was in the Atoka county jail Saturday night charged with murder in the death of his son, Harold Lee Motley, 2½ years old.

The child died of injuries which physicians said he received from a beating.

Arthur's brother Harold was a teacher, married, and had two children. Uncle Harold Motley was the family's tragedy.

In 1936 while visiting a friend's home he tried to discipline his son for not knowing how to recite his A, B, Cs and accidentally killed him.

I don't know what happened, but I've been trying to get a copy of the court records.

Governor Faces Contempt Case

OKLAHOMA CITY, Jan. 9. (U.P.) —Threat of a contempt of court action against Gov. Roy J. Turner and V. B. "Bill" Likins had the makings today of a major legal battle between the state and at least one district court judge.

First skirmish is expected in a few days, when Ewing C. Sadler, Sulphur attorney has promised to seek the contempt citation at Atoka against Turner and Likins, wealthy rancher and friend of the governor. Sadler said the action will be filed before District Judge Sam Sullivan, and Sullivan already has stated he will sustain it.

The dispute stems from the case of Harold Lee Motley, 43-year-old Negro man sentenced to a life term in the state penitentiary in 1936. Motley was convicted in the death of his 3-year-old son, who died shortly after being whipped by his father.

After serving nine years of his sentence, Motley went to Likins' ranch near Davis as a cook and house boy, on a leave of absence from the state penitentiary at McAlester.

Last October his attorney, Sadler, appealed to Judge Sullivan, who vacated the life sentence, on the grounds the trial court had been in error and the sentence was illegal.

(Motley has testified he was arraigned and sentenced on the same day, without being advised of his rights or having an attorney.)

After the judge's ruling, Motley left the Likins ranch and went to Davis, where he subsequently was arrested and taken back to the penitentiary when Turner revoked his leave of absence. He is still confined there.

I imagine that he was despondent and remorseful when he went to court without an attorney and he pleaded guilty and was sentenced to life in prison.

I found documents where Harold petitioned the Governor of Oklahoma for a pardon: he was paroled and returned back to prison and eventually pardoned. I'm unsure of the dates as I'm still researching.

Parole Granted Negro Under Life Term in Slaying

Governor Kerr Wednesday granted a parole to Harold Lee Motley. Negro under life sentence for murder in Atoka county, who has been employed as a cook at the Flying L ranch of V. B. Likins, near Davis, while on 65-day leave of absence.

The Negro has served nine years on his sentence.

Ethel would have left correspondence, photographs, graduation records of Arthur, but like most young people out here they often see it as junk and toss it into the trash not realizing how priceless the stuff is. I know that my mother had black and white pictures of my great grandmother, Ethel and I believe that my sister tossed them too - not the pictures but the boxes they were in.

Ethel's family may have been able to help finance Arthur's studies in Edinburgh: her father graduated from college. There's another angle that I'm looking into - the Dinwiddie family (European) were the enslavers of Dr Motley's great grandmother Caroline Dinwiddie 1825-1891. William Jasper Dinwiddle 1817-1873 was the father of her children. The Dinwiddie's helped Caroline to buy farmland in Clarksville. The Dinwiddie's (European) have a very large family and I noticed that in every generation there are a couple of doctors - maybe they helped?

I don't know if Annette Junior visited her relatives in McAlester City but I hope that she did. I wonder why she was in New York? I'm looking into i. I know that my father didn't know about Annette.

I don't know, but I believe Dr Motley didn't ever return to McAlester City, but I'm looking for records of travel to see if he returned.

Two Roads Diverged

'...Two roads diverged in a wood, and I—

I took the one less traveled by,

And that has made all the difference.'

Robert Frost

Dr Arthur Philip Motley died in the Edinburgh Royal Infirmary - where he had once worked - according to my diary on the 10th November 1989, eight years after Annette: in Scotland's People it states that he was 82, but of course he was actually 84 - an enigma to the end.

Two Worlds tells the remarkable story of Arthur Philip Motley a Black American who as a young man left his home in McAlester City Oklahoma in 1928 to travel the 4351 miles across America and the Atlantic Ocean to come to Edinburgh Scotland to fulfil his dream to become a doctor who over the course of six decades went on to make an astonishing community contribution in a working class area of the capital going on to become a legendary figure whose story deserves a wider audience.

Along the way as I searched out his trail, there were several mis-directions and several journeys down cul-de-sacs and several leaps of faith too: I suspect further information will yet come through the ether if not out of the closet.

In the description on the book cover it mentions a dark secret - the one that I first became aware of before starting writing about Arthur Philip Motley - that he had fathered an illegitimate son, Lewie Motley, who was born in McAlester City Oklahoma in 1925.

But as I followed in his footsteps and on his trail other revelations yet awaited me. His adored wife Annette had fallen pregnant to him with Annette Junior when she was only seventeen and whilst four months expectant their partnership was formalised in what may have been a shotgun wedding.

It came as a big surprise and a revelation to me too that Arthur had failed his medical examinations and didn't graduate from the University of Edinburgh – in conversations he certainly didn't mention this to my mother who in later years he sometimes took along to the university's lunch club for former students. He of course was quite within his rights to do so, but I do wonder if he was slightly economical with the truth.

Reading between the lines I believe he also kept his marriage and the birth of his daughter Annette Junior secret from his parents for over a decade.

But the biggest surprise of all came as I was beginning to write the conclusion to the book when I heard that his brother Harold, who given their proximity in age and to whom he must have been very close to at one stage had been imprisoned for accidentally killing his three year old son, 'whipping' him to death.

It's difficult if not impossible to put into words what this meant for all the family and how it impacted on them for the rest of their lives – a very painful episode etched into the psyche of all concerned.

For Arthur and Harold's mother, Ethel, it's perhaps something she never quite got over – essentially in 1936 she had lost three boys – her grandson – her son Harold now ensconced behind prison bars – and Arthur who had failed his medical exams and had left the University of Edinburgh.

That year, 1936, was very hard for her to bear especially after being such a good mother and given all that she had invested in her two boys - her high hopes were dashed after such a promising start with Harold qualifying as a teacher and Arthur studying medicine at the finest school in the world.

It would take a few years for her world to become a little bit brighter.

I have to assume Arthur would have written to her in 1939 with the wonderful news that he had at last qualified as a doctor.

And then in later years Harold was paroled so she would begin to see him regularly once again.

As for Dr Arthur Philip Motley, as the years and the decades passed the issue of Annette falling pregnant before they wed would have been long forgotten.

As for Lewie, he too would have been forgotten in the main but surely, as his father, he thought of the son whom he never acknowledged or ever saw at least occasionally. As for his brother Harold's tragedy, who knows how that affected Arthur – was that another reason for him distancing himself from his family back home in Oklahoma?

We'll never know.

A frail Dr Motley in hospital: photograph courtesy Vicky Mount

In terms of purely medical skills Dr Motley wasn't of the first rank.

Undoubtedly and like every General Practitioner out there he made mistakes some of which were more costly than others which at the extreme end may even have cost lives.

From our stair he may have mis-diagnosed Mrs Helen Blades at number 6/6 who very sadly died of cancer; my good friend Paul Forbes says that when he was a baby his mother took him to see Dr Motley who said all he had was colic – fortunately his mother didn't believe the diagnosis and instead took him to hospital where he ended up being hospitalised perhaps saving his life.

My own experience is another example close to hand - with a poisoned leg, but for his partner Dr Shepherd I would have lost my leg and my life would have been very different with no international athletics career awaiting me.

Neither was he well-regarded by such stakeholders as the local Lothian Health Board nor within the hospital service either.

But of course for some of his patients – including me - he was always good for a sick line to take time off work – the health board were probably unimpressed at him handing these out like confetti.

But then again, that we were asking for such a thing, perhaps he was ahead of his time in taking a 360 degree view of our well-being, including our mental health, but that's perhaps being slightly generous!

As Richard Cropper who is very complimentary about him says earlier in the book '...but I recall his diagnoses could be somewhat hit or miss'.

But of course when you are in doubt about a diagnosis, unless you are referring every single patient to a hospital, thereby playing it safe, I do have a certain sympathy for him on this front.

'Well, you got a recipe for a get along scene
Oh, what a beautiful dream
If it could only come true, you know, you know...'

Cooke & Greenaway

Another untold hero of this story is the community of Oxgangs.

For whatever reason this wasn't anything like the civic society of 1920s Edinburgh which a young Arthur Philip Motley had arrived into what with colour bars in small isolated parts of the city, but more endemically where there might be prejudice at play and in its active form – through discrimination against coloured people - but instead was quite the opposite, embracing the 1970 Blue Mink pop song *'Melting Pot'*.

With regard to Dr Motley I don't ever recall even a hint of racism at play. And instead he was quite simply an integral and key and loved member of the community – he was one of our own.

Partly this may well have been because he was so long established as one of the early dweller's in the area moving to Colinton Mains in the mid 1930s and of course the Oxgangs community grew exponentially from the 1950s onward with hundreds of young families moving in to create new and happy lives for themselves.

We were young with young sensibilities and young attitudes.

And then as we moved toward the 1960s which was a very different world this somehow enhanced, embraced and reinforced such positive attitudes in this brave new world – a colourful mix of elements in our overall socialisation process and group psyche.

But of course in the city of Dr Jekyll and Mr Hyde there still remained the sense of duality but more often in the form of snobbery whereby alongside what school you went to or didn't go to defined you, but the other way of categorising you was whether you resided in an affluent part of the city or not – say home-owning Morningside as opposed to the council flats which were rented out in Oxgangs – and yet for those who might be quite judgemental about our area perhaps expecting it to be an area of racism and bigotry, they would have been very surprised - no, it was quite the opposite and I find myself feeling very proud of this aspect of the community in which I grew up.

In drawing Dr Motley's remarkable life story and route of travel to a conclusion - from growing up in the American South between 1904 and 1928 to providing medical care to thousands of patients half-way round the globe in an Edinburgh suburb in the decades between the 1930s and the 1980s with the War sandwiched in between - is an extraordinary tale of an extraordinary life and an extraordinary man who as reflected through the prism of the recent Black Lives Matter movement, in his own quiet way did as much to improve race relations as perhaps anyone in Scotland.

It was a life lived and led during a period of great social change and conflict within both a peaceful world and one at war too.

His approach was one of King's maxim – judge me not by the colour of my skin but by the content of my character.

And what a character!

Edinburgh is the city of duality – the dark wynds of the Old Town and the sun-lit avenues of the New Town - the haunt of the doppelgänger - the home of Deacon Brodie and Dr Jekyll and Mr Hyde – and this story tells such a twin tale - of Black and white and of Dr Motley's journey and my journey in search of him. And like us all his was a nuanced life with some dark secrets at its heart and in this respect Edinburgh was a perfect environment for him to study, to work and to dwell in.

And whilst it wasn't something that he thought about, at its heart there remained this dark secret that he had fathered two children with two very different stories and two very different outcomes separated by a great ocean - for the two worlds of his son and his daughter - Lewie Motley, an American boy who was never acknowledged and then Annette Motley Junior who grew up in relative luxury.

And whilst it is understandable at the time - 1925 - why he didn't acknowledge Lewie for nuanced reasons he instead took off - most probably engineered and propelled by his father the Reverend Frank Motley - to pursue his academic studies to eventually become a doctor, did he ever reflect upon all of this in his later years and wish to make up for not taking responsibility or did he instead think it was best not to rock the boat. After all it would have caused upset and meant there were financial and inheritance implications too.

Lewie's voice is the unheard and silent other story within this book. And as the decades passed it must have been very hurtful for him to have been so abandoned by his father.

For Dr Motley, given the nature of those twin experiences and the nature of his work dealing with such sensitive and life changing dilemmas he could at least draw upon and deploy both experiences when patients visited him wondering what to do when confronted by a young lady who had similarly fallen pregnant. It helped him to see that there were different routes forward and that life could still work out well no matter the route of travel chosen.

As for the two Annettes, whilst it's based on limited information my overall feeling is that neither of them were happy and I surmise this was partly down to the impact of a mixed marriage with similar but different experiences for both women.

For Annette being married to a Black man meant she lived a very different life to what she might have anticipated when young.

Whereas for Annette Junior, having a Black father and a white mother meant that she too was caught up in this world of Edinburgh and beyond duality.

As for Arthur amongst it all he did go on to fulfil his – and his mother Ethel's sweet dream *'...to become a polished doctor...'* but at what cost to them both?

Was it a Pyrrhic Victory in that the two of them would only ever meet up one more time in the course of the half century from the day young Arthur waved goodbye to Ethel and Frank on the doorstep of 902 Monroe Avenue and set out with his luggage and his dreams on that early 1928 autumn day in McAlester City to come to the capital of Scotland to study, to work and to live for the rest of his life.

Or perhaps and much more likely as his grandson Harold Motley writes in the Out of Left Field e mail to me that he doesn't think Dr Motley ever returned to McAlester City nor ever saw his mother Ethel again.

My heart goes out to Ethel – having invested so much in her two boys, Harold and Arthur, she lived for many years with her heart broken, what with Harold behind bars and Arthur halfway around the world.

But at least come the 1950s there were happier times for her after Harold was released and also knowing that her husband had visited her boy – Arthur – now Dr Motley – in far off Scotland and in her winter years it warmed her sweet heart to see how well he was doing in life.

In his last moments did Dr Arthur Philip Motley 'travel' between two worlds for one last visit back to McAlester City for a final stroll along and around the streets of his youth – a dying man's last slow walk down East Monroe Avenue stopping by number 902 for a final moment – to glance at his former home to reflect on how this is where it all began – that it was here – it was here that I set out 60 years before on the most wondrous journey.

And on that 'last journey' did he revisit Miss Freddie Royster his childhood sweetheart who he was driven apart from by his father the Reverend Frank Motley – I like to think so - and if they couldn't be joined together in life I've brought them together in death.

Arthur Motley was a very gentle man – in many respects a gentleman – and like a shepherd – the good shepherd - with a fine unhurried and genuine interest in the welfare of his flock and an excellent bedside manner - he was endlessly positive, empathetic and sympathetic to his patients.

And despite the gravity of the profession – dealing with both new life and recent death - he was endlessly positive and well-meaning. You felt better for seeing him.

Whenever I recall Dr Motley it is with great fondness.

The mere mention of his name brings a smile to my face and a warmth to my heart.

He was a kind and a caring family doctor.

He had an appetite for life and you felt better for spending a few minutes in his happy company.

He was a remarkable and a great man - such an extraordinary and yet very ordinary character too.

He was a good supportive friend to our family and to the rest of his extended Colinton Mains, Firrhill and Oxgangs family.

He was a community leader in young Oxgangs.

And we were truly blessed and fortunate to have grown up under his sweet pastoral care helping to ensure our ongoing emotional and physical well-being.